Routledge Revivals

Guards Imprisoned

First published in 1989, this book provides an in-depth look into the work and working life of prison guards as they perceive and experience it. The author, a teacher at Auburn Prison, New York, discovered that little was known about the guard's perceptions of his "place" in the prison community and set out to explore the dynamics of this key correctional occupation from the perspective of those who do it. The raw data was provided by over 160 hours of interviews with guards and is presented in the order of a "natural history" — from their prerecruitment images of prison to the search for satisfaction as experienced guards. The book also includes a follow-up with the officers who were originally interviewed in 1976, assessing patterns of change and stability in their attitudes and behaviours.

Guards Imprisoned

Correctional Officers at Work

Lucien X. Lombardo

Routledge
Taylor & Francis Group

First published in 1989
by Anderson Publishing Co.

This edition first published in 2017 by Routledge
2 Park Square, Milton Park, Abingdon, Oxon, OX14 4RN
and by Routledge
711 Third Avenue, New York, NY 10017

Routledge is an imprint of the Taylor & Francis Group, an informa business

Publisher's Note

The publisher has gone to great lengths to ensure the quality of this reprint but points out that some imperfections in the original copies may be apparent.

Disclaimer

The publisher has made every effort to trace copyright holders and welcomes correspondence from those they have been unable to contact.

A Library of Congress record exists under LC control number: 8980456

ISBN 13: 978-1-138-22078-2 (hbk)
ISBN 13: 978-1-315-41185-9 (ebk)

Foreword to 2016 Routledge Revival Edition of

Guards Imprisoned: Correctional Officers at Work

The year twenty-sixteen marks Auburn (Prison) Correctional Institution's two hundredth consecutive year of operation. During these two hundred years the pendulum of prison reform has taken many trips back and forth in its journey between humanistic concerns and stark oppression. In the early twenty-first century we seem to be emerging from the era of "mass incarceration"[1] to the development of alternatives to incarceration that were so much discussed in the early 1970's.[2]

While the search for alternatives to criminal prosecution, sentencing, and 'new' programs continues, life as it is lived inside of prisons continues as it has for two centuries. People in the uniforms of correctional officers and technological and bureaucratic systems seek to monitor, care for and control prisoners.[3] Prisoners continue to seek to cope with the 'pains of imprisonment', minimize their stress and find ways to occupy their time. It is at the intersection of these two worlds that the questions asked and the answers discovered in the first two editions of *Guards Imprisoned* continue to find their relevance. As was noted in the preface to the First Edition, public policy debates about sentencing, alternatives and treatment vs. punishment "...tend to obscure the realities of prisons as places where people live and work." This reality must not be forgotten; it continues to need exploration.

The world of the correctional officers at Auburn Prison continues to reflect the essentials of prison life in any prison no matter what the politics of incarceration demand. Correctional officers continue to carry out their human services, security, order maintenance, supervision and rule enforcement functions. Correctional officers must still find ways of blending the human and bureaucratic components of their work often with an increasingly recognized

---

[1] Michelle Alexander, *The New Jim Crow: Mass Incarceration in the Age of Colorblindness*. NY: The New Press, 2012.
[2] Office of National Drug Control Policy, *Alternatives to Incarceration*. 2011. https://www.whitehouse.gov/ondcp/alternatives-to-incarceration.
[3] Alison Liebling, David Price and Guy Shefer, The Prison Officer. NY: Willan Publishers, 2011.

multi-problem population of prisoners.[4] They must deal not only with prisoners, but also with the prison administration, state level bureaucracies and legal changes that seek to structure correctional officer discretion and maintain accountability in institutions where transparency and visibility are not part of the regime. Correctional officers like all workers still experience stress and satisfaction from the work, and they still find ways of coping with their experiences and work environments. They do this almost always out of the public eye.

Occasionally correctional officers gain visibility, most often from failures and when they reflect the stereotypes for which *Guards Imprisoned* provides broader contexts of understanding. The escape of two prisoners from Clinton Correctional Facility in Dannemora, NY, in 2015[5] and the recent reports of correctional officer brutality in New York State's prisons[6] point to the need to continue to give voice to the diversity of correctional officer experiences and to the reality beyond the stereotypes whose voices are often the loudest. These situations also reflect the importance of thoughtful and diverse training for correctional workers whose day-to-day work is almost always invisible and much more complicated then even the officers recognize. The human dimensions of officer-prisoner-administrator interactions must be revisited if correctional practice is to reflect the human concerns current public policy discussions are trying to bring about in the use and practice of incarceration. Nearly thirty years after the publication of its second edition, *Guards Imprisoned* continues to provide a baseline for understanding the diverse (documented in the first edition) and slowly changing (documented in the second edition) work world and experience of the correctional officer. Hopefully its revival will stimulate new and thoughtful research and discussions of life as it is lived and experienced in prisons.

Lucien X. Lombardo

May 1, 2016

---

[4]Fred Osher, David A. D'Amora, Martha Plotkin, Nicole Jarrett, Alexa Eggleston, "Adults with Behavioral Health Needs Under Correctional Supervision: A Shared Framework for Reducing Recidivism and Promoting Recovery", Council of State Governments Justice Center Criminal Justice/Mental Health Consensus Project, 2012. https://csgjusticecenter.org/wp-content/uploads/2013/05/9-24-12_Behavioral-Health-Framework-final.pdf

[5] "Joseph Spector, "New York Eyes Reforms after Dannemora Escape" Press and Sun Bulletin, June 29, 2015. http://www.pressconnects.com/story/news/local/new-york/2015/06/29/new-york-prison-reforms/29481501/

[6] Tom Robbins, *Attica's Ghosts*, https://www.themarshallproject.org/2015/02/28/attica-s-ghosts#.zYc7UsQFQ

GUARDS IMPRISONED
Correctional Officers at Work
Second Edition

Lucien X. Lombardo

GUARDS IMPRISONED Correctional Officers at Work, Second Edition

ISBN 0-932930-79-4
Library of Congress Catalog Number 89-80456

Kelly Humble *Managing Editor*

Preface to First Edition

The purpose of this book is to provide the reader with an in-depth look into the work and working life of prison guards as they perceive and experience it. Beginning with some speculations about the relationship between large-scale prison violence and guard/inmate interactions, I soon discovered that little was known about the guard's perceptions of his "place" in the prison community. Therefore, I put aside my interest in the violence and set out to explore the dynamics of this key correctional occupation from the perspective of those whose job it is to guard the men who are confined in a maximum security prison.

As an exploratory study, this book is intended as a foundation for future investigations into the guard's role in the life of the prison community. In defining the boundaries and shape of the work and by describing what is important and problematic to some of those who perform it, I hope to raise new questions as well as provide tentative answers to some old ones.

One hundred sixty hours of interviews provide my raw data, but these discussions were interpreted through personal experiences and observations. As a teacher in the Osborne School at Auburn Prison, I had the opportunity to observe guards as an "insider" and to experience much of what the guards experience. Though this book is in no way autobiographical, its organization and structural framework are derived in part from my personal sense of the order in which the experience of working in prison is itself experienced. Thus, the order in which topics are presented is intended to provide a sort of "natural history" of prison guards as workers: from their prerecruitment images of the prison to their search for satisfaction as experienced guards.

One personal bias that underlies this study must be mentioned. My basic perspective is essentially a humanistic one. I view the prison guards, not as guards or correctors, but simply as people—people coping with the trials and tribulations of their occupations, deriving satisfactions and struggling to stay above water. In these everyday struggles there is no drama, no mythical heroes or villains, simply people in situations, people who are real, not abstractions.

If I learned one overarching lesson from writing this book and from working at Auburn, it is that public policy debates concerning rehabilitation and just deserts, treatment and punishment—while important—tend to obscure the reality of prisons as places where people live and work. It is my hope that this book will help draw the focus of policy to the more immediate human concerns that dominate the life of prisons, and in the process contribute to bettering the lot of the incarcerated and their keepers.

By way of acknowledgment, I wish to thank the officers of Auburn Correctional Facility for their time and patience. Members of the New York State Department of Correctional Services and Auburn's Superintendent, Robert J.

Henderson, also deserve special thanks for their generous cooperation in providing access to the officers and other relevant information.

I owe a special debt of gratitude to Professor Hans Toch whose gentle guidance allowed me to pursue this research in an independent fashion and whose attention to detail and insightful observations helped me clarify what I had discovered. Professors Donald J. Newman and Marguerite Warren of the School of Criminal Justice, SUNY, Albany, also provided valuable assistance when I tended to give a topic less attention than it deserved. The assistance of Jo Anne DeSilva, who typed, edited and otherwise handled early drafts of the book, was invaluable. My colleagues and the staff at Old Dominion University also provided much needed support, especially Judy Silver, who struggled with my handwriting, spelling and punctuation to produce a readable final draft. Finally, I wish to thank my mother, brother and sister for their understanding when I would demand quiet—and my father for his constant inspiration.

Preface to Second Edition

This Second Edition of *Guards Imprisoned* updates the original study by following the careers and impressions of the officers whose experiences and insights in 1976 provided the raw material for the First Edition. Interviewing the same officers again after ten years provided an opportunity to assess patterns of change and stability in the attitudes and behaviors of these men. It allowed them to describe what changes in their working environment they believe have had an impact on what they do and the ways they do it. It also provided an opportunity to learn how they have responded to changes in the Department of Corrections and at Auburn Correctional Facility. In the original interviews it was apparent that the "past was better" for many officers, but one did not have any way of knowing about that past. In studying the 1986 interviews, the 1976 material in the first edition provides a clear baseline for understanding their views of their present situation and change, for now we know what the past was like.

Such longitudinal information allows us to gain insight into the correctional policy implementation process and the ways in which new developments become transformed and transform the day-to-day operational world of the correctional officer. In addition, we see how generational changes in the correctional officer corps and the inmate population and culture project themselves into the working life of the men who staff the prison. Perhaps more importantly, we can reflect with these men on their careers and the impact their work has had on them.

Data for this update comes from 60 hours spent interviewing 17 of the original officers, some of whom had retired (3 of 11), been promoted to sergeant (3 of 11), or who have remained as correctional officers (11 of 31), some on the same job assignments (5 of 37 responding to questionnaires or interviews). In addition, 15 hours were spent interviewing 5 officers who were hired since the original study (officers with less than ten years' experience). Their perspective provides some insight into the process of generational integration into a correctional officer subculture. Though it would have been ideal to have interviewed *all* of the officers in the original sample, time limitations (only 2 months rather than the year it took to complete the original interviews) made this impossible. Though this smaller sample size may limit the nuances of perception that might have been provided by the larger group, I believe the consistency found in the responses of the reinterviewed officers portrays the basic reality of the correctional officer's working life as it has changed over ten years at Auburn. In any event, I was attempting to assess the collective experience of organizational change rather than individual change.

What I have tried to do in this second edition is to describe how these officers perceived their work in 1986. In the process, I will describe changes perceived by the officers and the ways they see these changes having an impact on their work. In the present edition, the original 1981 edition has been kept intact and new material has been added to the end of each chapter to portray the experience of change.

From this research I have learned that correctional institutions and correctional officer work and work environment does change and can be changed for the better. These officers tell us how structural and procedural organizational change affects people's conceptions of their work and the ways they do it. General change in the expectations and dynamics of officer/inmate and officer/officer relations is documented. We also see how changes in the inmates' environment have an impact on officer work strategies and how changes in administrative communication and recognition practices can improve officers' identification with their work in positive ways.

However, as I see some better conditions for correctional officers, I can only wonder how these changes are being experienced by inmates. From the data collected on rule violations, it appears that Auburn is certainly a more dangerous place for inmates than it was in 1976. It is clear to me that the lack of contact with the inmates' world (something I had in 1976 when I was a teacher at Auburn) regrettably leaves out an important part of the overall institutional picture.

Once again, I would like to thank the officers of Auburn Correctional Facility for their cooperation and time; Robert L. Henderson and his administrative staff for their assistance and access to data and space to work. As always, the spectre of Hans Toch leaning over my shoulder has provided a useful stream of questions and perspectives and must be acknowledged. Also thanks to my colleagues Steve Light and Janet Katz for the time they devoted to discussing this research and to Frank Cullen and Rob Johnson for their interest and support. Debra Laufersweiler who conducted an analysis of rule violation data and Jon Dorman who reviewed recent correctional officer literature were of great assistance. Ilona Tonelson's assistance in preparing the new manuscript was invaluable. I also wish to thank especially Betty and John Lombardo for their assistance in coding and learning about the world of Auburn Prison and for their constant support and patience. Also Old Dominion University, which supported this research with a University Faculty Summer Research Fellowship, deserves special mention.

Foreword

"Stone walls," we proclaim, "do not a prison make." The adage is a half-truth, of course, unless it is translated. The principle only holds if we mean that an institution can be a convincing prison without being architecturally obvious about it, or that the human climate of a prison is more critical than its physical attributes. But walls *do* define a prison in the sense that a prison is an insulated, circumscribed world. This means not only that prisons are a world unto themselves, but that most of us are effectively closed off from this world.

The wall that separates us from prisoners has occasionally been breached, but Lombardo's book may be the first opportunity that is furnished us to enter the world of imprisoned staff. The experience Lombardo offers us contains real surprises. In fact, the book is an embarrassment to a generation of us.

In retrospect, what becomes clear is that guards have suffered from two idiosyncrasies of prison experts: One is our practice of always viewing prison staff through inmates' eyes; the other involves filtering through, and projection of, pet theories, which yield fashionable caricatures such as Guards as Corrupt Wielders of Power, Guards as Police Surrogates, Guards as Agents of Custody Goals, Guards as Enemies of Inmates, Guards as Enemies of Progress and Guards as Members of a Subculture. (Professors who originate such stereotypes have been similarly described by unfriendly observers, but social science has never been played by the golden rule.)

What makes Lombardo's work better than previous studies of prison guards? Why do I accord him clarity of vision not given his predecessors? The answer is partly simple and partly complex. The simple answer is, "He talked to the guards." Unlike most prison students, Lombardo let correction officers describe themselves, their work and their world. He went among the officers, won their confidence, sought their perceptions and thoughts, their expectations and observations, concerns, worries and feelings. He explored matters that meant a great deal to the officers but about which no one had asked them before. The officers responded to Lombardo's interest by being unsurprisingly forthcoming. Also in retrospect unsurprisingly, they proved themselves aware, involved, eloquent, thoughtful, observant and honest.

If there is an "average guard," Lombardo's informants were probably reasonably average. Officers differ, of course: Some are more educated, some less so; some hail from farms, others from factories. Prisons also differ, and Lombardo's prison (Auburn) is more progressive than most. But when it comes to essentials such as officer background (working class), job assignments (diverse) and basic mission (ambiguous), Lombardo's officers resemble most prison guards in the United States and abroad.

On a complex level, the question "What makes Lombardo's book better?" is more subtle. We must consider the following facts:

1. Lombardo is a long-term prison worker and was an insider-outsider. What I mean is that this book belongs among studies in the social sciences done by men and women who could almost qualify as their own subjects. Such studies are always more true-to-life and, when they are good, offer sharper insights and greater depth. This is the case because membership in a milieu—as opposed to tourism or hit-and-run visits— sharpens perceptions. The insider-outsider hears more: He speaks language colloquially and responds to overtones and undercurrents in the milieu, whereas the outsider chases appearances and must have everything spelled out.
2. Lombardo's inquiry was exploratory. Good exploratory research combines humility—the realization that there is something to be learned that one does not know—with maturity—the willingness to inquire, listen and learn. Exploration minimizes bias: The people we talk to are not guided by our approving smiles when they happen to confirm our hypotheses, or by our frowns in response to the "wrong" answers. More importantly, our analysis is less jacketed by pre-existing categories whose fit may be restrained.
3. Lombardo's portrait of prison guards is traced with sensitivity to human individuality and diversity. As past officer-stereotypes are discarded, no new ones emerge. Rather, the correctional officers—like other categories of humanity—are ordinary people whom we see as differing from each other in their goals, values, predilections and views of their jobs. They vaguely share a common fate, but it is a fate with substantial and meaningful variations occasioned by personality and environment. The composite of such human variations makes up the world of the guard—a world just as complex as that of the inmate, or— for that matter—that of academia.

A book on correctional officers is inevitably a timely book, and a *good* book on correctional officers, such as Professor Lombardo's, is an *important* book. Fewer occupational groups in our society are more maligned than that of the guards; fewer are faced with more difficult challenges and are more misunderstood, mismanaged and alienated. The officer's job is *grossly* mislabeled: The officer has much room for exercising his judgment, but is nominally militarily constrained; he deals with urgent and manifold inmate needs, but is officially charged with standing and watching, escorting and waiting, opening and closing prison gates;

he solves problems and dispenses justice, but is seen as administering punishment; he serves the oppressed, and is seen as oppressor. In doing work, theofficer faces all sorts of obstacles and obtains few rewards. And while the officer is enjoined to be "professional," it is implied that he is much too undereducated, unsophisticated and biased to rise to the challenge.

The need to ponder the officer's fate—a fate that is convincingly documented in Lombardo's pages—is just as urgent as the need for reforming inmate life. It is ironic that while assembly line workers today are charged with planning and rethinking their work, correctional officers—whose assignments are infinitely more complicated—are treated in Stone Age management terms. It is also ironic that civilian prison staff are classified as "helpers," whereas officers—who do most of the helping in prisons—are categorized as "custodial." It is even more ironic that when officers demand a meaningful role in the correctional enterprise (or some organizational support for the roles they already play) we mistake their demand for a reactionary desire to regain irresponsible dominance and power.

The title of this book is no hyperbole. Prison guards are truly imprisoned: They are not only physically confined but are locked into movie caricatures, into pejorative prophecies (sometimes self-fulfilling), into anachronistic supervision patterns, into unfair civil service definitions, into undeserved hostilities and prejudgments of their actions. Officers are imprisoned by our ignorance of who they are and what they do, which is the price they pay for working behind walls, a price that officers need not pay because observers like Professor Lombardo can free them from the burdens of our ignorance. The rest is up to the readers of this book, especially those who are active in public life and who, after hearing the testimony of these guards, may devise ways of improving their conditions and enhancing their dignity. To "professionalize" prison guards does more than ameliorate their fate. It makes prisons more fair, safe and humane for the inmates, and reflects favorably on us as a civilized nation.

Hans Toch

Table of Contents

Exploring the Work and Work World of Prison Guards: Perspectives and Processes

1

One of the most curious features of the whole history of modern imprisonment is the way the custodial officer, the key figure in the penal equation, the man on whom the whole edifice of the penitentiary depends, has with astonishing consistency either been ignored or traduced or idealized but almost never considered seriously.

Gordon Hawkins
The Prison: Policy and Practice, *p. 105*

There is no dearth of literature on the inmate. Academicians for the last generation have been fascinated with the discovery of inmate types, cultures and more recently, inmate political groups. However, precious little is known about the guard himself.

David Fogel
"...We are the Living Proof...," *p. 70*

Why has the guard been ignored for so long? Hawkins says that it may be because criminologists have tended to rely on reports of inmates to discuss guards and Fogel suggests that it is because guards do not write books. I suspect, however, that it is because researchers have often felt the guard to be "unapproachable." It may be that those of us interested in the community life of prisons can more easily identify with the prisoner. At times, I am sure, we all feel that our lives are "like living in prison." We feel confined and controlled by bureaucratic rules and regulations. We face anonymity and alienation in our daily lives. Few of us, however, readily identify with the "controller." We feel uncomfortable with power and have a difficult time understanding those we believe wield power. We generally do not speak the same language as the controller. This inability or lack of desire to understand the guard from the guard's perspective may, in part, account for the lack of substantive knowledge about prison guards and their work.

With these observations in mind, Chapter 1 describes my approach to the prison's controllers, the prison guards. I describe my perspectives, research processes and special considerations and try to show that the guard is indeed approachable and his perspectives understandable.

HISTORICAL PERSPECTIVES ON THE GUARD'S* WORK

Historically, the name given to the correction officer has always been rich in metaphor, a metaphor often varying with the purpose ascribed to the institution within which the officer carried out his duties. Early in prison history the correction officer was known as a "watchman," whose role was similar to that of his early policeman counterpart.

> One or more of them shall patrol the yard, carefully examining every portion of it in the course of their rounds; see that all is safe; and should necessity require it, they shall, upon any emergency, apprise the night overseers.[1]

This early "watchman" watched for breaches of the peace in institutions where corrupted inmates could find the peace, tranquility and order necessary to restore them to their precorrupt state.[2]

"Keeper" was another name given to the early correction officer. The "keeper" was literally the "keeper of the keys," which was considered a significant task:

> Every night they have in charge the keys of the whole institution; and upon their watchfulness depends its safety, from fire, from nocturnal incursions of discharged convicts, or daring villains from without.[3]

For those of a religious bent the "keeper" was "his brother's keeper":

> But the improvement in the character of the subordinate officers is extensive and important; and we trust the time is not distant, when a man must possess an established character, to be concerned even as an underkeeper in keeping his fellowmen.[4]

When the early correction officer was viewed as playing a more active part in enforcing the institution's discipline, not merely maintaining by his presence and watchfulness the order established by the prison's structure, a military metaphor was adopted. He was called subordinate officer or guard. An 1868 New York Report thus disapprovingly notes that "A military or naval officer who has to deal with a refractory prisoner, will probably consider it his duty to break the man's spirit by punishment."[5]

Though the term "keeper," referring to correction officer, survived in some areas into the 20th century, the terms guard and prison officer were gradually

*I refer to both guards and correction officers throughout this book. The men who do the work refer to themselves by both titles and when I change from one title to the other I do so to reflect the most "natural" title in a particular context.

replaced by the term "correctional officer" during the struggle for "professionalization" in corrections. With the advent of professionalization, custodial personnel were generally lumped together in a group called the "correctional workers" or "correctional staff." Professionalization and civil service status were urged to remove "politics" from correctional personnel selection.

In the 1920s the "profession of corrections" was a mixture of religion, medicine and education. One observer described the prison official as "...a moral instructor, the oracle of justice; a teacher in ethics."[6] Those working in corrections were professionals by analogy: Their work involved "curing the criminal" as a doctor (a professional) cured his patients. The occupational boundaries of this emerging profession are difficult to trace; however, in the mind of at least one observer, they included criminologists, wardens, prison chaplain, doctors and dentists, social workers, the eye, ear and nose specialists, psychiatrists and an amorphous staff.[7] It seems that anyone who dealt with prisoners or the institutions fell into the "correctional profession."

In the 1950s the debate surrounding correctional personnel and their status as professionals or amateurs was still alive. A. A. Evans observed:

> The core of the correctional tasks—changing human behavior through modifying attitude—influences every decision and action of employees and staff in this work.
>
> Those who "...possess professional skill in working with others, whether this skill is inherent in his personality, brought to the position from other experience or acquired by training and development on the job," ...were professionals.[8]

Professionals were men who gained status by comparison to those who imposed "Prussian discipline, orderliness, and mass subordination."[9] The latter were "amateurs."

In the late 1960s the President's Commission Task Force on Corrections drew a distinction between professional and non-professional correctional functions. Correction officers' duties appeared to fall into the latter category, because officers were not directly involved in the "professional treatment" aspects of correctional programming. Correction officers were seen as custodial personnel, who "man the walls, supervise living units, escort inmates to and from work and supervise all group movement in the institutions."[10]

A "Work" Perspective

In these historical descriptions the guard force is unidimensional, with all guards following the party line prescribed in their job title and job description. Although a title, job description and workplace may serve to identify an occupation, these general characteristics are incapable of capturing the diversity, subtleties and shades of meaning represented in the occupations of individual practitioners. My colleagues and I are professors. We teach, perform research and otherwise serve the university community, but there the similarity ends. Each of us shapes his tasks, priorities and techniques out of the raw materials of individual interests, students, books and university resources. The same might be said for those who perform any other occupation in any setting. The same might be said of prison guards.

I employ this approach to the prison guards' work for three reasons. First, it allows a useful and convenient framework for analysis. It allows a focus upon the *person* of the guard, a person capable of standing alongside others who work for a living. Viewing the guard as a "worker," I assume that he is an ordinary person, living an ordinary life, different from his fellows only in his work.

Secondly, a work perspective makes it unnecessary to adopt an ideological position on correctional policy. In conducting this research, I did not want to decide beforehand that guards *should be* "change agents" or "correctors" or mere custodians. I wanted to permit the guards to define themselves. In the approach adopted here, preclassifications reflective of correctional policy choices become only one factor among many that enter into the complex equation that organizes the forces which shape the reality of the individual prison guard's work experience.

Finally, a "work" perspective draws attention to the need to explore the impact of the "work environment" on the individual. Whether this impact results in satisfaction, dissatisfaction or stress, its relationship to worker morale and behavior is important to describe the development of knowledge concerning the guard's attempts to cope with the prison environment. This emerges as significant information capable of adding to our understanding of the life of the prison community.

The work perspective employed here is an interactionist perspective. I assume that the guard is an active participant in prison life, an individual interacting with his tasks, inmates, fellow officers and administrators, as well as his own needs and desires. By exploring these diverse interactions, I expected a realistic portrait of the prison guard to emerge.

VIEWS OF CORRECTIONS OFFICERS IN THE PRISON COMMUNITY[11]

Many studies of correctional institutions deal with the correction officer in terms of his social role in the prison community vis-à-vis inmates and the "treatment staff." Here it is the characteristics of a vaguely defined group, not the individuals' unique ways of performing their roles, that are presumed to matter. Sykes writes about the "Regime of the Custodians" as if all guards played the same role in that regime.[12] Sykes also describes the "Defects of Total Power" and points out that reciprocal relations between guards and inmates add to the corruption of the guard's authority.[13]

Cressy examines the administrative context in which the guard works and describes officer responses to contradictory administrative directives. Guards are told to get the most discipline with the least friction and, according to Cressey, they respond by becoming apathetic, deliberately concealing inmate misconduct or engaging in misconduct themselves.[14]

A more systematic approach to describing correctional workers is provided by Hall, Williams and Tomiano. This approach redefines the guard as a "change agent." Utilizing a managerial grid, they describe five categories of "change agent," whose characteristics are determined by the degree to which they concern themselves with "commitment" and "conformity" on the part of the target" of change.[15]

Matheisen draws on his own observations and inmate perceptions of guards to identify four types of officers: "the persistent guard," the "good guard," the "kind guard" and the "weak guard."[16]

These attempts to describe alternative approaches to the prison guard's job have relied on either unsystematic observations or inmate impressions of guard behavior (Sykes, Cressey and Matheisen) or have assumed the ideal-type work goals which may or may not be those of the officers themselves (Hall, Williams and Tomiano). However, underlying all of these descriptions is the officer's approach to the enforcement of institutional rules and attempts at maintaining discipline. A second feature is their focus upon how officers personally relate to inmates. Here we find "good guys" who care, "bad guys" who let inmates know they do not care and the "apathetic" who act as indifferently as circumstances allow.

These analyses of correction officer work behavior also generally fail to allow for any internal motivation on the part of the guard. Here the officer is a non-actor, moved to behave as he does only by the corrupting influence of inmates, the conflicting directions of administrators and the conflicting demands of his role.

THE GUARD AS "PEOPLE WORKER" AND "BUREAUCRAT"

By viewing the prison guard as a worker, the "custodian" versus "treater," "professional" versus "amateur," debates recede into the background and more general perspectives that relate individuals to their work can be applied. In developing substantive areas for research, two theoretical perspectives were most fruitful sources of ideas: Goffman's concept of "people work"[17] and Merton's description of the "bureaucrat."[18] As "people worker" the guard must cope with the statuses and relationships with which inmates come to prison, and he develops human feelings toward those in charge. These aspects of "people work" force guards to deal with the human problems of inmates on a personal level. "People work" also involves finding ways to obtain inmate compliance with officer and institutional directives. As rule enforcer or supervisor, the guard interacts with inmates not only as an individual but as the institution's and society's symbol of authority as well.

The guard also functions as a member of a complex, bureaucratic organization and thus performs "bureaucratic work" as well. In terms of his relationships with clients this means the guard should provide impersonal and stereotyped responses to individual problems, adhering strictly to formal procedures. Thus, while the officer's "people work" role involves treating inmates individually, his official bureaucratic role pulls him in the opposite direction. By viewing the guard as a bureaucrat, the dynamics of his relationship to the prison organization for which he works become an important concern. Here Katz's and Kahn's description of the "role taking" process in complex organizations proved most helpful in focusing my research and in drawing my attention to the multiplicity of forces at work on individual workers.[19]

These two perspectives of the correction officer as worker are tied together by the changing ideological currents of politics and society which affect the goals and procedures of the criminal justice system.[20] Thus the correction officer works in an organization whose place in the "proper scheme of things" is constantly subject to redefinition. With these perspectives in mind, my inquiry was designed with the following specific objectives:

1. to explore the shape of the prison guards' tasks as they experience and perform them;
2. to explore the dynamics of correction officer—inmate relations, giving particular attention to rule enforcement situations and personal relationships between officers and inmates (Here, the officer's experience of authority and social distance would receive special emphasis.);
3. to discover those aspects of their work which correction officers find dissatisfying (Here, techniques for coping with these problems would be particularly important.);
4. to describe those aspects of their work from which prison guards derive satisfaction;
5. to discover the dynamics of correction officer "group" relationships, how guards relate to and deal with one another;
6. to shed some light on how selected aspects of the correction officers' work experience interact.

SELECTING A RESEARCH SITE

This book is based on the results of an experience survey conducted with a sample of correction officers drawn from one maximum security institution, New York State's Auburn Correctional Facility (see Appendix E for a discussion of sampling procedures). To the extent that the "unique" characteristics of an individual maximum security institution (the number of inmate programs available, the management approach of the superintendent, the age, racial composition and turnover in the inmate populations, etc.) provide a "unique" context within which correction officers work, it presents findings that do not apply elsewhere. However, if the general perspective and methods employed are judged successful in enhancing our understanding of prison guards and the place of the guard in the prison community, the "work perspective" employed here may have more general applicability.

Auburn Correctional Facility was chosen as a research site because of its accessibility over a period of time and the likelihood that cooperation from all concerned could be obtained. I had served as a teacher in the prison school from 1969 to 1972 and again from 1974 to 1977, the years during which this research was conducted. As an employee, I had opportunities to observe and experience officer behavior in a natural setting, minimizing any tendency officers might have had to "put on an act" for an "outside" researcher. Even while research was being conducted at the institution, I was a fellow employee, not a researcher. Although I did not disguise the fact that I was conducting a survey of prison guards, I made no attempt to heighten the visibility of my research activities. The progress of the research was discussed at the institution only at the initiation of an interested officer, and only in general terms. That the officers did not know I was a graduate student became evident when a guard who worked in the school met me at a newsstand two weeks before I was to return to my teaching duties after a two-year absence. He remarked, "Hey, I haven't seen you in a while, been sick?" It wasn't until I had nearly completed the research that the inmates discovered my second life. This occurred when another researcher commented to one of my classes about what I was doing.

The fact that I was known to the departmental staff and institutional personnel at Auburn enhanced the cooperation of those involved in the study. At the state level the deputy commissioner for security and the deputy commissioner for research and evaluation responded favorably to my initial proposals and the superintendent at Auburn provided much valuable assistance. The officer serving as the state vice-president of the correction officers' union and president of the local chapter contacted all officers at the institution, requesting their cooperation. Only these men knew what part my "insider" status played in their decisions to support my research efforts.

Timing of the Research

Since the overall goal of my research was to explore the day-to-day attitudes and behaviors of correction officers, I hoped that I could do so during a period of relative institutional "normalcy." Having observed correction officer behavior and attitudes both during contract negotiations and before and after incidents of large-scale violence, I felt that the occurrence of either situation during the interview period would distract the officers from their everyday work world and thus contaminate the nature of their responses. Luckily 1976 was not a contract-negotiation year, thus avoiding an increase in the saliency of contract-related issues in the minds of officers. Although prison riots were beyond my control, I was fortunate that 1976 saw no major incidents at Auburn or any other of New York State's correctional institutions. I was thus able to study prison guards during a time when officers had to contend only with those situations they "normally" encountered in their work.

Auburn Correctional Facility

Auburn Correctional Facility, a maximum security institution administered by the New York State Department of Correctional Services, is a 160-year-old institution that has figured prominently in the history of corrections, a history not lost on the institutional staff. Centrally located in a community of 35,000 people, the prison has lent its name to the "Auburn system" of congregate labor and segregated housing that developed in the early 1800s and it provided the site of the world's first death penalty electrocution in 1890. Auburn prison also served as the training ground for Thomas Mott Osborne, the well-known prison reformer of the early 1900s. In 1929 Auburn Prison experienced two major riots which claimed the lives of 11 inmates and the prison's principal keeper. In 1970, a year before the Attica experience, the institution experienced another major disturbance in which many of the officers who participated in this study, as well as the author, were involved.

The prison is built on approximately 25 acres of land, and inside its 30-foot walls it is divided into two sections. In front, a central recreation yard is bounded to the north and south by cell blocks, to the east by the prison's administration building dating from 1940, and to the west by the kitchens, mess halls and an auditorium first used in 1936. Inside the main recreation yard, adjacent to the administration building, is a relatively new structure housing a Media Center—Gymnasium complex which was completed in 1971. The western half of the institution houses the prison's industrial shops and the school. Behind the southern cell block is a second inmate recreation area which contains facilities for weight lifting, handball and a miniature golf course.

Auburn has been designated a "transfer" facility; that is, it generally does not receive inmates directly from the courts. Rather, inmates are assigned to Auburn only after they have served part of their sentences in other state facilities. The institution generally houses between 1,500 and 1,600 inmates, with an average ethnic distribution of 60% black, 30% white and 10% of Latin American origin. The majority of the prisoners come from the New York City area and other large metropolitan areas, though there are also a number from the state's rural regions.

For many years the turnover rate in the inmate population was relatively low—according to some estimates in the neighborhood of 15-25% per year. However, in recent years the state's expanded use of medium and minimum security facilities for adults has increased turnover substantially, to approximately 75-80% for 1976, the year in which my research activities took place.

The most significant characteristic of the institution is its heavy emphasis on inmate programming. The day school program offers academic courses for students from the primary grade level through high school and vocational training in a variety of trade-related areas. Evening educational programs were begun in 1971, offering similar courses for inmates who are unable to attend day school, as well as college courses and "special subjects." A neighboring university provides a full-time college program to selected inmates. These educational programs involved over 700 inmates at the time of this study.

Industrial training at the facility includes five areas of production: license plate manufacture, furniture, metal fabrication, silk screening and auto body repair. These programs generally occupy 450 to 500 men.

In addition, inmates are actively involved in the Logan JC's (the first Junior Chamber of Commerce chapter chartered in a New York State correctional institution), the NAACP, religious groups (such as the Quakers and various Muslim sects) and other groups who participate in weekly programming on a volunteer basis.

The inmate-elected Inmate Liaison Committee regularly meets with the prison administration to offer suggestions for improving institutional policy and procedures. In addition, inmates have an opportunity to influence policy through the use of an Inmate Grievance Committee, put into effect January 1976, as this study began. The Committee consists of two inmates who are elected by the inmate population, two staff members (either officers or civilians appointed by the superintendent) and a chairman (either an inmate or staff) selected by the Committee from a list of submitted names. This committee hears complaints covering all facets of institutional life, and its decisions are appealable to the institutional superintendent, the department's commission and, ultimately, to an independent State Commission on Corrections.

Other inmate activities include family visits and furlough programs. A large number of inmate-organized cultural events are annually sponsored by various ethnic groups, and involve the participation of members of the noninstitutional community and inmate families.

The Officers at Auburn

When this research began, there were 359 correction officers at Auburn. Of these, approximately 290 were on active assignments on any given day, the remainder being on vacation or having regular days off. The men work eight-hour shifts, beginning at 6:50, 7:10, 8:00, 9:00 and 10:00 a.m. and at 3:00 and 11:00 p.m. The officers are supervised by 19 sergeants and seven lieutenants. The supervisors report to two captains, and the entire custodial staff is the responsibility of the institution's deputy superintendent for security. Officer work assignments are often self-selected, in that officers with sufficient experience are able to "bid" on jobs as they become vacant. (This bidding system was put into effect in 1970. Prior to 1970, officers were assigned work locations by administrative personnel.)

All but three of the officers at Auburn belong to the correction officers' union, which represents them and correction officers throughout the state in contract negotiations, labor management meetings and in grievances against the local correctional administration and the state. The Auburn chapter is generally considered one of the more militant chapters of those operating in New York State's correctional institutions, having engaged in picketing activities designed to gain public recognition for their concerns and, in 1970, holding a two-day strike in violation of state law prohibiting public employee strikes. Officers at Auburn dress in standardized nonmilitary apparel. They wear blazers during months appropriate to the weather, or jackets, making them look like "bus drivers." They carry no paraphernalia associated with police work such as night sticks, guns or handcuffs. They enter the institution without the trappings usually associated with police-style authority.

Auburn has been a relatively stable prison in terms of its correction officer corps, as well as its inmate population. Turnover in staff is generally low, only 7.6% for 1976, the year in which this research was conducted. The stability among the inmate and staff populations is important, indicating that both inmates and officers have a larger stake at coming to terms with their environment and each other than at institutions where the turnover of both staff and inmates is relatively high.

Finding Officers to Talk

Given the nature of my research questions, I wanted to maximize the variety of work experiences to be found among the men I might interview. To do this, length of service as an officer and job assignment within the institution were the primary criteria utilized in selecting officers with whom I would talk. Selecting a sample was relatively easy (see Appendix E for a discussion of sampling techniques), but getting to talk to those selected was a complicated, time-consuming and tedious process. In January the president of the local union sent a letter at my request introducing me to all the officers at the institution, requesting officer cooperation (see Appendix A). This letter was sent to "break the ice," informing officers that "something was going on" should they be selected for an interview.

In April I sent a letter to each officer in the original sample of 52, plus an additional 20 officers most likely to be contacted should substitutions be needed, explaining the nature of the research, requesting participation and the most appropriate time and location for an interview (see Appendix B). After three weeks only three offices responded. Since this procedure required the officer to respond actively, a high rate of return was not anticipated. During my tenure as a prison teacher I had frequently seen requests for information ignored. However, I felt that this letter would give subsequent contacts a basis from which to proceed. Failing to get responses to my letter, I proceeded to contact officers individually, either in person during working hours or by phone.

To reduce feelings of "being pressured into something" and to minimize the number of refusals from the original sample, those officers who could not agree on a time for an interview were contacted only once every two or three weeks. I maintained this nonthreatening and nonpushy attitude to avoid alienating the entire officer population, thus threatening the entire research project by alienating just *one* officer. This process continued until a total of 50 officers were interviewed. These officers represented approximately 15% of the entire complement of officers at Auburn. They had from two to 30 years experience and represented every institutional job assignment (see Tables 1 and 2, Appendix D for distribution and comparisons with the entire population of officers at Auburn).

In all, only 13 of the 52 officers originally selected were not interviewed. Some of the nonparticipants said that they held negative attitudes toward their work and did not want to discuss it. As one officer bluntly told me, "I don't have any regard for the job. I never did and I don't want to talk about it." Others were "retreatists" who generally "didn't get involved" either in correction officer activities or with inmates (three worked in the administration building, away from the inmates). A third group of six officers was "too busy" with outside activities. Repeatedly frustrated by failure to "find the time for an interview," they requested that I contact someone else.

The Interview Process

All interviews were conducted outside the prison, usually in my home or in that of the officer. Noninstitutional settings were chosen to provide a relaxed atmosphere and to avoid "institutional contamination" that makes trivial questions seem more irritating or important than they are. The interviews averaged two and one-half hours. The intensity of the experience caused me to schedule not more than three interviews during any one week. I limited myself to this number to avoid developing "interviewer's fatigue," which might be interpreted as a sign of lack of interest and an excuse for noncooperation.

Note-taking served as an effective method of preserving officer responses for later analysis. When an officer's reply outpaced my ability to write, the officer reacted by slowing or repeating his replies, often with greater introspection.[21]

In constructing the interview schedule (see Appendix C) and in carrying out the interviews themselves, I constantly kept in mind the idea that interviews are a social process, involving not only the purposes of the researcher, but also the meanings and purposes brought to the interactions by the officers.[22]

Questions on the "Background Data Sheet" were intended not only to elicit information, but also to "anchor" the interview subject in the "work-oriented" nature of the inquiry. The items "number of weeks training before put on the job" and "previous job assignments" were designed to allow the officer to think back to the beginnings of his career and to remove his focus from specific "gripes" of the moment. Items asking for "preferred job" and "preferred shift" were intended to start the officer thinking about "what his work means to him." Following the completion of the Background Data Sheet, issues of recruitment and initial expectations were explored to encourage the officer to perceive the interview as a discussion of his "personal history" as an officer and the meaning of that history to him.

Next, each interview subject was asked to describe his work, talking about inmate behavior and the difficulties and problems associated with the job. In this way I hoped to bring up issues that would be examined more directly later. Following this introductory material, general job satisfaction themes were explored and specific areas associated with job satisfaction were examined. Upon completing our inquiry into job satisfaction, the officer was then informed that the discussion would shift to the "bad things" about the job, things found "dissatisfying." Upon hearing this, many officers remarked, "I thought we just did that," and laughed.

As with job satisfaction, officers were first asked open-ended questions, allowing them to indicate which issues were most problematic with their perspective. Specific issues often associated with job dissatisfaction were explored in turn.

Our interview next focused on two "work behaviors" that are most often associated with the correction officer's work: rule enforcement and the handling of inmate problems.

Finally, interpersonal aspects of the correction officers' work were explored.

To provide closure for the interview, each officer was asked to describe his perceptions of the reactions of various "publics" to his work: his family, the general public and the inmates. He was also asked if he had any suggestions for improving the questionnaire.

To a greater degree than we originally anticipated, the interviews proceeded smoothly. Rapport with the officers was excellent in all cases. Many officers indicated their disbelief that their job was "interesting," commenting that the interview was a "learning experience" for them. Upon completing the interview phase of our research, each participating officer was contacted to acknowledge the significance of his contribution.

By employing content analysis, interview material dealing with individual questions was organized into categories broad enough to encompass the individual themes officers associated with their work, yet specific enough to provide meaningful distinctions. Though the material could be organized in a number of ways, the purpose of *describing the correction officer's work world as he experiences it* served as a guiding principle throughout.

Interview material was supplemented by data gathered from "The Daily Journal: A Daily Report of Every Infraction of the Rules and Regulations of the Facility by Officers and Inmates and Actions Taken in Each Case and Memorandum of Any Complaint by Inmates of Bad or Insufficient Food, Want of Clothing, or Cruel and Unjust Treatment by an Officer" (hereafter referred to as "The Daily Journal of Infractions"). From this source I obtained both the number and nature of infraction reports written by each officer interviewed.

EXPLORING CHANGE: 1986

New Perspectives

When I began in 1974 to plan the research which resulted in the first edition of this book, the literature on correctional officers was extremely sparse and perspectives on correctional officer work needed to be drawn from a variety of related sources. Even by 1979 when the preparation of the first edition manuscript was under way, academic interest in correctional officers was only beginning to surface. Now, however, many of the areas discussed in the first edition have received more detailed study. In a recent review of correctional officer literature, Philliber summarizes and analyzes what we know (from over 120 sources) about the characteristics of correctional officers and the relationship of these characteristics (education, gender, race, age, length of time on the job) to various work-related attitudes.[23] She describes recruitment practices, changes in task definition and strategies, role conflict and correctional officer subculture. While finding methodological weakness in much of the more quantitative research, she summarizes this literature by writing:

> One of the strengths of this literature is the degree to which it succeeds in giving its readers a strong "feel" and "gut-level knowledge" about CO's, their everyday work world, and the problems they face. Whereas other subdisciplines in the social sciences are replete with sophisticated statistics, this area might be congratulated on capturing the reality behind the numbers.[24]

In pointing to areas in need of exploration, Philliber identifies the need for longitudinal studies and studies emphasizing the environmental and organizational settings in which they take place. This second edition seeks to contribute to those areas. By emphasizing change, rather than time-bound description, new perspectives have been added to those of the original study to make the picture of officer working life over time more complete.

In his classic historical-sociological-institutional study of Stateville, Jacobs[25] provides a fascinating picture of the ways outside social and political forces affect and transform the "prison community." In describing the "transition of the guard force"[26] Jacobs demonstrates how a "professional reform" administration, the racial integration of the guard force and the introduction of public employee unionism altered the social organization and interaction among Stateville's staff and between the staff, the administration, and the inmates.

In a much more limited way, this edition of *Guards Imprisoned* attempts to describe in detail the forces and conditions and events that have had an impact on the attitudes, perceptions and behaviors of officer corps at Auburn. Though the time frame and location are certainly different, Jacobs' work was extremely important in drawing my attention to social, political and ideological forces which were reflected in the data provided in my interviews. Such forces include the now-direct impact of the state bureaucracy on officer behavior and their attitudes toward prison administration; the impact of education, training and attitudes toward work affecting intergenerational relationships among officers; and changes in the relative importance of ethnic identity and local community ties as factors in the structuring of correctional officer peer group relations.

In addition, Gareth Morgan's *Images of Organization*[27] provides a wide variety of perspectives for interpreting and understanding the organizational implications of the ten years of collective correctional officer experience. In particular, his discussion of "organization as flux and transformation"[28] draws attention to the ways organizations transform their environments to maintain their historical identities.[29] This perspective helps us to understand how correctional officers change their self-definitions of their tasks, their perceptions of their role in the correctional system, and their definition of the unique character of Auburn Prison. It also helps us to understand how officers incorporate these changing interpretations of salient forces in the external environment into the context of their working lives.

Morgan also highlights the importance of understanding mutual causality and positive and negative feedback[30] in organizational change. Information processing and communication characteristics of organizations help determine the direction of change and the degree to which change is accepted. This perspective helps in understanding how correctional officer relations with inmates, implementation by and adaptation of officers to new rule-enforcement practices, a variety of new policy and procedures and improved communication, involvement, and opportunities for recognition are influenced by previously successful or failed experiences with change. *Thus, the cumulative impact of all of these changes becomes important to understand and not simply the individual episodes of change.*

Changes at Auburn Correctional Facility 1976-1986

During the ten years that passed much about Auburn Correctional Facility has remained the same. Auburn remains a maximum security transfer institution whose tradition of being a program intensive institution has remained intact. Many of the programs that existed in 1976 have been expanded and some new programs have been added. The yard is now open until 10:30 p.m.; a weekend family visiting program (including conjugal visits in trailers inside the walls of the institution) is available for inmates; unscheduled inmate access to telephones for collect calls is provided. Phones are in the yard, and in the library-gymnasium building, and are available to inmates whenever these areas are open.

Over the years, the average daily population of the institution has increased by about 100 inmates (from 1,572 inmates in 1976 to 1,673 in 1985). This increase was made possible when previously unused cell space was renovated to provide a new mental health unit within Auburn's walls during 1981. This level of increase is rather small when compared to the New York State total increase from 17,000 inmates in 1976 to nearly 41,000 in 1988. Inmates at Auburn are still housed in single cells and the impact in terms of population levels of the state-wide prisoner increase has been minimal. The ethnic and racial composition of the population has changed somewhat with 25% white, 54% black and 20% Hispanic in 1984. The age distribution reportedly has tended to lower the average mean age for the overall population.

Though Auburn still houses inmates with a wide variety of criminal histories, it now almost exclusively houses inmates with extremely high security classifications. This has resulted, for example, in the need to "import" inmates from nearby low security camps to do maintenance work around the perimeter of the facility.

Despite the rapid increase in the number and variety of New York State's correctional institutions, the inmate population turnover at Auburn has not varied a great deal over the past ten years (See Table 15, Appendix D) [between 12.2%/month in 1982 to 18.4%/month in 1977, with a mean of 14.6%/month for the ten years]. Reportedly these figures are a great deal higher than they were in the 1950s and 1960s.

The administration at Auburn has also remained fairly stable. Robert J. Henderson, who was named superintendent at Auburn in 1972 remains as Auburn's superintendent today. The organizational structure has been expanded over the years to include a new "super-deputy superintendent" in addition to the deputies for security, programs and administration.

Though the upper level administration has remained relatively constant, what has changed drastically, however, is the increase in middle level supervisory personnel. Where there were two captains, there are now three; 7 lieutenants have become 20; and 19 sergeants have become 35. Changes in the location and levels of responsibility of these supervisors have had a significant impact on the line-level officers.

The Officers at Auburn

While the administration of Auburn has changed very little, the size and composition of the officer corps at Auburn has changed drastically. An analysis of available seniority lists for the years 1976—1985 shows that the number of correctional officers has grown steadily from 357 in 1976 to 516 in 1985 (see Table 16, Appendix D). With this increase has come a dramatic shift in the experience distribution of the Auburn officers.

In 1976, 23% of the officers at Auburn had 19 or more years' experience; by 1985 that percentage had dropped to 13.5%. Change among the less experienced cadre was more dramatic. In 1976, only 19% of the officers had less than 6 years on the job. By 1985, that percentage had increased to nearly 55%. This means that nearly 50% of the officers working at Auburn in 1986 were hired since 1980. For an institution which has experienced relatively little turnover in terms of resignations, forced resignations and other outflow patterns, this increase means that a relatively new generation of officers has joined the still-existing force of well-experienced veterans. This generational change was a major concern of the officers interviewed.

While other institutions have experienced dramatic changes in the racial and gender composition of their officer corps over the past decade, these changes have not reached Auburn. In 1987, there were only 4 female officers, and only 12 black officers on the staff.

Officers' General View of What Had Changed

In the Spring of 1986 each of the officers in the original sample was sent an open-ended questionnaire asking them to identify those changes that occurred at Auburn and in the Department of Corrections over the previous ten years that had the greatest impact on the work officers do. They were also asked to identify the significant events or incidents that had the greatest impact on how officers feel about their work. Responses to this questionnaire provided new areas to supplement those covered in the original 1976 interview schedule which formed the basis for the 1986 research as well. In addition, interviews with the Warden,

Deputy Superintendent for Security and other administrative personnel, and a review of the NYS DOC Annual Report for 1976-1986 provided perspective on changes in the State system. Below I describe what the officers feel has changed. Much of what they report is documented in other sources.

Changes at Auburn

Inmate Community, Many of the officers felt that the nature of Auburn's mission was changing. For decades Auburn had the tradition of being the state's model educational penal institution. Officers always felt that inmates who wanted a good education would be sent to Auburn and the officers took pride in that feeling. However, with the opening of many minimum and medium security facilities during the past ten years, the "good" educationally-oriented inmates were now going elsewhere. For many officers, Auburn is now developing a reputation as the institution that handles the state's most troublesome inmates with the lowest number of problems while maintaining its reputation as a "high program" institution. That the inmate population has "gotten worse" is a common perception among these experienced officers. For some, this means that the inmates are more demanding; for others, worse reflects increased drug usage inside the walls, and increased inter-inmate violence and the accompanying growth of extortion rackets and related violence (See Chapter 5).

Changing Nature of the Officer Corps

A second change salient to these officers is the changing character and quality of the correctional officers at Auburn. The experienced officers were concerned about the influx of younger and less experienced officers. At the same time, they perceived experienced officers leaving, either by retiring "earlier than they used to" or by transferring to the newer medium and minimum security institutions where they believed the tasks were less demanding. This they believed reduced the general level of experience available in the institution. For others the level of officer experience was less a problem than the different attitudes. Newer officers were perceived by many of the older officers as feeling that the state owed them a living and that it was not necessary for the new officers to give their best work in return. Overall, these changes have led to increased stress and some intergenerational conflict, at least in the eyes of these more experienced officers.

Supervision

Many of these officers felt that increases in the number of supervisors and changes in the scope of their responsibilities have diluted the authority of supervisors. Changes in supervisor recruitment requirements which reduced the amount of experience necessary to be promoted to sergeant to three years ("and not even three years in a maximum security institution") made officers feel that some supervisors were not as able to give advice and less able to handle problems. For many, this change compounds the problems created by the rising numbers of new and inexperienced officers. For others, the increased number of supervisors has improved communication and has opened up many more opportunities for advancement.

Liberalization

Finally, changes in rule enforcement practices and Adjustment Committee policies and procedures were signs of increasing liberalization. Some officers tied liberalization to increases in inmate programming and other freedoms within the walls. Often cited as examples of new freedoms were the open yard, conjugal visits and inmate access to telephones.

Increased Penetration of the State-Level Bureaucracy

Many of the changes identified for Auburn were also attributed to and found to be occurring in the State Department of Corrections. For the officers hired before 1976, this *change* has been an incremental but perceptible process, slowly altering their relationship with their work environment. For those officers hired since 1980, this penetration by the State DOC in terms of "policy and procedure" and directives is the norm and forms the backdrop for their prison cultural experience (see Jacobs: 1977 for a description of this process at Stateville in the early 1970s). For these new officers "state-level involvement" has always been there and does not cause conflict. Such generational differences and change seem to have softened officer reaction to DOC policy. Although the courts were seen as hearing more cases from inmates, and the department was seen as liberalizing inmate grievance procedures, these changes were seen less as threats, and more as shifts in the relative ability of individual officer discretion and state and court ordered procedures to control the inmate. This distinction is important for it shows how officers have come to accept the inevitability of increased due process protections for inmates, and the increased role of the inmate in controlling his own fate. Though the 1976 interviews saw a "fatalistic acceptance" of such changes, such "liberalization" was much resented and the Commissioner of the DOC much criticized. Now, however, many officers referred to the Commissioner as an individual who was doing a good job. As one officer wrote:

> The grievance committee is good, but it is one aspect that does deteriorate the officers authority, although it does resolve many of the problems.

Increased programming for inmates was also seen in the same light. No longer was there the resentful "Why should the inmates go to school for free and my children have to pay?" type attitude characteristic of 1976. Now programs are seen as a necessary part of correctional work and as opportunities for obtaining increased numbers of correctional officers to provide adequate supervision.

This perception that the number of programs being offered to the inmates has increased since 1976 is interesting for it comes during a time when the end of rehabilitation had formally been announced and a conservative "lock 'em up and throw away the key" philosophy seemingly dominated the correctional debate.[32] Viewing the correctional world from the grass roots is different from viewing it from the political world of ideology. In 1981 I wrote that the "purposes of incarceration debate" made little difference for the working correctional officer. Apparently, at least for the officers at Auburn viewing the State DOC agenda, such academic debates still have little relevance.

Finally, these officers also pointed to an increased sense of professionalism throughout the DOC. This is evidenced by a greater attention to written policies and procedures, and an accompanying demand for accountability required by both the institutional administration and the state-level bureaucracy. Though these changes have seemingly reduced the officers' discretion and, therefore, the officers' personal control over inmates, increased structure and predictability coupled with the power of written rules and procedures have removed much of the unpredictability and individual responsibility with which officers previously had to cope. [This phenomenon will be discussed in more detail at the end of Chapter 5.]

In the salience of these changes and officers' perceptions of them, a central theme which runs through the 1986 interviews begins to emerge; i.e., *the increased penetration of the state bureaucracy* into the day-to-day life of the institution and its general acceptance by the officers. Though older and more experienced officers (pre-Attica—1971) can remember when the "warden and the PK ran the institution" they now understand that legal and administrative environment has changed, and that the behavior and decisions of prison administrators and often their own decisions are reflections of broader state policy. Jacobs describes this penetration by the state-level bureaucracy as it relates to the changes at Stateville during the early 1970s. There, the creation of the Department of Corrections, the emergence of university-educated administrators, increase of civilians in treatment roles with a concomitant narrowing of responsibilities of other staff ushered in the era of professionalism."[33] From the perspective of Auburn's correctional officers, many of these same trends have come to Auburn, and the material added to these chapters shows how officers have adapted.[34]

Significant Events Between 1976 and 1986

In the preliminary survey officers were also asked to indicate what events or incidents which occurred between 1976 and 1986 had the greatest impact on what officers think or feel about their work. Though most officers referred to developing conditions rather than events or incidents, the information shows the entrance of new circumstances into correctional officer consciousness.

The 1979 Strike

The event mentioned most frequently by these officers was the two-week strike that occurred in 1979. This was a statewide walkout by correctional officers who had to be replaced by the National Guard. Opinions concerning the success of the strike varied from "It was great. We showed the administration and the state," to "The strike was needed, but we were sold out by the union and the State. It brought the officers together though." Such references to increased officer solidarity were balanced by individual cases of hard feelings and exclusionary practices often directed at probationary officers who were forced to work during the strike or face dismissal and more experienced officers who stayed at their posts (in institutions other than Auburn) and were now shunned by their colleagues.

All officers reported no difficulties when they returned to work after the strike. Most felt that the inmates looked forward to their return. With routines disrupted "...they had their fun, and now they wanted to get back to normal. They were a little rowdy at first, but things settled into the old routine in a couple of days."[35]

Prosecuting Inmates

A second series of incidents noticed by the officers involved the local district attorney's increased prosecution of inmates for crimes committed within the prison. For officers, this penetration by the outside legal system is a positive practice which holds inmates as responsible for their behavior as free citizens. It also provides a sense of understanding and support from those in the outside community. Reflected here also is a willingness on the part of the wider community and the state to share in the problems officers face on a routine basis. Here we see a second way the walls of Auburn were penetrated by outside agencies.

Officers' Treatment by DOC

Initial discussions with the warden and other administrative staff, and a review of Annual Reports of the Department of Corrections for the years 1976—1985 described the development by the state of a number of employee-related initiatives. These were also mentioned by several officers. Following the 1979 strike, the state established a program addressing the Quality of Work Life in Corrections. As part of this program officers and other correctional personnel are involved in the assessment and development of programs to support correctional workers. In addition, Employee Assistance programs have been established at each institution to assist correctional employees with individual personal problems. These programs were mentioned by several officers as having a positive impact on how officers feel about their work.

Finally, the development by the state of a sick-leave abuse program for all state civil service employees was cited by many officers as a program that was applied by the state without common sense. Several officers pointed to examples where individuals with exemplary attendance records were reprimanded for legitimate sick time use. This program seemed to be the most salient negative factor in a generally more positive atmosphere of employer-employee relations as experienced by the officers.

SUMMARY—1986

This description of the changes that occurred for the officers and the institution from 1977—1986 provide a contextual backdrop for interpreting the material added to each chapter of the original edition. It describes the recent events and new circumstances which appear significant to these men as they carry out their tasks.

NOTES

[1]Teeters, Negley K. and Shearer, John D. *The Prison at Philadelphia, Cherry Hill: A Separate System of Penal Discipline, 1829-1913.* New York: Columbia and Company, 1971, p. 139.

[2]See Rothman, David J. *Discovery of the Asylum.* Boston, MA: Little, Brown and Company, 1971, pp. 68-71.

[3]*Annual Reports of the Prison Discipline Society of Boston, Report No. 4, 1824.* Montclair, NJ: Patterson Smith, 1972, p. 85.

[4]Ibid.

[5]*Twenty-fourth Annual Report of the Executive Committee of the Prison Association of New York and Accompanying Documents, 1868.* Albany, NY: Argus Company, 1869, p. 123.

[6]Stutsman, Jesse O. *Curing the Criminal: A Treatise on the Philosophy and Practice of Modern Correctional Methods.* New York: Macmillan, 1926, p. 54.

[7]Ibid., p. 62.

[8]Evans, A. A. "Correctional Institution Personnel—Amateurs or Professionals," *Annals*, Vol. 293, May (1954), p. 75.

[9]Ibid., p. 75.

[10]President's Commission on Law Enforcement and the Administration of Justice, *Task Force Report: Corrections.* Washington, DC: U.S. Government Printing Office, 1967, pp. 95, 96.

[11]For more thorough reviews of the literature on prison guards see Hawkins, Gordon. *The Prison: Policy and Practice*. Chicago, IL: University of Chicago Press, 1976, pp. 81-109; Fogel, David. *"...We are the Living Proof..."* Cincinnati, OH: Anderson Publishing Company, 1975, pp. 69-109; Shover, Noel. *A Sociology of American Corrections*. Homewood, IL: Dorsey Press, 1979, pp. 154-171; Lombardo, Lucien X. "The Correction Officer: A Study of a Criminal Justice Worker in His Workplace," unpublished Ph.D. thesis, SUNY, Albany, NY, 1978, pp. 13-62.

[12]*Sykes, Gresham. The Society of Captives*. New York: Atheneum, 1970, pp. 13-39.

[13]*Ibid., pp. 40-62.*

[14]*Cressey, Donald. "Contradictory Directives in Complex Organizations: The Case of the Prison," in Prison in Society*, edited by Lawrence Hazelrigg. New York: Anchor Books, 1968, pp. 477-496.

[15]*Hall, Jay, Williams, Martha and Tomiano, Louis. "The Challenge of Correctional Change: The Interface of Conformity and Commitment," in Prison in Society*, edited by Lawrence Hazelrigg. New York: Anchor Books, 1968.

[16]*Mathiesen, Thomas. Defences of the Weak*. London: Tavistock Publications, 1965, pp. 337, 338.

[17]*Goffman, Erving. Asylums*. Garden City, NY: Anchor Books, 1961, pp. 74-83, passim.

[18]*Merton, Robert K. "Bureaucratic Structure and Personality,"* in *Complex Organizations*, edited by Amitai Etzioni. New York: Holt, Rinehart and Winston, 1961, pp. 9-57, passim.

[19]*Katz, Daniel and Kahn, Robert L. The Social Psychology of Organizations*. New York: John Wiley and Sons, 1968, pp. 171-198.

[20]*See Miller, Walter B. "Ideology and Criminal Justice Policy. Some Current Issues," in Classes, Conflict and Control*, edited by Jim Munro. Cincinnati, OH: Anderson Publishing Company, 1976, pp. 3-38.

[21]*Tape recording would have been an ideal method of preserving the interviews. However, the time and cost involved in transcribing 150 hours of interview tapes was prohibitive. In addition, I felt that tape recording would inject a "threatening" element into the interview process. My experience as a correctional employee and the fact that officers often asked, "Are these interviews being taped?" when contacted for an appointment, lead me to believe that this was a wise decision.*

[22]*Goode, William J. and Hatt, Paul K. Methods in Social Research*. New York: McGraw-Hill Book Company, 1952, pp. 186-208.

[23]*Susan Philliber. "Thy Brother's Keeper: A Review of the Literature on Correctional Officers," Justice Quarterly*, Vol. 4, no. 1, 1987, pp. 9-37.

[24]*Ibid., p. 11.*

[25]*J. Jacobs. Stateville*. Chicago, IL: University of Chicago Press, 1977.

[26]*Ibid., pp. 175-199.*

[27]*Gareth Morgan. Images of Organization*. Beverly Hills, CA: Sage, 1986.

[28]*Ibid., pp. 233-272.*

[29]*Ibid., pp. 243-247.*

[30]*Ibid., pp. 247-255.*

[31]*Turnover rate was calculated using data from the monthly population movement reports for 1976-1876. The following formula was utilized:*

$$\frac{\text{(Total in + total out)}}{\text{Total Population at Beginning of Month}} \times 100$$

[32]*See F. Cullen. Reaffirming Rehabilitation*. Cincinnati, OH: Anderson Publishing Co., 1983.

[33]*Jacobs (1977), op. cit.*, 73-127.

[34]*See John J. DiIulio, Governing Prisons*. New York: The Free Press, 1987.

[35]See James Jacobs and Lynn Zimmer. "Collective Bargaining and Labor Unrest" in J. Jacobs (ed.), *New Perspectives on Prisons and Imprisonment*. Ithaca, NY: Cornell University Press, 1983. Pp. 143-159 for an analysis of this strike.

AN INTRODUCTION TO PRISON GUARDS AND THEIR WORK

I

In order to understand the manner in which individual correctional officers define and give meaning to the details of their work, it is important to understand how these people came to this particular occupation. Their pre-correctional officer experiences in the community of Auburn, their perceptions of the prison and the "convicts" it houses shape the way they interpret and give meaning to their work environment. The correctional officers' initial training experiences, their first face-to-face meetings with inmates, other correctional officers and the administrative structure of the prison provide benchmarks which serve to measure the various experiences they will have throughout their careers. As correctional officers "learn the prison," they come to understand its different environments and the variety of tasks and problems, skills and techniques that each separate environment demands. In learning the prison, they also learn where in the prison they are most comfortable and the tasks they can best perform. The chapters in this section are designed to describe the variety of impressions and experiences these officers brought to their work, their initial reactions to their work and the work environment, and the tasks and problems they associate with the variety of work settings which are part of Auburn Prison.

Becoming a Correction Officer: The Invisible Prison Becomes a Place to Work

2

The men who stand guard over the prisoners at Auburn are, for the most part, men with strong ties to the local community. Although born in the Auburn area and sometimes raised in the shadow of the prison's walls, it was as if the prison was not there and few turned to the prison as their initial place of employment. After completing high school, some college or a stint in the military, most spent a number of years working as factory laborers, construction workers, truckers (see Table 4, Appendix D). In these jobs they gained experience and began to define themselves as men who worked for a living, earning their way and providing for their growing families. The guards' preprison occupations usually required hard, physical labor and permitted the completion of specific tasks, characteristics they would soon learn not to expect in their new careers as prison guards.

Why, in their middle or late 20s, did these men leave the outside economy to seek employment inside the prison? Was there something in the work they believed prison guards performed that attracted them, or did other considerations lead them there?

PUSHED INTO PRISON

Jacobs and Retsky found that some correction officers in an Illinois prison took their jobs after periods of unemployment, layoffs or because an injury prevented them from pursuing their former occupations.[1] This sequence appears to hold for many of the Auburn officers as well, with one-half indicating that job security was a primary factor in their recruitment (see Table 5, Appendix D). After experiencing the ups and downs of the local private sector economy, these men were willing to take a chance on an unknown occupation to obtain the long-term security and fringe benefits attached to a state civil service position. As some officers described their situations:

> I saw myself as a young man with a family, but I couldn't see any future in the local factories with the strikes and such. I talked with people about the civil service. I had some friends in the department and they mentioned the job. Back in the 60s the pay wasn't that good, but it had security.

* * *

> I was getting more money on my other job in 1968, but I was only working six to nine months a year. The guard's job only paid $5,600 when I started, but you got a check every two weeks.
>
> * * *
>
> We were on strike (at the plant) and I took the test then and wound up as a correction officer. I've never had a worry since then about layoffs. It takes a load off your mind. I'm secure now. I can go out and do the things I've always wanted to do.

The strength of "job security" as an incentive in recruitment becomes more obvious when one considers that it was frequently necessary for these officers to sacrifice immediate family life for the long-term promise of security. When first appointed, departmental policy forced many men to begin their careers at a prison other than Auburn. Before returning, officers spent from six months to three years away from home. Their willingness to accept a job under such conditions reflects an initial long-term commitment to their new careers.[2]

Although being a prison guard in many jurisdictions is not rewarding financially, pay and related benefits were the second most frequently mentioned factors that attracted these men to become guards at Auburn. Surprisingly, this is as true for some of the officers who began their careers in the early 1950s as for those who began after 1970. One officer with 26 years experience recalls:

> I went to college for three years and began interviewing for jobs. At that time (1949) the top-paying job I interviewed for paid $2,600 per year. The prison paid $4,200 per year. The pay was good, so I took it.

Another officer with two years experience reports:

> I flunked out of college and was in the dumps. I just played around for three years, worked in a factory and got married. I hated the factory; not much money, hot and rotten. They were hiring guards in 1972-1973 and the pay was good; $12,000 per year and overtime. I took the test, sat around for a year and got called.

That these men came to the prison in search of security and financial rewards *after* employment in the outside economy is significant. It indicates that they perceived other employment alternatives to be closed. When a warden says, "If the guards don't like it here they can leave," he is technically correct. But, psychologically and financially, many guards at Auburn are imprisoned, dependant on the prison for their new, secure lifestyle. Being imprisoned, guards, like inmates, are forced to adapt to their work and the working conditions.

For a smaller group of officers a job at the prison was an acceptable alternative to a job in the police field (another job offering civil service security) that they would rather have had. Some reported having taken the State Police examination at the same time that they took the correction officers test. According to one officer:

> I never really was interested in the job. I was interested in police work, the troopers. I'm still trying to get in there. When I got out of the army I took the troopers test and the correction officers test at the same time. I didn't score high enough on the troopers test, but I did do better on the guards' exam. We got good money for the education. Maybe later I'll get out of the prison and into police work. But I never grew up with the idea of working in the prison.

Surprisingly, the nature of prison work influenced few of these men to become prison guards. Even for these few, it was not that prison work was attractive, rather, becoming a guard was an escape from the dirt and drudgery of their former occupations. One officer said:

> I had two uncles and a cousin who worked (at Auburn Prison). They came home clean, no dirt. They said you didn't really have to work. I thought it was easier to work there than in the print shop, so I got in.

This man thought it would be easier to work in the prison, but he was yet to experience the "realities" of prison work and the demands it would make on him.

PRERECRUITMENT IMAGES

When taking a job, most people have some expectations about their work and the environment in which they will do it. The images one has of such workplaces as factories, offices and hospitals are often derived from personal experience. Though not the technical orientations of an insider, these images serve as practical reference points as one begins one's new employment. But unless one has either worked in or served time in a prison, one's ability to experience the tasks and atmosphere of prison work is usually limited to movies, paperback novels or the frequently sensational accounts of prison violence that appear in the popular press. Personal experience directly related to prison is something no one has until one finds himself within the walls.

For a new employee, a new occupation generally means a dose of "reality shock," a conflict between his expectations and the "reality" of the job.[3] Both Neiderhoffer and Westley discuss the "reality shock" experienced by the urban policeman when he first encounters a hostile public that he expected to be cooperative and he learns that police work is not always done "by the book."[4] To better understand these Auburn guards, the way they perform their duties and the ways they perceive and experience their work environment described in subsequent chapters, it is necessary to describe more fully the process of becoming a guard. This is a process that begins with images and expectations about the prison that develop long before the decision to file a civil service application. Drawn by job security, financial rewards and related benefits, these men decided to apply for and accept positions as prison guards. But what did these would-be guards think they were getting into? What images of their new work, guarding prisoners; their workplace, the prison; and their charges, the convicts, filled their minds before they began?

The Invisibility of the Prison

It was during their early years living in Auburn that the vast majority of these men began to develop images of their new work, the prison and its inhabitants. Before these men became guards, any consideration of the intrinsic realities of the correction officer's job, such as "helping people," "rehabilitating" or even "being firm with prisoners," was precluded by the invisibility of the job. This theme of invisibility emerged when the guards described what they thought the correction officer's job was like before they started as guards. At this point few had any idea what guards did. "I had no idea, I just didn't know," and "All I knew was that I was getting a job," were typical responses. This is remarkable in that 75% of these men were born in the community surrounding the prison and two-thirds had relatives working in prisons.

Those officers who did recall having some expectations were surprised at how uninformed they were:

> I thought (officers) all worked in towers. I had no conception of the program. I thought all inmates were in one building and all the officers were on the walls.
>
> * * *
>
> Just watch and do nothing. I envisioned catwalks above the inmates. I didn't envision being mixed in with the inmates. I thought you were separated from inmates.

Even those men with relatives working as officers betrayed an uncertainty about what sort of work guards do:

> I didn't know much about it. Just asked my brother-in-law about inmates, their cells. He said it was okay. I just saw the guys on the front gate and the walls.
>
> * * *

> I had some help having a cousin down there. He got me a copy of some old rule books and other things. Even these didn't give a full understanding of what you're getting into. Again, just ideas from the movies. Guards, not pushing inmates, but still the bad guys. But I knew some guards and knew they weren't like that. I was willing to take a chance.

This seeming inability to obtain thorough information about the job from regular employees may reflect a reluctance on the part of prison employees to talk about their job with outsiders, a reluctance that seems to have extended even to the officer's immediate family. Many officers whose fathers were guards reported that their fathers almost never talked to them about their work, at least until the sons became officers. Then, as one officer put it, "That's all we did talk about."

Evidence that these prospective prison employees discovered little about prison work from those employed there is supported by their own silence about what they do.

When an interview took place in an officer's home, the officer's wife would often locate herself in a nearby room, apparently to overhear the conversation. Frequently the wife would comment that she wondered what it was her husband did. As one wife remarked, "He's been an officer for 20 years and this is the first time I've ever heard him talk about his work."

One officer explained his reluctance to discuss his work with his wife by saying, "What am I going to say? Gee, honey, I looked in three guys' assholes for contraband today; or, boy, I wrote a guy up for taking an extra pork chop. Hardly exciting stuff."

Rather than reflecting a work group norm of secrecy designed to hide the inner workings of the prison from the public, my own experience as a prison employee and the comments of these officers leads me to believe that this seemingly secretive behavior has its roots in the officer's feeling that it is impossible for an outsider to understand what he experiences. Since the public and even one's family have no first-hand experience with prison life and its meaning, the officer feels there is no shared experience upon which he can base communication. He knows outsiders to be as ignorant of prison life as he was before he began working in prison. Communication with outsiders about the job is viewed as futile and is best avoided. When outsiders ask them about their work, many officers respond by saying that they are out of touch with what goes on inside because they work on the tower. By responding in this way, they avoid the "Oh, come on's" of a disbelieving public.

With the nature of their prospective employment hidden from them by the silence of those who worked within the walls, these potential guards were merely residents of the city of Auburn. The expectations and images of the prison that developed in their minds reflect the place of the prison in the minds of those townspeople not associated with it. As with the nature of their work, the dominant theme is again one of invisibility. When asked what they thought about the prison before they began working there, nearly 80% of the officers said they "...never really thought about the subject." The comments of those who did think about it portray the prison as a sometime curiosity, but not a major focal point of community interest:

> I don't think I really gave it much thought. I saw it every day and didn't really know it was there. It's an obvious thing, but I paid no attention to it.
>
> * * *
>
> I never gave it a thought. Like the Seward Mansion (home of the former Secretary of State, William Seward of Seward's Folly fame). I've never gone to it. I was brought up in a prison city and never really thought about it. There were no riots or escapes in my lifetime.
>
> * * *
>
> I didn't know much about what went on. I knew it was a place of punishment, that's all. If I got caught doing something, I might end up there. I played softball in there once, but never really thought about it.
>
> * * *
>
> My dad told me about the bullet holes he got in his hat in 1929. He was just standing outside during the riot then. When I was a kid we use to climb the trees on Wall Street (a street bordering the prison) and try to look in. The women's prison was there then. But usually I didn't pay any attention to it.

One possible explanation for the invisibility of the prison to those living around it is that the prison had become a deterrent. In the comments of some officers, one sees the prison as that terrible place one discovers only when one has transgressed enough to be sent there. At least that is what they reported being told by their parents and teachers who threatened them with "the college on State Street" if they did not mend their ways:

> I thought it was a place where all the guys who were criminals or who had committed crime were sent.
>
> * * *

> That's where they send the bad guys. I'd go there if I didn't straighten out. At least that's what I was told.
>
> * * *
>
> I had a completely different idea from what it is. I had the old idea of a place of corporal punishment. I picked that up from the T.V. and the movies more than from my father (who was a guard).

These would-be guards learned to think about the prison only to keep out of it. With the idea of prison as deterrent firmly in mind, it is possible that the need to avoid consciously thinking about the shape of the deterrent threat had diminished. The prison could thus easily be ignored, even as one passed it day after day.

Images of the "Cons"

Though these officers had few definite images of their prospective workplace, their expectations of inmates were more sharply defined. A mixture of local mythology and popular movies, their conceptions of convicts were less than favorable. Before they first entered the world behind the walls for the first time, the vast majority expected to find anything but normal people residing there:

> *What did you expect the inmates (convicts) would be like?*
>
> I thought they were all bad killers. The worst people on earth. I thought they'd kill you as soon as look at you.
>
> * * *
>
> I more or less though they'd be like the movies, like Cagney or Bogart.
>
> * * *
>
> I thought from watching the movies that they were surly, secretive and not very open.
>
> * * *
>
> I thought they were a different breed of people, all sitting on the ground with little caps on, looking out from under these caps with a sneaky look and talking out of the sides of their mouths.

One officer ignored the possibility of threats from murderers and rapists and concentrated on another more mundane problem:

> I always had the feeling that somebody would swipe my wallet. So I seldom take cash. I know it's crazy, but I always had the feeling that they were a bunch of pickpockets, not thinking about the murderers and rapists. I still find myself checking to see if my wallet's there.

A few officers who grew up in working-class sections of larger cities had different expectations of inmates. They expected inmates to be regular neighborhood people who had gotten into trouble. For these officers, reminiscences of ill-fated schoolmates replace the caricature of the "hard con," generally held by officers raised in Auburn:[5]

> I was raised among these guys in New York City. The fact that a guy's a convicted felon and went to prison made no difference to me. I've seen them and lived with them and shot pool with them. I've known their families. A guy in prison was just some guy that got caught.

* * *

> I used to see inmates every day. Undereducated, in trouble when kids. Growing up in a larger city, I saw a lot of guys go away to (training schools). Their family life wasn't the best, clothes not the cleanest, slow in school, family didn't care. Not all are like that, but the ones I knew from my neighborhood were.

Contact with the "Reality"

With these few and rather jaundiced expectations, the men who were new correctional officers met the "reality" of the prison world. While the rookie policeman often expected but failed to find a cooperative public, the new correction officer was more apt to have been pleasantly surprised by what he found.

Seeing and having contact with the criminal behind walls for the first time, the vivid images of convicts manufactured from local mythology and the media quickly began to disintegrate. The sordid, vicious characters of movies and television became "just like people on the street." Anxieties about working with convicts dissolved with the "underwhelming" realization that "it's not as bad as I expected." When asked if their expectations of inmates were confirmed by their initial contacts, most officers described their newly found "reality" with relief:

> No, I was amazed. I found out that they were somewhat normal people, not two heads, eight feet tall and grotesque. There's every kind in there.

* * *

> After I was in, I saw a bunch of guys of all races, nationalities and backgrounds and religions. One day I asked a guy what he was doing. I thought maybe it was Morse code. He was making something in braille. Just doing their time, occupying themselves. Probably no different from the rest of us, only more nerve.

* * *

> No. I always expected they'd have a different look. Like a murderer would be a mean and tough guy. A lot of them have baby faces and you look at their records and see murder. What you expect doesn't always go with the person you see. You expect lifers trying to escape, but they get in and they're the opposite. The big timer is the best inmate. They do time the best as they can and the easiest way. I always had the "nothing to lose" idea of a lifer.

* * *

> When I first went to Sing-Sing I was working 8-4 and I would see guys throw 300 pounds over their heads. I thought they were all killers and tough and difficult to talk to, but I don't think that way now. The majority you can talk to and get to know. He'll come to you with problems, and sometimes he can help you out.

From his initial encounter with this "prison reality," the new officer draws a number of lessons. First he learns that appearances are deceptive—that a murderer, after all, does not have a special look. The officer also learns that convicts are not alike; that where he may have had a stereotyped image of a convict, the stereotype broke down with the diversity of human character. Finally, the new officer learns that convicts, rather than being aloof and unapproachable, are people with whom one can communicate.[6]

BEING TRAINED TO GUARD PRISONERS

Approaching the prison for their first day's work as prison guards, these men generally did not have the benefit of formal training to introduce them to their new profession and, as described above, they were generally uncertain about what they were getting into. Most who entered the prison service prior to 1972, when a training academy was established, reported that they were simply issued "a badge, a club and a hat," shown the yard and told to go to work:

> I took the physical and went into the lineup room. They called off the officers and the jobs. I was supposed to go to A block in the morning

> and C block in the afternoon. I asked where these places were and the P.K. (Principal Keeper, now Deputy Superintendent for Security) went crazy. He even threw his hat on the floor. I asked him how I could be expected to do my job with no training and he just said, "That's the way it is."
>
> * * *
>
> I had two days' notice that I was to start. I went in and got sent to a wall post. The guy in the tower didn't throw me the key. I yelled for about five minutes. I thought it was my fault, but there was nobody there. Then I had to go to the sergeant and tell him.
>
> * * *
>
> The first day, I go in. They give me a badge and a new white stick. I was sent to the yard to check passes, it was great. Then at 11:30 the whistle blew and all of a sudden all the shops let out at once. Nobody told me about that, and I'm trying to check all the passes. It was ridiculous.

From these confusing, often bewildering, experiences the new officer quickly drew the conclusion that he was on his own to discover and deal with the complexities of his new occupation. He was quick to feel that he was in a subordinate position and that he would be told not what he needed to know, but what others wanted him to know. He would have to discover the shape of his job in his own way and from whoever would offer assistance.

Training by More Experienced Officers

In describing the experiences of rookie police officers, Westley and others found close, apprenticeship relationships developing between rookies and older officers.[7] For the new guards at Auburn, a close relationship between the recruit and the experienced officer was the exception rather than the rule. Officers who began their careers prior to 1970 reported that their reception was generally less than cordial, at times bordering on hostility.[8] Though a rookie was sometimes placed with an older officer for a day or two, most reported receiving little help or positive advice. What advice they received was often general. Such phrases as "treat everyone as a human being and they'll treat you the same way," "do what you're told," "they'll be watching," represent the amount of instruction that the older guards provided.

However, even such limited positive advice was not the normal reception for the rookie. Often the rookie was told, "Learn for yourself, the way I did." He was instructed in the art of unlocking lock boxes and releasing inmates from their cells; even then the information he received was not always complete:

> ...you automatically got the cold shoulder. You'd get introduced and the guy walks away. No cooperation from the older officers. You had to be there a couple of years and go through the crappy jobs.

Some officers learned to move with caution with older officers because they feared (often with reason) that any mistakes they made would be reported to supervisors.

> In the past they'd say, "Learn for yourself the way I did." Then, if you goofed up, they'd blow you in to a sergeant.

* * *

> The system here was that if you had an uncle who worked there or a relation, you were a good guy. If not, they didn't know you. They'd put you in a position where you might be buried. When I first started here, they put me on the front gate. A new P.K. was starting that day and they figured I'd let him in without asking for his I.D. and I'd get burned.
>
> Well, I called the guy who usually worked the gate and asked him what you do on that job. He told me to ask everybody for their I.D. He must have known what was going on. Well, the new P.K. came and I asked him for his I.D. He showed it, no problem. The P.K. recognized about burying guys, and later I asked him about a machine operator's job. I got a good one on construction with a half hour a day overtime. It worked out beautiful.

From a functional standpoint the reaction of the old-timer to the recruit was more practical than ceremonial. For the old-timer the recruit was reportedly a threat, and his treatment of the recruit a defensive reaction designed to protect "a good job assignment" he might have worked years to obtain. Being moved out of his job could thus be a blow to the officer's institutional sense of self.[9]

Prior to 1970, job assignments within the institution were dispensed by supervisors. For the officer, this meant that his place within the institution was often subject to the whim of friendship and institutional politics. Not to instruct a recruit or to discredit him were actions that could slow the recruit's progress toward prime institutional jobs. An officer stated:

> Then there wasn't job bidding and the older officers didn't want a young guy coming in to take their jobs. Then a good young officer could move in. It was harder to break in then than now. Now there's not as much competition.

After 1970 the relations between the recruit and the older officer appear to have improved as competition for jobs was reduced by the introduction of a job-bidding system based on seniority. One officer who began work in 1973 describes his experience:

> It was easy. A lot of officers would tell you "this is the job" and offer help. They'd tell you how to handle problems. Even now, if I work a different shift somebody will tell me what to do if I'm not sure.

Another officer, after five years on the job, found his initial experience with older officers satisfactory, though he felt he had been treated like a child:

> New officers are accepted right away. A new bunch of officers came in two or three weeks ago. If not for the officers, they would have been lost. These officers had no idea what to do until the other officers helped. I had no problems personally with the officers or the administration. But they treat you as a kid. I'm not a kid. But there's no waiting to see how you'll do. Nothing like that. They'd help you. Bend over backwards.

Competition for jobs, however, was not the only factor in the recruit-experienced officer relationship. Uncertainty concerning proper ways of handling given situations at times made even old-timers reluctant to provide a new man with advice. If the experienced officer was wrong and a supervisor observed the recruit's mistakes, the old-timer could "lose face":

> I've often asked myself why the new guy often got the cold shoulder, but I haven't found an answer. With my experience, I've got no desire to tell a new guy what's going on. But I don't know why. You just worry about what you're doing. It's hard to tell a new guy how to do things. I might tell him and he gets a reprimand. What does that make me look like?

The temporary nature of the rookie's initial institutional placement might also have acted against the development of close relations between the rookie and the experienced officer. No matter where the officers began their careers, they felt it was generally known that they would not remain there. Many officers felt the older officers who greeted them saw little value in providing information and in establishing close relationships with men who would soon leave. The fact that the new man was becoming an *officer* seemed to make little difference in this context.

From an analytical perspective, the treatment of rookie officers prior to 1970 resembles the "degradation" ceremonies undergone by inmates upon their entrance into prison. In this regard, Erving Goffman points to "role dispossession" that occurs for inmates, as their confinement prevents them from maintaining roles in which they were previously involved.[10] Although the officer is not sequestered behind prison walls 24 hours a day, his role attachment to the outside was disrupted. Being forced to leave his home to take a job in another area for a length of time, for instance, forced him to relinquish, at least temporarily, activities and friendships in which he had previously participated. And, upon the officer's return to his hometown, irregular shift schedules and workday schedules often prevented him from establishing a regulated life of customary activities. Some officers thus found themselves having to abandon college programs they had started until they had obtained a regular job on a regular shift.

Even though he was firmly committed to his job, the treatment the rookie received at the hands of older officers would seem to work against his comfortably committing himself to his new role as "officer." As the officer learned that his preconceptions of inmates were unrealistic, he learned that his preconceptions of other officers were also in error. Where he previously considered officers to be "pretty good guys," his fellow workers began to look differently once he encountered them inside the institution. In spite of the recruit's apparent long-term commitment to his new job, this cold treatment at the hands of experienced officers tended to reduce his commitment to a guard fraternity. Though he must seem sure of himself vis-à-vis the inmate, the recruit may not make a strong investment of self in the officer role. In this way he becomes deprived of a personal role, though he does have a job. Remarks such as "I can't speak for other officers, I can only speak for myself," and the frequent use of "they" rather than "we" to refer to correction officers underscore the separation of the individual from the group, even among the experienced officers. At least at Auburn Prison there seems to be a tendency for individual officers not to perceive their "work group" as a "reference group."[11]

Training by Inmates

Although the Department of Corrections and the local prison administration provided little training, and with the reluctance on the part of the experienced officers to instruct the rookie correction officers, new men were in many cases forced to turn for advice to the inmates over whom they had authority. Prior to the introduction of job bidding in 1970 and of the academy in 1972, inmates appear to have played a large part in orienting the new officer in his job. Many officers reported that when a rookie officer was sent to an area of the institution with which he was unfamiliar, there always seemed to be an inmate there who knew what was supposed to happen. The inmate filled a void in orientation, enabling officers to proceed on their new jobs in a more or less comfortable way. Indeed, the new officer had virtually nowhere else to turn to discover what was going on in the prison but to the inmates.

The fact that the inmate did not conform to stereotyped expectations may help to explain the readiness with which the officer accepted (though sometimes uncomfortably) the inmate's advice. In turn, the fact that inmates could actually help served to reinforce the officer's discovery that the inmates were, after all, "like the rest of us":

> When I started, after seeing prison movies, I was scared shitless. I started on a Saturday as a temporary employee. I thought they were criminals and that's it.
>
> *Did you find what you expected?*
>
> They all looked like people. I couldn't tell them from people on the street. The guy that broke me in the mess hall was a murderer. You couldn't work for a nicer guy. When I started, the inmates checked everything out in the mess hall to see if things were clean. An inmate broke me in. Inmates trained officers. Really! He told me to stand back and he showed me how and where to frisk. He hit the table top to sound it out. Rap the bars to see if they were solid. Many times when you're running companies, or you're a new officer in a factory, there's an inmate that shows you the right way. On Sunday they let out the wing waiter to mop and clean cells. Now they have four or five at a time. The wing waiter guided you right so there's no confusion. An inmate doesn't want to have any more problems than he has.

A number of points about this officer's experience should be noted. First, there is the paradox of an inmate instructing the officer in security procedures, showing the officer how and where to frisk. Such an experience must have made the new officer wonder about the primacy of the security aspect of his job. How important can security be if the instruction concerning security comes from those over whom one is to maintain security?

A second point is the officer's belief that the inmate does not want any more problems than he already has. This attitude might lead an officer to place more trust in the inmate than in the administration or in his fellow officers, both of whom failed to provide him with much guidance.

A third aspect of the officer's experience is his attitude toward the criminality of the inmate: "The guy that broke me in was a murderer. You couldn't work for a nicer guy." This statement illustrates a typical correctional officer attitude toward inmates. From the officer's perspective, when deviants exist in a population that is deviant by definition, deviance ceases to be important and behavior in the new environment comes to be the most important factor by which a man is judged. Though the officers were not specifically asked about this topic, most officers left the impression that invoking an inmate's prior criminal behavior on the job makes their task more difficult. They feel that it is more difficult to relate personally to the inmates as individuals and make judgments based only on the inmate's immediate behavior if they know what the individual might have been like on the outside. While being trained by the inmates, the new guard quickly realizes that the inmate's current, on-the-spot behavior—not his criminal record—is the most relevant and important indicator of an inmate's character:

> I remember my first day at Attica. I met Willie Sutton. He came up to me and said, "You're new here," and he asked me if I knew who he was. I told him I didn't know and I didn't care. I never ask why they're in. My job is to see that they stay here and keep them working.
>
> * * *
>
> I probably thought the same as everybody else. They were madmen. Turn your head and you get a knife in the back—all murderers and rapists. But that's not true. You only run into it once in a while. They're probably all a little mentally unstable. I don't worry about that now, I take it for granted. I don't worry if this guy killed a couple of people, I just don't care.
>
> * * *
>
> In this prison, you used to get a file on the guy if you had him in the shop. They kept cards and you knew what he was in for. They took that away. They didn't want you to prejudge anybody. The hardest thing was and is to have guys and get intimate with them and find out what he's in for. It's hard to associate the man with the crime.

The Training Academy Experience

In 1972 New York State established the Correctional Services Training Academy. This academy was designed to provide pre-service and in-service training for parole and institutional management personnel, as well as correction officers. As part of this overall training effort, a 13-week training program was designed for incoming correction officers. This program consisted of ten weeks of classroom instruction and three weeks of on-the-job training. Eight of the officers interviewed participated in this program. Their reactions to the program and the lessons they derived from it after one to three years on the job were not consistent. Where one officer found the whole training program "a big farce," another said he could not imagine beginning his job without it. In fact, the latter officer indicated that he would like to repeat the experience if the chance were offered.

Some officers found classroom instruction concerning the attitudes and behaviors of inmates most beneficial. Others saw value in such courses as "report writing." Another officer found all classroom work useless and felt he gained the most from his on-the-job training.

Though there is little consistency among the officers in their evaluations of particular segments of the training program, there appears to be some consensus in the officers' perceptions of departmental motivation and in the image of the job they felt their training instructors were attempting to convey. After two or three years' experience as officers, the men felt that the training academy experience was designed to make them feel like inmates. Most felt that they were talked down to and treated like children. The regimentation, haircuts, curfews and redundancy were perceived as designed to "push" them to see how much stress they could take before they "lost their cool."

Looking back, one officer interpreted this treatment as an exercise in empathy through role-playing, rather than as an attempt to develop a disciplined, professional correction officer. He felt that the training enabled him to better understand and appreciate the feelings and emotional reactions of inmates in the prison environment.

One recruit perceived in the training academy experience an attempt at building a sense of comradeship among officers and a feeling of pride in their new profession:

> There was lots of competition. They broke us into groups of about 30 each and had competition in the physical fitness program. There's the feeling like you're joining the group of correction officers. Something to be proud of. They tell you that people don't think much of you, but try to show you how correction officers stick together. They look at it as a profession and stress its importance. After all, not anybody can do that job. The strain, they don't hide it.

This officer's reaction to perceived attempts to build group identification and pride is atypical. Most of the state-trained officers are cynical in interpreting this aspect of their training. While acknowledging the professional image of the correction officer presented by the instructors in the academy, they feel that the image is not reinforced by administrative support:

> They tried to talk it up like you're a professional and that you should act like one. But then it's 90° weather and you're standing there in wool pants and a baseball cap. The whole orientation of the uniform is unprofessional. They kind of built it up, glorified it and tried to compare it to the troopers throughout the program, but I never heard of anyone blowing the (corrections) academy. They caught one guy

> with a girl three times, twice at the academy, and they still kept him. They never did do anything to guys who refused to get haircuts.

The recruit grew to expect that the Department of Corrections did not always do what it said it would do. Cynicism toward the organization and its policies and weak identification with a "profession" were two lessons derived from the academy in these retrospective views.

These, however, were not the only lessons of training. In a more positive vein, the recruits reported learning an important principle for dealing with inmates: "Be firm, fair and consistent." They also learned, however, that this principle was laden with contradictions. They learned that there is no one way to do things and that each man has to develop a style that suits him. As one officer describes it:

> At the academy they tell you rules have to be enforced, but they give you no specific way to do it. They realize that each man has to handle it in his own way, by the book or loose. They try to get you to develop your own personality. Some blow up quick, others are patient.

SUMMARY—1976

As the naive citizens of Auburn became the guards of the prison community, they accepted jobs but did not readily identify with their new titles. They quickly learned to identify with and appreciate the convicts over whom they would stand guard and learned that convicts had to be judged by behavior and not as stereotypes.

They also developed a skepticism and cynicism toward those who administer the prisons and even toward their fellow officers. Their identification with their new "corrections profession" was weak; the search for group definitions of "proper" behavior proved fruitless as the individual guard had to struggle to make his way on his own in the new world of the prison. Generally scorned by older guards and accepted by some inmates, his loyalties became confused. With this beginning, the new guard fell into his routine and began learning the tasks associated with the running of the prison.

THE NEW GENERATION: 1976-1986

Interviews (N=5) and questionnaires (N=18) completed by officers who were hired since 1976 provide information on the changing recruitment patterns and initial experiences of the new cadre of officers who make up over half of the officer corps at Auburn. These new officers have tended to start their new occupations at a younger age ($\bar{X}=24.6$ for new sample compared to $\bar{X}=26.5$ for 1976 sample). While 70% of the 23 officers in the new sample began before they were 25, only 40% of the original sample did so. In addition, nearly 50% of these new officers were born and lived most of their lives in communities outside of Cayuga County, coming to Auburn only as they became correctional officers; this compares to only 10% of the original sample.

One of the recently retired officers (hired in 1959) remarked how he was born and raised in a community about 25 miles from Auburn and how he had never really been accepted by Auburn officers even though he had been heavily involved in local scouting and other community activities. The strength of this "Auburn native" ingroup/outgroup definition in defining officer relationships may be breaking down as increasing numbers of officers come from communities outside of the local area.

The occupational background of the new officers also differs from that of their original sample fellow officers and reflects the dwindling industrial base of upstate New York and the expansion of service sector employment. While the majority of the original 1976 sample (56%) came to correctional work from factory work, only 35% (N=8) of the new sample had such experience. Sales work accounted for 26% (N=6) of the new officers while none of the original 1976 sample were employed in such occupations. Overall only 24% of the 1976 sample of officers were previously employed in service sector jobs. For the post-1976 sample, that proportion rose to 60%.

The newer sample is more likely to have had some college-level educational experience (60% pre-1976, 83% 1986 sample). Three of these officers indicated that they had educational experience in the criminal justice or corrections area and that their new job gave them an opportunity to put their degree into practice.

For the group hired since 1976, the motivations for becoming correctional officers also differ substantially from those hired before 1976. Whereas lack of job security in the local industrial economy was a major factor driving officers to the prison as a source of steady employment in the years before 1976, this factor was identified as salient for only 35% of the post-1976 sample. For the new sample, pay and benefits dominate (70%) while this was a major factor for only 30% of the original sample. Also emerging as a new factor was the idea that working in corrections might be an interesting occupation with 26% of the new sample group indicating that this was one of the main reasons they became correctional officers.

What we see now is that the people coming to Auburn Correctional Facility as correctional officers are doing so at a younger age, with slightly more education, with fewer and qualitatively different previous work experiences than their more experienced counterparts. In addition, their motivations for coming into correctional work are substantially different. Whereas the ups and downs of the local industrial economy drove many of the officers hired during the 1950s,

1960s, and early 1970s into correctional work, these new offices, not having experienced the cyclical and physical nature of industrial work, were drawn to corrections for the money and the benefits available in state employment. Rather than relating their new employment choice to dissatisfaction with the civilian economy and comparing their new positions with the demands of factory work, these new officers appear to be making more positive decisions to seek employment in the prison for what that employment provides.

Expectations and Reality

In general the invisibility of the prison sitting in the middle of the city of Auburn so evident in the 1976, appears to be less so in the new group. One of these new officers reports that he "never thought about" the prison, the work of correctional officers or about inmates. A couple of others thought that inmates were locked up almost all the time. However, the themes which emerge from their descriptions of prerecruitment images demonstrate some sense of expectations and familiarity with prison issues even if these expectations were not always accurate. References to expected "limited inmate rights"; "continuous fighting"; officers having "a lot of authority and controlling people"; reports of "physical abuse by guards" demonstrate that general knowledge of prison life and concerns has become more commonplace than it was ten years ago.

For these new officers, having somewhat realistic expectations meant that their exposure to reality of prison life might be different than the "underwhelming experience" described by those officers of the previous generation who entered prison work with stereotypical expectations of inmates as superhuman and a knowledge of prisons gained from movies made in the 1940s. Indeed, the perceptions of these new officers tend to focus on "negative" rather than positive characteristics of inmates. They also seem to experience the "reality shock" that was missing when their older counterparts began their jobs 15, 20 and 30 years ago.

> I thought there was fighting every day and I had no idea that I could go through a day and not get involved and hurt. I also thought that officers had a lot of authority and controlled peoples lives totally when they got out of line. They spit at us, throw cigarettes and as long as we can't prove it, there's nothing we can do. My first day at Sing-Sing I almost got sick. You can't ever let your guard down.
>
> *How was it different from what you expected?*
>
> I was amazed at the way inmates can talk to officers. The insolence. The old-timers must be going crazy. I was also amazed by the things they get. Hard and soft contact lenses, the best sports equipment,

> things high schools can't afford. They get the best food, and the stuff they throw away is amazing.

* * *

> When I started, I saw a city within a city. They're doing the same things in here as they're doing on the street, hustling, fashion. I didn't feel they'd be as violent as they are. The weapons, being degrading toward others as they are.

Another officer, with three years' experience demonstrates a more complex analysis of inmate behavior and officer response than was evident in the younger officers ten years ago. For this officer, the "games inmates play" and the *manipulative world* of prison becomes salient, whereas for his counterparts hired 15 to 30 years ago, the *human* contact between officer and inmate was more apparent.

> Inmates help out because they want you as a friend on their level. But it's all a game. Inmates want to help because they can't get things without you. They'll do without you if you let them, but you have to be in control and have the upper hand. Not physical but mental. Where I work I could go all day and never say ten words. I just shake my hand and point. Use body language. If you talk they'll argue.

Training

All of the officers in the new sample had the experience of going through the state's 16-week training program as well as on-the-job training. Lacking from their descriptions of their training process is the training they received from inmates (a dominant theme for officers hired before 1976). Because of the permeation of the training academy experience in the younger cadre, the impact of state-level policy and directives is becoming more salient to a much larger proportion of the institution's officers. The individualistic experiences (though shared by many) which were evident in the training experiences of officers hired during the 1950s, 1960s and early 1970s, appear to be giving way to a more collective experience of training.

> The training academy experience was to teach you the administration's way, the state's way, Albany's way. But you find that things don't work that way. The facilities aren't staffed to do it that way.
>
> *How would you do training differently?*
>
> I would listen to the inmates more carefully. You get the impression in training that the inmates are bad, that they play games. Even

> though they tell you that the inmates are people and you should deal with them as people and not as objects, they don't tell you it's an environment of people. But they tell you it's a jail, and this is done this way and you'll walk in and tell people what to do. People don't like to be told what to do 24 hours a day.

An officer with seven years experience who went to the academy in 1979 after seven years of working with mentally ill for the Department of Mental Health describes his perceptions of the impact of academy training on younger officers.

> What they teach at the academy doesn't really correlate. Some of the ideas. We train OJT's now and you have to laugh at the way they feel. They teach things at the academy with hypothetical stuff written by people without experience. Most young officers are gung-ho—like the Marines. They have that "I'm invulnerable, I wear a blue shirt" attitude. After a while they learn they're not invulnerable.
>
> I was 33 when I was at the academy. They teach you to be strong, fair, impartial, but to let them know who's boss. But an 18- or 20-year-old takes that kind of thing differently than a 33-year-old. An 18-year-old is impressionable. Just like the inmates.

These new officers appear to enjoy the benefits of having older, more experienced officers available at Auburn. While officers hired prior to the 1970s experienced the "cold shoulder" from the veterans, those entering in the 1980s appear to get support.

> It's not like the old style training. The older officers will tell you how no one would tell you anything in the old days. Now with the turnover and the academy people are better trained and the officers are more willing to train others.
>
> * * *
>
> Auburn's lucky with seniority. So newer officers can learn from officers with 15 years in. At Sing-Sing I was fresh out of the academy and after a few weeks I was a senior officer helping to train the rookies.

One other aspect of training that deserves mention is the younger officers' observations that training in legal matters, inmates' rights and officer rights and report writing were among the most beneficial aspects of the training experience. This signifies the salience of procedural regularity and accountability that has entered into the previously rather secluded world of Auburn prison.

SUMMARY—1986

New officers coming to work at Auburn reflect the changing economic character of the general central New York area. Coming to prison work at a younger age, with less work experience, more likely to have more education and more likely to be from out of the county surrounding the prison, these officers are also arriving in much larger cohorts. While their more experienced counterparts readily established human relationships with inmates, these new officers are more likely to find inmate hostility and resort to stereotypes in establishing their initial relationships with inmates. In addition, their sense of awareness of prison issues coupled with changes in the character of the inmate culture are more likely to lead them to experience a "negative reality shock," when their experienced counterparts were "underwhelmed" by their initial prison experiences.

NOTES

[1]Jacobs, James B. and Retsky, Harold G. "Prison Guard," *Urban Life*, Vol. 4, April (1975), p. 9.

[2]In fact, 46 of the 50 officers interviewed were living in the Auburn area when they became officers, but only six began their correctional careers at Auburn. Each of these six had less than four years experience.

[3]Ritzer, George. *Working: Conflict and Change*, second edition. Englewood Cliffs, NJ: Prentice-Hall, 1977, p. 23.

[4]Neiderhoffer, Arthur. *Behind the Shield: The Police in Urban Society*. Garden City, NY: Doubleday and Company, 1967, pp. 151-154; Westley, William A. *Violence and the Police*. Cambridge, MA: Massachusetts Institute of Technology Press, 1970, p. 159.

[5]These differences between the men raised in Auburn and their "Big City" counterparts may point to significant differences in the practical experiences of correction officer forces working in prisons located in large urban areas and those located in rural areas whose inmate populations come largely from urban areas. Although this question is beyond the scope of this study, this difference might merit further research.

[6]Upon entering the prison world, the correction officer recruit seemingly undergoes the staff version of the "fraternalization process" undergone by new inmates described by Goffman: "The new [inmate] recruit frequently starts out with something like the staff's popular misconception of inmates; he comes to find that most of his fellows [inmates] have all the properties of ordinary, occasionally decent human beings...the offenses that inmates are known to have committed outside cease to prove an effective means for judging their personal qualities." Goffman, Erving. "On the Characteristics of Total Institutions: The Inmate World," in *The Prison: Studies in Institutional and Organizational Change*, edited by Donald Cressey. New York: Holt, Rinehart and Winston, 1961, p. 54.

[7]Westley, W. A. *Violence and the Police*, Cambridge, MA: Massachusetts Institute of Technology Press, 1970, p. 158; Maanen, John Van. "Observations on the Making of Policemen," in *Policing: A View from the Street*. Santa Monica, CA: Goodyear, 1978, pp. 293-308.

[8]The choice of 1970 as a dividing line is not arbitrary. Many experienced officers suggest that the introduction of a bidding system for institutional job assignments significantly altered recruit-experienced officers. An examination of interview data tends to support this conclusion.

Question: What was it like when you began, as far as being accepted by other officers?

Entered Correctional Service	Initial Experience Positive		Initial Experience Negative		
	Percent	*N*	Percent	*N*	Total
Before 1970	38	12	62	20	32
After 1970	82	9	18	2	11

[9]When specific officers come to identify themselves with certain jobs, they exhibit the secondary adjustments that Goffman ascribes to inmates. From the officer's perspective the job provides him with control over his environment. See Goffman, Erving. *Asylums*. Garden City, NY: Anchor Books, 1961, p. 55.

[10]Goffman, Erving. "On the Characteristics of Total Institutions: The Inmate World," in *The Prison: Studies in Institutional and Organizational Change*, edited by Donald Cressey. New York: Holt, Rinehart and Winston, 1961, p. 23.

[11]This situation is described by Sherif when he says:

> ...we frequently find a discrepancy between the individual's membership group and his reference group. Of course, the very fact of existing in a group setting, within an organization with its values and goals and pressures toward conformity, is significant. Psychologically, however, there are profound differences between the inwardly cherished values and goals and conformity merely for the sake of surviving in a setting while inwardly relating oneself to other values.

Sherif, Muzafir. *Social Interaction*. Chicago, IL. Aldine Publishing Company, 1967, p. 229.

The Men and their Tasks

3

The traditional portrait of the prison guard has him standing in the prison yard, night stick in hand, or sitting in a tower with his machine gun, observing inmates as they go about their daily routines below. However, such media stereotypes mask the great variety of tasks and work environments that occupy and surround the working guard. The correction officer's tasks are not so simple or so singular. As in any community, a large number of functions need to be performed if the prison community is to run smoothly. In prison it is the correction officer who performs many of these functions or who supervises the inmates who perform them.

The variety of tasks correction officers perform is compounded by a variety of work environments. He may never come into contact with inmates or they may constantly surround him. His work environment may be highly structured or it may be relatively uncontrolled.

Combinations of these variables create a variety of work environments, each with different demands and expectations regarding the behavior of both inmates and officers. For officers it is less important that they meet inmates in prison than it is *where* in the prison they meet. It is clear that the distribution of tasks and environmental considerations faced by an individual officer depends on his particular job assignment.[1]

THE VARIETY OF JOB ASSIGNMENTS

Job assignments at Auburn may be classified into seven general categories according to their location within the institution, the duties required and the character of contact with the inmate population. These seven categories are

1. block officers,
2. work detail supervisors,
3. industrial shop and school officers,
4. yard officers,
5. administration building assignments,
6. wall posts, and
7. relief officers.

Each of these assignments has its own duties and its own problems, and it is the men and their tasks that occupy the rest of this chapter.

Block Officers

Perhaps the busiest and most demanding job assignment is that of the block officer. In cell blocks housing between 300 and 400 men, the block officer supervises and cares for inmates and supervises other officers who are assigned to gallery duty within the blocks. During the evening shifts, when inmates are locked in their cells, the tasks of the block officer are fairly routine: making rounds to inspect cells for fires, watching for signs of self-destructive behavior and handling inmate problems as they arise. On day shifts the block officer's tasks become much more complex: a combination of security, supervision, housekeeping and human services:

> In the block my job is to keep the block running orderly and on schedule. Special things to do during the school week and others on weekends. Let them in and out on time, make regular counts. Let those in coming from work. Give out medication. Lock them in and count again. Then let them out into the yard. All the while I have to handle all kinds of problems, personal, plumbing or electrical. I hand out newspapers and mail. I make check rounds to make sure there's no two in a cell. Let some in at seven o'clock and after eight o'clock let those in from the yard. Then I make the final count. There's call-outs and everything else in between. Anything can happen and always does.

Block officers are busy keeping track of 300 to 400 men, solving many personal problems, supervising inmate cleanup crews, all the while attempting to maintain some degree of security. The atmosphere is frequently quite hectic with the officer often sitting at his desk surrounded by five to ten inmates all wanting their own personal problems handled immediately. Requests for passes to other parts of the institution, inquiries about rules or personal concerns are put to block officers in rapid-fire fashion, often creating an atmosphere of confusion. Because of the responsibility they carry and the management and organizational skills they demonstrate, block officers are generally respected by most other officers.

In the block, problems for the officer arise from a lack of stability and consistency, not from the inmates, but from the administration. Changes in rules and regulations create confusion for officers and inmates alike. As one block officer explains:

> [The biggest problem] is the conflict within the administration itself. There's a constant changing of orders brought on by directives from the central office. It creates a state of confusion in the blocks. Among the inmates it's dangerous, among the officers it's chaos. The constant state of turmoil drives everyone crazy. Like the letter writ-

> ing business, three directives in three days. Everything just keeps changing.

Work Detail Supervisors

Assignments in the clothing room, commissary, hobby shop or store house involve ordering and distributing goods to inmates, supervising a crew of inmates (usually six or seven men), managing inventory and keeping account books. Because these officers often control inmate access to scarce resources and staff access to favors, these positions carry with them both power and frustration. But working with a smaller group of inmates also provides opportunities for satisfaction. One work detail supervisor explains:

> I get a lot of hassle as clothing room officer. I have to issue clothing and I have to refuse to issue it sometimes too. I get sworn at all the time. I could lock guys up every hour. I have to put up with verbal abuse: I'm always a "mother———!" I take it as part of the job. I've got to decide whether to turn inmates down or not. They take my name at least once a day because they don't like it. If I stay one more year, I'll set a record for staying in the clothing room the longest. Sergeants call and want me to do favors for some inmate hassling them. I've got to turn them down, and they get an attitude toward me. It's a hassle job: fighting and arguing with the inmates. Some days I dread it because certain guys are coming up. But it's all in a day's work. I've got eight guys working for me, seven black and one Puerto Rican. I have a good working relationship with these men. They know what they can and can't do. With some I have a more personal relationship, with others a more officer—inmate relationship.

Supervising work details can be hectic or relaxed. While the pace in the clothing room varies with inmate schedules, cleanup crews can regularly be observed taking their time, often enjoying pleasant weather.

Industrial Shop and School Officers

Officers in these areas perform order maintenance and security functions. However, in these locations they are not alone. Two or three officers are assigned to these areas, where they are in charge of a smaller group of inmates than in the blocks (30 to 40 in an industrial shop and 200 to 300 in the school). Here they must also work with civilian foremen, industrial supervisors and, in the school, with teachers, counselors and school administrative personnel. In addition to taking counts and checking the whereabouts of absentees, the officers, at times, must design and maintain record-keeping systems for inmate payrolls, and at times they must assign inmates to specific tasks and, together with civilians, manage the interactions of the inmate work group. Just as block officers or work detail supervisors, they must handle inmate problems and complaints as well:

> The [license plate shop] where I work is like a factory. We tell the men reasons why we do things. We [have the men] punch time cards and try to make it like real conditions. Security-type things? If there's a question, my job is to let the inmate know why. Sometimes they think it's petty, but I'm in charge of knowing where everybody is and how many there are.
>
> * * *
>
> ...as a new guy comes into the shop that's where they start. If we get two or three guys at a time, the one with the highest number gets the porter's job. It just so happened that two black guys got the toilet area and a white guy got put further up. The black guy asked about this and asked about that. I showed them the number system and they accepted it.
>
> * * *
>
> On my job in the school, guys come up to you with personal problems like sickness, a death in the family, and he wants to see a counselor. It might take three to five days before he does. You have to deal with this then and there. You have to pacify. A lot of men are babies, always asking, "Why do I have to do that?" You say, "Rules and regulations say do it like this." The guy blows his top and starts giving you a lot of grief. Now you've got to soft-talk him. Try to keep it calm and keep peace in the school area.
>
> *What is the biggest problem you have doing your job?*
>
> [In the school] getting them to go back to classes. On my job right now, the inmates aren't going along with the program. They're assigned to the school, but constantly skipping. I get a hassle because I have to account for them. If I can't, I have to put in an infraction. Then they come to me and ask, "Why did you put an infraction report on me? I was here." I say, "No, you weren't." This gets repetitious. Same thing day after day, but it's my job. I have to know where they are.

> When school teachers are out sick, this creates a problem. There are no relief teachers and there might be free periods. They might not be supervised for an hour and a half and I can't get him back to the block. I might get 30 to 50 guys like that and they're hanging around my back with nothing to do. I've got to supervise them and do my routine work at the same time.

Yard Officers

In the blocks inmates are at home; in the school, shops and on work details they are at work; but in the yard inmates are "on the street." For the correction officer, the work environment of the yard is the least structured and provides the inmate the most freedom of action. In the yard the behavioral norms established are those of the inmates and not those dictated by a task, the administration or the officers. Officers working the yard are generally those with the least seniority. They have no specific groups of inmates to supervise nor tasks to complete. Consequently, they spend most of their time concerned with security and maintaining order. Occasionally they may be called upon to direct inmates to the proper channels so that inmate problems can be resolved:

> In the yard it's mainly the observation of key individuals—the supposed troublemakers. You keep an eye on them so they're not causing any trouble that the prison doesn't need or I don't need.
>
> There's very little physical labor in the yard, but much mental labor. You've got to be alert to what's going on around you. Inmates are constantly trying to beat you. You have to keep your eyes and ears open to observe them in different situations. You're paid to watch, listen and control.

The yard officer's tasks are characterized by the suspicion that inmates are breaking rules or plotting something devious. The problems of the yard officers are different from those of the officers described above and derive from the unique environment of their assignment:

> My biggest problem is trying to decide if a guy's breaking a rule. Then if I think he is, it's figuring out how to enforce it.

Administration Building Assignments

Correction officers with job assignments in the administration building work under a set of circumstances totally different from that of most other officers. For the most part, these officers have few, if any, contacts with inmates. They are only indirectly concerned with security, having primary responsibility for handling routine administrative tasks. Some of these officers open doors, close doors, check passes in and out of the institution. Others handle routine administrative tasks, often working with civilians. An officer who works in the institution's arsenal describes his work:

> I keep the keys and weapons. Mostly an administrative job. I work the switchboard, handle finances, money that comes to the front hall from the visitors for inmates. I process drafts [inmates transferring to or from other institutions], furloughs and courtmen. You're a doorman, a telephone answerer, you do everything.

An officer who works the night shift in the administration building explains:

> I work with the lieutenant and the watch commander, I cover them when they're out. I answer the phone. [The biggest problem] is answering the phone for outside calls. Relatives and friends of inmates, employees calling in sick. They tell you one thing and a couple of days later they change their story completely and you get stuck in the middle.

For officers in the administration building the day-to-day operations of the prison that affect inmates are of little concern, since they generally have more contact with the public than with inmates. Often they can be seen explaining institutional rules and regulations to complaining, bothered and upset civilian visitors.

Wall Posts

Officers who work on wall towers are concerned almost exclusively with outer-perimeter security. They live in their guard towers for eight hours each day, caring for their equipment, making scheduled security check-ins, eating their meals and otherwise occupying their time. Almost completely removed from the prison's ongoing activities, they readily carry on conversations with inmates or officers passing by on the inside, and often with civilians passing on the outside.

Even upon the walls, out of the daily flow of institutional life, problems arise, but the problems are different from those of their inside counterparts:

> If something happens, it's most important to protect people. You can't shoot till you get the order. By the time you call up, somebody's dead. You're on your own there, actually. You don't know what's coming. You can tell by the climate if something's going to bust loose. I wonder about that. I guess you'll just have to wait till it

> happens. But I never worry about it. They're always looking for an answer. Today it's right, tomorrow maybe not.

On the wall one has time to philosophize and think deeply about one's situation.

Relief Officers

Relief officers perform a variety of tasks substituting for regular officers on their days off, vacations or sick days. They may have steady relief assignments, working the same two or three jobs on a rotating two-week basis, or they may work a much wider variety of jobs. Not being on any one job for an extended period of time, it is often difficult for relief officers to establish personal relationships with inmates. Moving throughout the institution, performing a variety of tasks, they have no personal identification with any one task and have a more generic definition of their job than does the average officer:

> Naming the biggest problem with this relief job is a tough question because of the varied jobs, I suppose, being a training relief officer, working two to four jobs in the course of a day and having to know what each job consists of. There's supposed to be a written description of every job a guy does in the institution. I've got to know every man's job. It's my choice. Not knowing fully what the job consists of, I struggle along, I play it by ear, unless the guy I'm relieving carries a notebook on what the guys do and could show me.

ON-THE-JOB MOTIVATIONS

Even though officers can now bid on the institutional job assignments they perform, it is not the specific duties that are involved in a particular job that seem to be the officer's primary concern. The motivations for working on a particular job assignment are, for the most part, a reflection of individual attempts to relate meaningfully to their work environment, rather than attempts to find positions from which they will be able to make meaningful contributions to the correctional task.

To explore more closely correction officer work motivations, each officer was asked to respond to the question: "If you could have any job in the institution, which job would you pick?" The officer was also asked to indicate why he would pick a particular job. From the responses to the latter question, a number of characteristic motivational concerns emerged.

The most frequently mentioned reason for choosing a particular assignment was that it provided the officer with *activity* and made time pass quickly. According to one officer who works in the kitchen area:

> It's one of the worst jobs and I've got to be crazy to work there. But I worked there before and it's a job where you keep busy. I thought it would make the job go faster.

Officers are not only concerned with putting in "fast" eight-hour days when they bid on "active" jobs, they also want their career as an officer (perceived by many as a "sentence") to pass quickly. One relief officer, for example, relates:

> [I] work a different job every two weeks and get around to see the whole joint. I get to know what the inmates can and can't have. And it also breaks up my 25-to-life "bit."

A second motivational concern is *autonomy*—a desire to obtain some measure of control over their personal work environment. In order to avoid being subject to perceived inconsistencies of supervisory and administrative directives, some officers want assignments that allow them to make decisions concerning what they do and how they do it. Having autonomy in one's job assignment also means becoming independent of other segments of the institution:

> I worked all the other jobs and didn't want all the hassles. [There are] not as many bosses here. I've got one sergeant to answer to and I take care of most of my problems myself.

Another common concern reflects officers' *desires to contribute* either to the well-being of the inmates or to the overall running of the institution. Although this concern contains some elements of "activity," it is primarily focused upon the positive contribution the activity allows, and not on the activity per se:

> I like working with the misfits. Here [in segregation] you get a good chance to work with the inmates.

* * *

> I thought I could be more helpful [in the mess hall]. They requested that I go there. An inmate told a sergeant [that] if he wanted it clean, he should get me.

Another work concern voiced by officers reflects a preference for *privacy* or a *desire to remove themselves* from danger or conflict. Having experienced frustration and conflict in encounters with inmates, the prison administration and supervisors, some officers bid on jobs and shifts that effectively take them out of the action:

> I wanted nights. It's safer than days. No headaches from the brass or from the inmates, but you still have your jobs to do.

A final work concern relates less to the work of the officer inside the prison than to his *life outside* the walls. Arranging shifts to fit family responsibilities and obtaining assignments to obtain weekends off regularly also prompts some officers to bid on certain jobs.

This list of motives is similar to "profiles" of "prison concerns" found among inmates. Toch, in a study of the impact of prison environments, found that special inmate needs include concerns for activity, freedom, privacy, emotional feedback, support, safety and structure.[2] Like inmates, officers prefer job assignments that "match" their needs for special kinds of social environments.

There is also a discernible tendency for officers who have special motivational concerns to prefer specific job locations (see Table 6, Appendix D). Block jobs, for example, are the most likely to be associated with activity or the desire to help inmates than with any other need. Working in the blocks would thus seem to provide officers with opportunities to keep themselves busy and make the day go by, as well as with opportunities to render services.

For those officers who prefer to work with work gangs of inmates, the primary concern appears to be control over one's environment. The officer in such jobs is less encumbered by interference from supervisory personnel and less distracted by large groups of inmates. He is able to make decisions concerning his men in his own work and also to control specific goods and services to which other institutional personnel might want access. Most officers who express a concern for control do so, indicating they could be their own boss or that they had less interference from others. Work gang jobs also provide a degree of activity, lessening boredom.

Officers expressing a preference for jobs located in the administration building or upon the walls are primarily concerned with decreasing their contact with inmates. Jobs in the administration building are also associated with activity and control over one's environment. For those officers who preferred to work on the wall, getting away meant not only getting away from inmates, but also administrative personnel. On the wall the chances of being bothered by anyone are virtually nil.

Other data also point to the importance of these motivational concerns to the officers. When asked if they had received their present job by bidding and if so, why they bid on that particular job, those officers who bid on their jobs (see Table 7, Appendix D) indicate that control over their environment and shift were their primary concerns.[3]

The job locations of the 21 officers who did not bid on their jobs again emphasize the importance of special motivational concerns (see Table 8, Appendix D). These officers obtained their jobs by assignment, often prior to the introduction of the bidding system, and they wanted to retain their present jobs. Others who began work and received assignments after the introduction of the bidding system decided to stay with their assignments. From these data it is evident that officers have tended to stay on jobs without bidding on others when their jobs allow for "activity" and "control," such as the assignments of block officer and administration building officers. For younger officers who lack seniority, relief jobs provide for movement throughout the institution, a constant change of environment and diverse "activity," though such jobs are low on "control" since the officer is not permanently assigned to a fixed location.[4]

GENERAL THEMES IN THE GUARDS' WORK

The foregoing discussion of specific job assignments and motivational concerns described the range of prison guard duties and the variety of forces motivating these guards to perform them. However, the more general nature of the correction officer's job needs explanation. The variety of facets that form such a general definition provides a look into the operational reality of "being a guard" in more general terms.

In response to inquiries about the general nature of their work, correction officers provide a wide variety of perceptions and definitions with only one theme agreed upon by one-half of the officers (see Table 9, Appendix D). This diversity of definition would seem to indicate that definitions derived from individual experiences take precedence over social definitions provided by the guards as a group, again indicating the weakness of the officer—group tie. However, despite this lack of consensus on any one theme, a number of common themes are evident.

Human Services

The most frequently mentioned theme is that of the provider of human services. Though some officers approach the human service aspects of their work grudgingly, calling themselves "baby sitters" or "playground directors," complaining that "we do everything for the inmates and they never do anything for themselves," most approach the service aspect of their work with a positive attitude. At times officers feel they perform positive services for inmates in spite of perceived pressures against doing so. When they say, "A lot of officers don't like to hear about [providing for inmate needs]," "Others get on me for doing things for the inmates," and "If you try to do too much you get your ass chewed out," these guards underscore the officers' belief that "helping inmates" is not always looked upon favorably by their peers or supervisors, even though they view the human service function positively for themselves. This belief that to provide human services is somehow perceived negatively by others gives the officer a sense of being different from other officers and from supervisors, who in the process become "bad guys." It also provides the officer with a more positive sense of "self as officer" than he might otherwise have had.

As a human services worker, the correctional worker becomes involved with inmate problems and must listen to "sob stories" told to him on a personal level. He is expected to handle institutional adjustment problems and to deal with self-destructive behaviors.

Requests that he "cut red tape" are constantly put to him by inmates. With such, the officer either refers the inmate to a counselor or to a sergeant, or he handles the problem himself. However, no matter how he manages these varying situations, many a correction officer sees himself as the institution's frontline problem-solver and referral agency. And, indeed, it is the correction officer who initially encounters nearly every problem in the institution.

The human services theme, as it manifests itself in the correction officers' jobs, has three general aspects, each of which illustrates the characteristics of "people work" put forward by Goffman.[5] Primarily, some officers envision themselves as *providers of goods and services* who see to it that the inmates' basic needs are met. Food, clothing, medication and cleanliness are prime concerns. Inmates locked in their cells for disciplinary or medical reasons must be fed. Occasionally an officer encounters an inmate who refuses to bathe regularly; other inmates often complain to officers about such inmates and the officer will often attempt to have the offending inmate adjust his habits. If the officer can persuade the inmate to tidy up, he reduces the number of problems he must deal with on his gallery. Success in his efforts enhances his status in the eyes of inmates. He is viewed by inmates as an officer who can get things done, gaining more cooperation from those for whom he is responsible. Similar processes appear to be at work as the officer seeks to secure clothing, food or other "necessities of life" for inmates.

Most officers are quite aware of the necessity to keep their word if they say they will take care of a problem for an inmate. Failure to keep one's word is reported to diminish the confidence inmates have in the officer's ability to "take care of business." From the officer's point of view, failure to keep his word can demonstrate to the inmate that the officer does not really care and provides opportunities for what Mathiesen calls "censorious" behavior on the part of inmates.[6]

As one officer put it, "If you say you will do something for an inmate and you don't, you're marked. They'll see you every day and know who you are. You're in for trouble." Trouble here means that the officer's job becomes tougher. Rather than cooperate, inmates may linger on the gallery before moving into their cells, thus delaying a count. Reportedly, the officer who fails to fulfill his promise must hold back from making an issue of such incidents, lest his failure to live up to his word becomes known to others on the gallery. Here the important thing to note is not that refusal to do a favor causes the officer to lose some of his authority, but rather that failure to live up to one's word once it is given diminishes the value of the officer as a person.

A second aspect of the human service theme deals with the correction officers' handling of inmate institutional problems. Here the officer acts as a *referral agent or an advocate*, setting up appointments with counselors, calling the correspondence office or an office to check on the status of an inmate's account. It should be kept in mind that these officers are not required to make phone calls or otherwise intervene on behalf of inmates, and are often discouraged from doing so by administrators and supervisors. All they need to do is to tell the inmate to follow established procedures (i.e. drop a note to the appropriate office and wait for a written reply). Officers, however, know from experience that delay causes problems for them, hence they are motivated to move against the "institutional bureaucracy" in attempts to gain action. Some interview excerpts will illustrate:

> You're dealing with the inmates' everyday problems, money, packages, mail, visits, telephone calls. You've got to call right away and lots of times you can't get the right people. If a guy's borderline, you've got to be careful because he might go into a rage.

* * *

> I have a lot of inmates come to me with problems. I try to give help and helpful words. Maybe you call to see how a guy should make arrangements for something. Get the service unit or the chaplain to talk to him. Give some helpful advice. I find myself doing it a lot. A lot of guys come to me and say, "Mr.———, I've got a problem, maybe you can help." One guy was shaking and upset. He said he was in a big jam and he didn't want to go to the P.K. He gave me a check he'd gotten in the mail (correspondence had overlooked it). I took the check, gave the guy a receipt and put it in his account. It's not a big thing, just little things to take the edge off. Sometimes if you're helpful you can correct things and save trouble. When they can't handle it, they just swing out.

The third, possibly most important, aspect of the human service theme is the role the officer plays in the *institutional adjustment* of inmates. In this role many correction workers see themselves as psychiatrists, doctors, social workers or father figures. The "pains of imprisonment" have been described by Sykes,[7] but it is the correction officer who most closely observes the onset of these "pains" and who, if he desires, can most effectively deal with, or at least aid, the inmate in coping with these pains. When asked what they do when an inmate comes to them with a personal, *noninstitutional* problem, two-thirds of the officers indicated that they try to listen and offer advice, and that they would approach particular inmates if they thought they were having problems with which they might help.[8] Family problems, personal problems and mental health problems come to the attention of the correction officer. This is especially true of officers who work in blocks, industrial shops or with work gangs of inmates. In these situations, officers are involved with the same group of inmates on a day-to-day basis and mutual trust between officer and inmate is more likely to develop. The inmates become dependent on particular officers as sources of support and the officers become dependent on the inmates to provide them with opportunities to "help." In combatting boredom and in seeking to exercise personal control over at least their immediate environment, "helping" proves functional (beyond the benefits of the "help" itself) to both the inmate and the officer:[9]

> They've got problems. They get bad-news letters, they stay in and brood about it. I call the service unit and get a "it's none of your business." We took care of all these things before the service unit was set up. I can't see why it takes so long to get an answer, to make a decision. I had a guy working for me, a good worker, a Muslim. Everybody was down on him. They said he'd be a bum. I said let's see what he does. I asked what his problem was and he said that he got a bad letter. His little girl had had an operation. He didn't know how serious it was, but he was worried. I tried to make arrangements for him to make a phone call. I had a couple of friends up there, you make them after a while. This was like one of those situations you sometimes face yourself, not knowing about these things. He got his phone call and perked up.

This officer's ability to empathize with the inmate makes the offer of assistance less a calculated maneuver designed to secure cooperation and more simply the "human" thing to do.

Occasionally an officer is faced with inmates with serious psychological problems which occasionally become disruptive but must somehow be managed. In these situations officers sometimes enlist the help of inmates in trying to manage the situation:

> One group you have is the psychos. There are some in the school. One guy comes to school and takes off all the time. You can't keep him in the school. I didn't know where he was. I saw that he did talk with one of my porters a lot. I asked the porter about the guy and he said he was okay. After a while I teamed him up with the other porter and he stayed on the job. The guy was in [the mental facility for criminals] three or four times. The [other] inmate saw that he had a problem. The inmate tried to talk to this so-called nut, so I asked to see if he could do anything and it worked out pretty well.

Officers working in the Special Housing Unit (Segregation) are particularly aware of inmate problems, being in charge of security, mental health and self-protection cases. These officers are particularly attentive to the institutional adjustment aspects of their job:

> You never get two alike. Each guy is an individual in mind and thoughts. Different things make them do things. One guy was having problems with his wife and tied a sheet over the bars in back. He had one foot on the bed and one on the toilet and timed it so I was coming around. He didn't want to hang himself. I ran for help and when I came back he was untying the sheet and another officer was folding it up. He did it more for attention. His wife knew he'd be away for a long time and she was playing around and he couldn't stand that.
>
> It could be mail from home, wife, provoked by another inmate, by the staff, to keep from being moved. Sometimes you can't figure out why at the time. One guy stripped down and stood in the center of his cell with his eyes closed. He'd been on drugs and had mental problems. I tried to talk to the guy and he wouldn't answer. We figured out though that he was going back to the population the next day and he didn't want that.

Order Maintenance

This perspective of the correction officer's work is not to be confused with the "restraint" function of keeping inmates "in" or preventing them from getting out. Just as with the human services theme, when an officer acts to protect inmates from one another, he measures his duties in terms of beneficial effects that result for the inmates. Such phrases as "keep them in check," "keep them from going at one another," "keep inmates from killing each other," "keep stealing, gambling and homosexuality to a minimum," illustrate a positive as well as a negative control theme. One officer provided an excellent description of this perspective of his work:

> Security doesn't mean keep them from going over the wall. It means you try to make the guy feel secure, that he's not going to get killed or hurt. You keep the place clean on the block job. You make it so an inmate can sit next to another inmate in the mess hall or the auditorium and feel comfortable. So he doesn't have to worry about something happening. It's so compressed in there. Other than that it's just like the street. If they want to go out they'll find a way. It's not that kind of security.

In this respect, the correction officers see themselves as police officers who intervene in family quarrels to maintain social order:

> If a guy did something to you and you didn't like it, you'd hit him, right? It has nothing to do with prison. It's like a city within a city and we're the policemen. They won't rat on each other normally, unless something will hurt them. I had a guy two years ago, pacing in the shop all day long. Just before he went to the blocks he said, "(Officer), put me on the roof." He said he'd kill a guy in the block if he went back. I called the sergeant and he put him there. Another colored guy was trying to pick on him and he's trying to go along with the program and he wouldn't take any more baloney. He was going to prove he's a man, but he wouldn't do it because "it's not worth it for these animals," he said. He'd escaped from another prison and everyone said he's an escape artist. But I put in a good word for him and gave him a tool room job, only he could go in there. He said I had faith in him and he'd do the job. He respected me for trusting him and so he told me when he was going to do something. It saved him a new sentence and me a hassle.

Here one learns that it is not merely the officer's physical presence as an authority figure which serves to check inmates in their conflicts with one another, but the relationships that develop between an officer and an inmate. A positive relationship allows the inmate to approach the officer when a problem is developing, allowing the officer time to defuse it. Thus one finds a connection between the officer's abilities to maintain order and personal relationships between officers and inmates.

Security (Guard Function)

The security function of the correction officer's role most closely resembles the conventional picture of the "guard" as one who prevents escapes, but only one-sixth of these officers mentioned "keeping inmates in" as part of what they do. One officer saw security as his primary function:

> What do I do? Security. I'm not concerned with why they're in. I just make sure they stay here till the courts let them go. If they rap about their records, okay, but it's not my job to take care of them with talk. I don't push myself on them. I let them alone. If they want to talk or kid or joke, okay. If not, I leave them alone.

Where order-keeping and protecting inmates is in many respects an active function of the officer, security is essentially passive. Standing and watching, or sitting and watching, are the principal forms security takes.

Supervision

Correction officers are charged with seeing to it that inmates "do things": that they are ready to leave galleries on time, that they return to their cells on time, that they arrive and leave recreation areas on time. With 1,600 inmates in the institution and each inmate expecting that he will be able to use the limited facilities when he is scheduled to use them, delays in one area cause problems all along the line. This is especially important in an institution like Auburn, where programs for inmates are heavily stressed.

In addition to supervising inmate movement, correction officers also supervise inmates on their various work assignments. Institutional food must be prepared and served and dishes must be washed. Clothing and bedding have to be collected, cleaned and redistributed. Cleanup crews and construction crews must prepare institutional areas for the use of all concerned. It is the inmate who performs these chores and it is the officer who is responsible for seeing to it that he does.

Rule Enforcement (Police Function)

The enforcement aspect of the correction officer role involves not only citing inmates for rule infractions, but discovering contraband and gathering information concerning possible illicit activities inmates may be engaged in. Though this function receives much attention in prison literature,[10] only 22% of the men interviewed include it in their self-definition of the officer role, and none of these officers sees rule enforcement as their only function. Rule enforcement seems to be a concern primarily of younger, relatively less experienced officers. The salience of rule enforcement for those officers indicates that this aspect of their work is a problem with which they are trying to come to grips.

Prison rules say that correction officers must deal with everything from extra helpings of food and smoking in restricted areas to clothing regulations and sanitary conditions of both cells and inmates to fights, gambling and drugs. As the institution's policemen, officers not only enforce regulations, but are also involved in investigatory processes. The gathering of information concerning the entry of drugs or other contraband into the institution, the production of prison "wine" and the conduct of gambling are included within the correction officer's role definition. Skill in the use of inmate informants is seen as a necessary, though not respected, investigatory technique.

SUMMARY—1976

From the guard's perspective, prison guard tasks have nothing to do with rehabilitation, just deserts, corrections or punishments. These are issues for the policy planner and program designer—issues that focus upon the inmate's past or attempt to prepare him for the future. For the prison guard going about his day-to-day business, it is the immediate present that matters, life as it is lived and passes *within the prison community*; the outside has little relevance.

The guard attempts to find assignments that will accommodate his own needs, whether he seeks to make time pass, to control his work environment or to help or get away from inmates, the guard's work, as he performs it, is often a reflection of his personal preferences. In defining and developing tasks out of the raw materials at hand, guards manage personal conflicts to maintain order or to supervise inmates to get some work done. Most importantly, guards become human service workers dealing with the inmates' personal and institutional adjustment, assisting inmates to cope with the pains of imprisonment.

TASK REDEFINITION: 1976-1986

Over the course of the ten years since the 1976 study, the 32 officers from the original sample who provided information changed job assignment an average of three to four times. The average length of stay on any one assignment was 37 months. While eight of the officers moved from assignments *in* the population to *out* of population assignments, five of these eight and eleven overall moved to positions with increased responsibilities. For many, their new assignments have changed their lives: "I sleep better now"; "Now, I drink a lot less and never before I go to work," and "My family can stand me now" were commonly heard refrains from these experienced officers. Only three of the original sample officers remained on the same post and shifts for the entire ten years. For one officer who did so his assignment (block officer) and shift (11 p.m. to 7 a.m.) reportedly managed to keep him isolated from the changes that were taking place around him. On his preliminary information form he wrote:

> I am still on the night shift and not in contact with many of the programs and problems with the department or ACF. I'll be retiring in three years and am in the process of building up my outside business. As you can see, I'm not very interested in my state job but I will help you out if I can.

This officer, however, was unique. Most officers experienced and were forced to cope with new conditions and problems that were reshaping their approaches to their tasks and the tasks themselves.

Re-emergence of Custodial and Law Enforcement Functions

Though the basic outline of correctional officer tasks identified in 1976 has remained fairly constant, some subtle and other not-so-subtle changes have occurred in response to organizational changes and to changes in the inmate community. The most dramatic shift that has taken place is in the correctional officers' approach to their tasks. The Human Services functions of correctional officer work had a prominent place in the working lives of the officers in 1976. Though the importance of this function is still recognized, its prominence has been reduced as other functions appear to have gained in importance. As organizational changes have reduced opportunities for *helping* officer/inmate interactions (see Chapter 4), and as increased drug availability and violence have changed the dynamics of intra-inmate behavior (see Chapter 5), officer task emphasis has shifted to custodial and law enforcement functions.

> *Q: If you had to describe to someone who didn't know anything about the correctional officer's job, how would you describe it?*
>
> The basic thing is security. Make sure they don't get out and make sure they're a ward of the state. Protect themselves against themselves and other inmates. Against the dangers of the institution. Act as a counselor, father figure, chaplain, etc.
>
> * * *
>
> The amount of programs has grown enormously. And through the tier system there's more we have to know about the legal ramifications. The amount of legal knowledge that you have to have has grown enormously. Before we just had the facility rule book. Now there's the facility rule book, state and facility directives.
>
> *How has the job changed over the last ten years?*
>
> The CO today has to be more intelligent. More alert because of the legal issues. Where before the legal issues were not as important. In society and in the facility you have to explain why now. Before you had "yes, boss," "yes, Captain," "yes, sir." Now you have to explain, you can't just say, "I told you so."

Reduced Expectations

According to many of these officers the past ten years of correctional evolution have resulted in *reduced expectations* concerning the work of correctional officers. While "the early days" saw officers making individual discretionary decisions concerning a broad range of activities, the 1980's have seen the responsibilities of the officer become more circumscribed. *Redeployment* which required the development of job descriptions and justifications for each correctional officer post and position (a state mandated activity), helped contribute to this perception.

> With redeployment, every officer's job now has a description. The Sergeant can't say, "Hey, this is part of your job," because it's in the description and this is it. That's all you have. It's great because in the blocks and on other posts if you're working a vacation you don't have to go in blind, you just look up the job. You've got something to go by. The supervisors can't screw you up and have you do somebody else's job when they slough off.

> Before the officer was right and that was it. Now you have to show how and why you were right and you have to be right according to the directives. The inmates get copies of most of them so they're up to date.

Such specificity may breed structure and predictability and provide officers with clear direction. At the same time, however, specificity also reduces the officer's tendency to "creatively" approach the job. Before 1976, exercising discretion in determining the shape of one's tasks was done out of necessity. Such behavior was tacitly allowed and encouraged by the lack of direction. What appears to be happening now is that officers are coming to rely on "directives" and directions to determine job tasks and procedures. While it was relatively common for officers to alter verbal orders to fit individual situations and avoid problems, now the tendency appears to be one of following directives and using directives to justify one's actions to inmates and to superiors.

For other officers, reduced expectations relates to a reduced sense of officer self-discipline and is an indication of the lack of professionalism expected from officers.

> There's not really different expectations, if anything there's less. The administration doesn't deal harshly enough with problem officers. An officer who has brought booze into the institution, for example, within six months he might be back at work. There's less discipline for the officers now. I remember when you couldn't bring newspapers in. Now people bring them in and give them to the inmates. Now you catch officers horsing around with inmates in the yard and no one says anything.

Specialization

Another result of redeployment has been the development of more *specialists* as opposed to the generalist officers of the pre-1976 period.

> There's more specialization now. There are frisk officers, packing officers, the CERT team, hostage negotiations, with drug testing you can qualify with the FDA and get called as an expert witness. The officer of the year was a frisker.

An officer who is now a sergeant describes this increased specialization and the associated problems:

> Jobs we took for granted ten years ago are now done by specialist officers. Before all officers would be involved in taking care of drafts (movements of inmates in and out of the institution). Now we have special friskers and packers for these things. This has made it worse. I smell booze in one place and tell an officer to look, and he says that the frisker is supposed to do that.

Shift in Responsibilities

Another factor that has had an impact on the human services functions of the Auburn correctional officers is the increase in the number of supervisors and a subtle shift in the control of access to informal service networks from officers with connections to sergeants. Though many officers still report using the grassroots helping networks that they have developed over time, nearly all acknowledge that opportunities to put these networks into action (provided by inmate requests to officers) and officer tendency to utilize personal networks has decreased over time.

> From what I hear, ten years ago you had 14 Sergeants, now you have 38. I get lots of calls from officers to have a Sergeant call them to do the officer's job. To make decisions. Today the Sergeant has to make the decisions. The officer doesn't take as much on himself as ten years ago. He takes on very little.
>
> * * *
>
> Officers now are better trained than I was. But there's a lack of discipline among them. Why? Well, before you did what you were told. Officers with seniority were looked up to, and you followed the senior officers. Now they look to the Sergeants more, they don't look to the blue shirts.

An officer with three years' experience, however, has a different perspective:

> Now we're getting laxity. Auburn's lucky with seniority. So the newer officers can ask officers with 15 years in. At Sing-Sing I was out of the academy two weeks and I was almost a senior officer.

Transfer of Human Service Function to Inmates

Perhaps the change that has had the greatest negative impact on correctional officers' ability to perform human service functions has been the increase in the ability of the inmates to handle such problems themselves, particularly the more personal type of problems. Increased inmate access to telephones (nine in the yard, ten in the gym and ten outside the employees' mess providing virtually unlimited collect calls during the hours they are available) has made it possible for inmates to handle directly and in a timely manner many of the personal problems for which officers had previously served as intermediaries between the inmate and the chaplain and counselors who handled inmate contact with the outside world. Greater use of visitations and state-funded visitations for families living at a distance has closed the gap between family and inmate and made direct contact more likely. Hence, the correctional officers are less likely to play the go-between or personal counselor role that they once did.

This change may also be reinforcing trends in negative inmate behavior. While the pre-1976 world of Auburn reinforced inmates depending on officers, the changes described here appear to enhance inmate dependence. Hence, it should not be surprising to see inmates expressing independence in other areas as well (see increase in "order maintenance" rule violations, Table 19, Appendix D).

SUMMARY—1986

Though the basic components of correctional officer work have stayed essentially the same, changing conditions have led these officers to re-emphasize the security and law enforcement aspects of their work and to reduce their emphasis on human services activities. As sergeants have been given more responsibility and inmates more opportunity to handle inmate problems, as specialization and policy and procedure directives have provided more structure to correctional officer tasks, the individual officer's ability to shape his job has been reduced.

NOTES

[1]See Jacobs, James B. and Retsky, Harold G. "Prison Guard," *Urban Life*, Vol. 4, No. 1, April (1975), pp. 5-29 for a description of prison guard work at Stateville Penitentiary in Joliet, Illinois.

[2]Toch, Hans. *Living in Prison: The Ecology of Survival*. New York: Free Press, 1977.

[3]This variation in responses might also indicate that the individual officer is motivated to seek an assignment based on his personal interpretation of specific tasks, rather than on any idea of what officers in general consider "good" jobs.

[4]When preliminary information was being gathered for this study, the lieutenant in charge of officer job assignments indicated that officers were primarily concerned with their shift and with getting away from inmates when selecting a job. Based on this observation, each officer was asked: Realizing that you can only find certain jobs on certain shifts, which do you think would be your primary

concern in deciding what job you would bid on, the job itself or the shift? The 44 officers expressing a preference were equally divided between job and shift. When these are divided by preference there is a slight tendency for officers who view the job as most important to want to work with inmates. For those who view the shift as important there is a slight tendency to prefer work locations away from inmates.

[5]Goffman, Erving. *Asylums*. Garden City, NY: Anchor Books, 1961, pp. 74-83, passim.

[6]Mathiesen, Thomas. *The Defences of the Weak*. London: Tavistock, 1965, pp. 150-193.

[7]Sykes, Gresham. *The Society of Captives*. New York: Atheneum, 1970, pp. 63-83.

[8]That such helping activities do occur was verified by inmates. During the course of casual conversation between the author and inmate-students, several inmates were asked, "How are they treating you here?" One inmate known to the author from previous discussions as a man who had a generally skeptical attitude toward the prison administration related the following story:

> I've never seen a place like this. It's an easy place to do a bit if you can get used to it. The biggest thing is the officers. They say, "Yes, Mr.———, how can I help you?" I came up from New York City thinking it would be rough, cold and all that. On that bus trip I was building up all kinds of defenses. I was standoffish. But once I saw that, I came out of my defensive bag and relaxed.

Other inmates expressed similar opinions:

> These guys are mostly all right. You've got some assholes who try to act big, but most of the officers here, they treat you like a man. They'll help you out if they can. So you gotta respect them.

A "militant" inmate remarked:

> These guys here don't give you nothin' to fight against. (Sarcastically) They're so nice, always joking and doing things for you. I don't feel comfortable when they keep asking you how you're doing. There's something that ain't right about it.

Toch's findings concerning the environmental dimensions at Auburn support these observations in *Living in Prison*, p. 135.

[9]For other discussions of prison guards in helping roles, see Johnson, Robert. "Informal Helping Networks in Prisons: The Shape of Grass Roots Correctional Intervention." *Journal of Criminal Justice*, Vol. 7 (1979), pp. 53-70; Briggs, Dennie. "Chino California," in *Dealing with Deviants: The Treatment of Antisocial Behavior*, edited by Stuart Whitely, Dennie Briggs and Merfyn Turner. New York: Schocken Books, 1973, pp. 95-174; Cormier, Bruno M. *The Watcher and the Watched*. Plattsburg, NY: Tundra Books, 1975.

[10]See Sykes, Gresham. "The Corruption of Authority and Rehabilitation," *Social Forces*, Vol. XXXIV (1956), pp. 257-262; McCorkle, Lloyd W. "Guard-Inmate Relationships," in *The Sociology of Punishment and Corrections*, edited by N. Johnston, L. Savitz and M. Wolfgang. New York: John Wiley and Sons, 1970, pp. 419-422.

PRISON GUARDS AT WORK

II

Prison guards performing their tasks are always concerned about the nature of their relationships with the inmates in their charge. Previous discussions of guard-inmate relationships have drawn heavily on inmates as a source of information, focusing upon power, authority and some variant of the concept of "social distance" and the relationship of these concepts to the guard's role in rule enforcement. In Part II these themes will be examined from the perspective of the guard—placed in the context of the guard's daily activity. Alternative courses of action and the guard's perception of the forces that shape his choices among these alternatives are examined.

In Chapter 4, human service and helping relationships receive special attention. Here the concept of "sympathetic understanding," or social distance, is employed to explore the guard's "person-to-person" interactions with inmates. The correction officer's experience with his authority is examined in Chapter 5, along with the informal rule enforcement processes employed to manage and regulate inmate behaviors. Chapter 6 brings together the material in Chapters 4 and 5 in an attempt to re-examine the "corruption authority" perspective on guard-inmate relationships put forward by Sykes in his classic work *The Society of Captives*.

Guards and Inmates: Human and Helping Relationships

4

One of the most challenging aspects of the correction officer's work is the decision as to how he will relate in personal terms to the men in his charge. If he is to be a successful officer, he must establish and maintain what for him is a comfortable and appropriate degree of social distance between himself and the prison inmates.[1] To the extent that a guard defines himself as a human services provider, the character and dynamics of this aspect of the correction officer's work are most important.

One could argue that prison inmates are by definition somehow different from prison guards and that the amount of sympathetic understanding exhibited by guards toward inmates must be very small. The criminal, after all, is an individual who has somehow deviated from the rules that the rest of us seem to follow. The correction officer, however, represents the law-abiding segment of society and its legal system, whose norms the criminal has violated.[2]

The opposition to any reduction in prison security that is manifest in some of the communities where prisons are located demonstrates the general population's desire to keep the criminal at a safe distance.[3] In 1975 Auburn city officials voiced concern that a prison work release program was encouraging paroled inmates to remain in the Auburn area. These officials wanted to maintain extensive social distance between the "convict and the citizen" and argued that liberated inmates could change the nature of the Auburn community.[4]

Maintaining social distance between the "citizen" and the "criminal" outside prison walls is one thing; inside the walls it is quite another. For the citizen-turned-correction officer, the "criminal" ceases to be an abstraction. Association between the correction officer and the "criminal"-turned-"inmate" is impossible to avoid. Officers share space and time with inmates and in the process are forced to deal intensively with inmates and to establish characteristic ways of relating to them.

GENERAL INDICATORS OF SYMPATHETIC UNDERSTANDING

During the course of the interviews with the officers at Auburn, it became apparent that the "degree of understanding" felt to exist between the officers themselves and inmates varied among officers. For individual officers "social distance" often varied from inmate to inmate and situation to situation. It also became apparent that the degree of social distance officers maintained from inmates was, in general, not as great as one might expect.

When he was asked to indicate his preferred job assignment, one officer remarked:

> I don't mind working with inmates. In fact, sometimes they can really be okay. But at times I like to go to the wall or tower. That's not something I'd like to do forever. But inmates are the bottom of the barrel, constantly with problems. They can't take any responsibility and that gets to me. And they're 20 and 30 years old.

This comment illustrates some general points concerning officer-inmate social distance. First, it shows that even an officer who may like working with inmates may occasionally feel the need to remove himself from contact with them. Such an officer may succumb to the repetitiveness and frustrations of dealing with inmate needs and may view the wall post as a relief station, where he can physically, socially and psychologically remove himself from inmates and the everyday tensions of his job. Nearly all of the seven officers in our sample for whom wall duty is a regular assignment indicated that they chose that job because they felt they had "served their time" with inmates (these men averaged 24 years of service) and that it was appropriate for them to "retire" to the wall and away from the inmates.

The quote also illustrates that an officer can hold seemingly contradictory attitudes toward inmates. On the one hand, he refers to inmates as "really okay," indicating that he feels comfortable relating to them. On the other hand, he calls inmates "the bottom of the barrel," giving the impression that he does not care to associate with them at all. The fact that officers are capable of maintaining such contradictory attitudes about inmates reflects the nature of the "process" they employ in evaluating inmates. As with rule enforcement (see Chapter 5), correction officers tend to evaluate inmate behavior "situationally," rather than judging inmates on the basis of a generalized set. When things are going well, inmates are "okay"; with increased tension and frustration, inmates become "the bottom of the barrel."

If officers needed to maintain considerable social distance from inmates or lacked sympathetic understanding of the inmate situation, one might expect that officers would tend to describe inmates in terms of stereotypes and that their responses to inmate behavior and needs would reflect such stereotyped images. There is, however, little evidence in the interviews to support the existence of inmate stereotypes. There was almost no tendency for officers to refer to inmates as if all, or even most, inmates possessed similar characteristics. Indeed, as they became officers, what preprison stereotypes did exist were shattered. The above reference to inmates being "the bottom of the barrel" is a rare example of a stereotyped response. Nearly all of the officers, including the one cited above, qualified their references to inmates by such phrases as "some inmates" or "a few guys" or by giving a percentage of the inmates whom they felt behaved in a particular way.

When officers were asked to describe how inmates behave, it was virtually impossible to get an officer to describe general characteristics of inmate behavior. Even when pressed to give general characteristics, the response was inevitably something like "You can't talk about them as a group. Maybe there are some types, but I can't tell you about them in general." One officer's response summarizes the usual "situational" approach to evaluating inmates:

> *How would you describe the way inmates behave?*
>
> That's a hard question, because under the circumstances you expect that they have to adjust. Some act like high school kids. If there's a rule or a way they're supposed to act forced on them, they'll rebel and question it. Being in a hospital or a prison you're a captive audience. But there are different types. One is the loner. Even though the loner's good enough to make it on his own, he gets into trouble too if there's nobody to watch his back. Even the biggest of them.
>
> Another type travels with guys for protection. Like the Muslims. They're a group of men together to make their bit easier, to keep people off their backs, for group protection.
>
> Guys have to find ways to do their bits. The hardest part is putting up with people who mess with you. You don't have a choice. You get messed with, you draw the line or you can't make it. Most fights are for this reason. A guy might say something that's really nothing, like a fight I had in the mess hall over a mouse. A white guy says to the mouse, "Hey, brother in there." Both guys involved knew each other but the black guy took offense. The white guy didn't apologize and the other guy drew the line and had to fight.
>
> It's the weak and the strong, the loner and the group. A guy might be a punk (homosexual) to have protection. Some are greedy, some are ignorant. Except for the institution, you see the whole spectrum of the population. You find all the traits that you do on the outside. Maybe we're just more careful outside.

If this officer's description of inmate behavior or his ability to make meaningful distinctions among inmates demonstrates "sympathetic understanding" for some inmates, his choice of words in referring to inmates demonstrates another characteristic encountered in many interviews that is relevant here. In describing some ways "guys find to do their bits," this officer refers to inmates as "you" rather than "they." When he says, "The hardest part is putting up with people who mess with *you*," it is not exactly clear whether he is talking about the "hardest part" for officers or for inmates. This choice of words, typical of many officers we interviewed, can be interpreted as the officer's attempt to put the interviewer in the inmate's place, at least as the officer perceives it, and it is indicative of the officer's ability to identify with the inmates he watches.[5]

Another general indicator of the relatively low social distance officers maintain from inmates is frequent references by officers to incidents in which inmates displayed "human concerns" for officers. Quite often, without any prompting by the interviewer, officers proudly produced handmade Christmas cards and get-well cards they had received from particular inmates. As one officer displayed a get-well card signed by ten inmates, he remarked, "You know, these guys have feelings too. They know when you've got problems. If you care about them, they'll care about you." Though all officers are not the recipients of good wishes from all inmates, such inmate gestures are a well-known and appreciated part of the officer's work environment.

Another indication that correction officers generally do not maintain much social distance between themselves and inmates is the officers' tendency to compare themselves and their position in the institution to that of the inmates. After the initiation of an elaborate inmate grievance procedure, for example, many officers asked, "Why can't our grievances be responded to within fixed time limits like those of inmates; they [the administration] would probably have a lot less problems."

Comparisons between officers and inmates are made not only with reference to the relative availability of "individual rights," but references are also made to the comparability of the behavior of the two groups. The consensus among the Auburn guards is that there is a trend toward increasing permissiveness in the treatment of inmates. According to many officers, this change was accompanied by changes in the treatment of officers as well. Though specifically asked about inmates, one officer quickly drew a comparison between officers and inmates:

> It's really changed since I started. It reflects the outside. Before it was very military for the inmate and for the officer. Now both are slacked up. Now, with the younger type of inmate, court decisions, all the programs and the attitudes of the officers, laxity shows up in the inmates. Once there was regimentation of the inmates, marching and all that. There was also regimentation of the officers. Some guys (officers) blame their sloppy appearance on the state. But they've made a lot of things optional for the inmates and for the officers. Just like inmates aren't used to taking orders, neither are a lot of officers.

HELPING RELATIONSHIPS

While these general observations provide some indication of the degree of sympathetic understanding that officers hold towards inmates, it is in performing their human services tasks that this understanding gets put to the behavioral test.

Handling Inmate Institutional Problems

When a prison inmate has a problem relating to the institution, it is often a problem for the correction officer as well. Inmates unfamiliar with the workings of a bureaucracy and lacking faith in established procedures view officers as shortcuts to information, goods and services. Whether they have a question concerning a commissary or stamp account, a request to see a counselor or a desire to obtain a new clothing issue, the correction officer is called in as the inmate's intermediary.

Once the problem is brought to the officer's attention, a number of alternative courses of action are available to him. First, he may ignore the problem and tell the inmate to "put in a slip" or follow established procedures. Second, he may refer the inmate to a supervisor or sergeant. Finally, the officer may handle the problem himself by phoning someone who can provide the inmate with an answer or can otherwise become *personally* involved in solving the problem. The first two alternatives entail less personal involvement than the third, which demands affirmative "action" from the officer.

Though the administration desires that officers refer inmate institutional problems to supervisory personnel for solution or that inmates be told to follow normal procedures, only 12% of the officers indicated they normally dealt with institutional problems in this way. The remaining 88% indicated that they become directly involved in solving inmate institutional problems. Such personal involvement may take a variety of forms, depending on the nature of the problem. Most generally, officers will take advantage of their "connections" in various departments, making phone calls to get the information an inmate needs to know. Even though civilian personnel working in offices complain to the administration about receiving officer inquiries about inmate accounts and other matters, most officers continue this established informal practice. Though it is strictly against institutional regulations, one officer even indicated that he allowed the inmate to discuss his problems with his contacts on the phone.

Other officers reported helping inmates set up bookkeeping systems to allow them to adequately keep track of commissary and correspondence accounts. Cutting through red tape, officers also improve the inmate's chances of successfully contacting counselors and other personnel whom the inmate might wish to see. The fact that officers help inmates with their institutional problems, however, does not mean that they did so in every case. Often the officer has to judge the sincerity of the inmate and the "reality" of his problem. In deciding how to proceed, officers take into account their knowledge of the inmate's general attitude and reputation. As with rule enforcement, "knowing the guy" plays an important part in determining the outcome of an inmate-officer interaction.

Officers are motivated to intercede for inmates in institutional matters by three primary concerns that define the officer's understanding of the inmate's situation. Officers realize that for inmates, minor problems can become major concerns. Many officers observed that inmates do not always think things through, or that they often get excited and ignore significant details in trying to solve their problems. By intervening, the officer prevents what to him is a minor matter from escalating into a major problem.

Secondly, the importance of "time" to the inmate is almost unanimously acknowledged by the officers. Inmates, the officers feel, always need to know what they need to know right away. Failure to find answers quickly often leads to further "pestering" of the officer. Officers know that inmates do not readily take no for an answer. If they fail in their first attempt, they will often return with the same request. To avoid repeated inquiries, officers frequently relent early and satisfy the inmate's request.

A third motivation for officers' intervening in inmate institutional problems is their belief that other parts of the institutional bureaucracy fail to deal effectively with such problems. As one officer put it:

> Oh, brother. I feel sorry for some guys. The responses they get from different parts of the institution are terrible. They keep running you around, "See him," "See him," and nobody wants to be bothered. They say they're only inmates, but when you're with them you don't think that way. There are some good people.

Handling Inmate Personal Problems

As far as inmate personal problems are concerned, the tendency for the officers to become personally involved appears to be less pronounced than with institutional problems. Whereas only 12% of the officers generally did *not* become involved with inmate institutional problems, 42% of the officers indicated that they would mainly refer inmates to a supervisor, a service unit counselor or to a chaplain when the inmate approached the officer with a personal problem. There are a number of reasons for this strategy. Some officers feel that they are not competent to deal with inmates' personal problems such as a death in the family, "Dear John" letters or individual adjustment problems, and that it is therefore best to refer an inmate to someone better qualified. Typical of this attitude is the following incident:

> One guy said that his mother was sick, according to her last letter, and that he hadn't heard from her in over a week. I told the guy, "I'm not qualified to tell you how to handle the problem." I call the priest and told the inmate to contact him for advice. I tell him right away that I'm not qualified on it and that he should get to those trained to handle those problems. It's passing the buck, but that's the way I feel.

However, some officers try not to get involved with inmate personal problems because they do not want to be blamed for an inmate's action should the advice backfire. One officer related the following:

> Sergeant was telling me that when he was a young officer, he knew an inmate in his company real well. The guy tells him that he heard that his wife was running around on him and that a kid was involved and he didn't know what to do. The young officer said that he'd probably hit her in the mouth. The next time the guy's wife came up for a visit she was going to sit down and the guy belted her. They asked him why and he said that an officer told him to do it. So, I'd probably just refer the guy to a counselor or civilian. I can get myself in a lot of trouble sometimes if I give advice, even though it does sound like I'm passing the buck.

Though many officers do not get involved with inmate personal problems to the point of offering advice, others are less reticent. In fact, 58% of the officers indicated that they sometimes give inmates their opinions about personal situations. Officers who become involved in this way often feel that the inmates expect to receive personal help from the officer and that this expectation is legitimate. They also feel that inmates are reluctant to talk to other inmates about personal matters and that they, the officers, are a preferable alternative. One officer who does get involved with the personal problems of inmates looks at it this way:

> I listen. You find out you gain more respect if you listen. Give them your attention. It's appreciated. I spent half my career listening to personal problems.
>
> *Do you ever offer advice?*
>
> Sure. I wonder if it's right sometimes, but I do give it. You offer it on the level you live, not on how they live. They can't ask advice from another inmate who can't help him or is in the same boat. They'd rather ask a more normal-type person.

Evidence of sympathetic understanding of the officer for the inmate also includes the policy of keeping personal problems confidential—at least of not discussing them with other inmates. Though not specifically asked, many officers indicated that the fact that an inmate will bring a problem to an officer indicates to the officer that the inmate is placing trust in him and a violation of such trust is frowned upon by officers and is seen as potentially dangerous for inmates, who may become objects of joking or ridicule should word of their personal problem spread. The following incident illustrates the kind of encounters with officers that inmates are not desirous of having publicized:

> I went by a guy's cell and he was crying. He says for me to go, but if he tips, he might hurt six or seven people. I opened his cell, walked in and started talking and got him calmed down. I knew the guy long enough and convinced him good enough to stop crying. He punched the wall four or five times and I talked him into going to sick call and handled it alone. Once you run into a situation like this, don't say anything. Other inmates asked me what was happening when I went by. I told them "Nothing's going on." You don't spread the word on a thing like that. If the inmate knows this, it takes the edge off and he feels better.

Finding Out If Inmates Have Problems

Though many officers apparently get involved in dealing with inmate institutional and personal problems when such problems are brought to them by inmates, one might assume that more "sympathetic understanding," and therefore less "social distance," is evidenced by officers who *take affirmative steps to discover* if particular inmates in particular circumstances are having difficulties. This strategy requires the officer not only to be reactive, but to be the initiator of interactions involving "human services" intervention.

Forty percent of the officers interviewed indicated that they preferred *not* to initiate such interactions, preferring that inmates bring problems to them. Such officers generally tended not to get involved if a situation did not present itself to them. A majority of our officers, however, indicated that there are times when they must make an effort to discover if an inmate is having a problem. The situations when such inquiries are appropriate are circumscribed by a rather rigid set of circumstances. There is no universal "how ya doin'?" type of activity, and proactive officer intervention usually occurs only in specific cases.

The primary concern in an officer's initiating a proactive intervention is that he be somewhat well-acquainted with the inmate. The officer feels that if you have no standing relationship with an inmate and you ask the inmate about a problem, the inmate will resent your prying into his personal affairs, even if he has a problem.

Moreover, the existence of an established relationship between the inmate and officer permits the officer to observe the inmate's behavior over a period of time and to notice changes in the inmate's normal routine. It also allows officers to be solicitous without appearing to be nosey:

> I don't go out of my way to look for problems, but if I see guys I know and their attitude changes, I go up to them and see if they're having problems. Maybe I could help him. One guy on my company, he always looks drunk or "high," so I check his thermos every night. The guy says to me, "I'm high on life." Now if he says "get lost," then I'll talk to him. I might try to find out and help him out. If I get to know guys, I can notice changes.

A factor that appears to have special importance in contributing to the establishment of "human service" relationships between officers and inmates and in promoting their acceptance by inmates and officers is the "nonprofessional" character of such relationships. Officers and inmates both seem to believe that officers are paid to be "police," guards, security personnel. It follows from the logic of the situation that any personal relationships that develop between officers and inmates are developed out of personal choice, and not paid for by the state. Officers are not "paid" to solve inmate problems or to serve as their counselors. Service unit counselors, parole counselors and educational counselors are paid to counsel. The motives of these paid counselors therefore become immediately suspect, while guard help is viewed as *real*.

Officers Sharing Their Institutional Problems With Inmates

If an officer's willingness to become involved with inmate problems and to take steps to deal with these problems provides some indication of the closeness of "social distance" or "sympathetic understanding" that exists between officers and inmates, the officer's willingness to share *his* institutional and personal life with inmates may indicate an even greater degree of intimacy, lower social distance or a greater degree of "sympathetic understanding." Institutional procedures, problems officers have with other officers or supervisors and other frustrations with the job often lead officers to complain, and it is often inmates who hear their complaints.

Of the officers interviewed, 52% indicated that they avoided talking about their own institutional problems with inmates. Some of these officers cited their fear that they might divulge matters dealing with security. Others felt that becoming personally involved with inmates might later put them in a compromising position. If they criticized other officers or the administration to inmates, for example, the officers feared that the inmate might threaten to spread the information in exchange for a favor. Still other officers said they refrained from discussing their institutional problems with inmates because they felt that inmates had enough problems of their own and did not need to be bothered with those of the officers.

Nearly half of the officers, however, reported that they sometimes did discuss their own institutional problems, aggravations and frustrations with *some* inmates. Though they often recognized the dangers involved in confiding in inmates, these officers felt that complaining to inmates, or in the presence of inmates, was unavoidable:

> Probably everybody's guilty of that. You get so frustrated. Take last week; the temperature's in the 80s and we still have to wear shirts and ties. Somebody called Albany to see if we could deviate from the rule which says we can change to short-sleeve shirts on May 1st, but Albany said no. A lot of us probably bitched about that. It's not good to do, it's wrong, but probably everybody down there knows one or two inmates you feel you're close to, that you can confide in. We're more guilty of that than we'd like to admit.

In discussing their conversations with inmates, the officers made the point that they accept advice from inmates. When it came to institutional procedures or correctional policies, many officers admitted that they felt that inmates often made significant suggestions that the officers felt the administration should listen to:

> *Do you ever find yourself discussing your institutional problems with inmates?*
>
> Sure I do. It's not a good tendency, but you do it. It's all according to how long you've worked with the inmates. Just because he had some problems outside, caught his wife with some guy or something, that doesn't mean that he's not capable of giving you advice. He might be very capable. "Why, there's a problem here," he might say and you might not even be aware of it.

An officer can find himself discussing institutional problems with inmates because doing so serves an informational function, providing the officer with information concerning his work that he might otherwise not obtain:

> I carry on conversations with a few guys who get bulletins from Albany. The legal changes, things in the department. I get information from the inmates. It never comes from Albany to us, so we get it from them. They're more aware of what's going on than the officers.

Officers Sharing Outside Personal Problems With Inmates

If an officer were to share his personal life with inmates, this should indicate that he places little social distance between himself and the inmates. Eighty-eight percent of the officers indicated that they tried to keep their personal lives "out of the institution." Only six officers told me that they occasionally discussed their outside life with inmates.

The desire of officers to keep their personal life "outside" provides some indication that, for most, the feelings of closeness they felt for inmates is confined to the inmate as "inmate" and to their dealings with each other in the work setting of the prison. Some officers felt that bringing their extracurricular affairs into the institution was the worst thing an officer could do. This, they felt, would interfere with the officer's ability to deal with inmates in terms of the inmates' behavior and institutional climate. For most officers, their outside life threatened to inject an inappropriate or contaminating element into the equation of forces that balance officer-inmate relationships, in the same way as the officer's knowledge of inmates' outside criminal behavior, discussed above. As long as officer-inmate relationships are determined by officer and inmate knowledge of and mutual expectations concerning only institutional behaviors, relationships are easily managed, since both officer and inmate judge each other solely on the basis of observed behaviors. When knowledge of outside factors is considered, officers feel that both inmates and officers would manufacture fanciful pictures of each other and begin behaving toward each other on the basis of imagined realities rather than behavioral realities:

> I don't care for them to know my home life. Some of them find out as much as they can about an officer and then they throw it up to you. Sometimes they get the wrong idea if they hear about a guy's [officer's] marriage breaking up, or they might think the officer can't deal with people, and lose respect for him. It's bad enough trying to defend what you do *in* the place without having to deal with outside stuff too.

For a very few officers the sharing of their personal life with inmates is not taboo. Although these officers do not indiscriminately share intimacies with inmates, they see nothing wrong with discussing their outside interests, an occasional family or business problem. The officers may see such conversations as promotion reintegration of the inmate into the outside community upon his release. They refer to problems the inmate must someday face. One officer, for example, said:

> I talked to a couple of inmates about some problems I was having with a property transaction and zoning boards. It lets them know

> about the problems we have to go through on the street. It lets them know it's not peaches and cream on the street either. It lets them see that everybody's got problems.

SUMMARY—1976

The degree of sympathetic understanding guards feel for inmates is, at Auburn, much greater than one would normally expect. Rather than there being a "guard mentality" toward inmates, officers respond as individuals to inmates whom they judge as individuals. When helping inmates with problems, guards do so in the face of perceived peer and administrative condemnation. Not being *paid* to counsel makes guard assistance real. When officers share their institutional problems with inmates, a felt camaraderie bred by shared experience leads guards to accept inmate advice. Just as guards do not desire to know about an inmate's "outside" history lest it interfere with an "inside relationship," they do not readily share their outside lives with inmates. The walls of the prison emphasize divisions between guards and inmates, while they also draw the two groups together as people sharing a common environment.

FROM PERSONAL, HUMAN RELATIONSHIPS TO BUREAUCRATIC RELATIONSHIPS, 1976-1986

In general, 1986 data from both interviews and questionnaires demonstrate that correctional officers see themselves as being less likely to be involved in actively intervening in inmate institutional or personal problems and less likely to share their problems with inmates (except for officer personnel problems) than they were in 1976 (see Table 17, Appendix D). In addition, the data shows that officers hired since 1976 are much less likely than the more experienced officers in the original sample to get involved in handling inmate problems. With the proportion of officers in this less-than-ten-years-experience category having increased drastically, these findings point to the development of a new normative structure shaping officer/inmate relations as Auburn Correctional Facility approaches the 1990s.

Responses to questions concerning human and helping relationships revealed that many of the themes discovered in 1976 were still operative ten years later. Many officers would intervene by calling appropriate personnel to help rectify inmate institutional problems. Others would listen to personal problems and occasionally offer advice. Now, however, new themes show how organizational changes have tended to increase the social distance (degree of sympathetic understanding = degree of problem-sharing) between officers and inmates. In place of the personalized, informal, nonprofessional human relationships discussed in 1976, we now see the outlines of a more formalized set of relationships. Helping is now becoming "part of the job" but, helping is now limited by suspicion and concerns for procedure rather than being motivated by more general human concerns.

Handling Institutional Problems

One officer with 26 years' experience says that he still handles inmate problems as he always did and is proud of the reputation he developed among the inmates.

> I try to help. I always did that. As bad as the inmates are in my work area, I didn't like to have my leg pulled though. The older inmates would tell the younger ones to go see me if they had a problem, but they warned them not to try any bullshit. I never had the "b.s.'ers." They have all kinds of problems. One guy heard at night that his brother was shot. He waited until 8 a.m. to see me to talk about it. He didn't go to the Sergeant I called and got him to see the priest.

For others who still call and help make connections for inmates, a new concern for procedural regularity and working relationships has entered into the calculus of officer/inmate problem-solving interactions.

> Before I'd help out with a problem I'd try to see what he's tried on his own. If he's had no luck, and it depends on the inmate. If he's working for me and he did go through proper channels, I might tell him to wait a couple of days and then, if he doesn't hear, I'll check it out. If it's a money problem have him bring his printout and I'll go over it with him, and if there's a problem, I'll handle it. I take the time for a good worker because they can't pay him more than $1.55 and this is a benefit. Overall, there's a lot more formal procedures now, but I've been around, and I know where and how to get hold of people. Kind of going beyond just getting information. That's what happens when you've been here for 20 years. But I don't abuse it. It's a matter of habit, even though it's not policy. Procedures were set up because of the constant abuse, to keep people [officers] under control.

The substitution of the new policies and procedures for individual contacts in problem-solving was a recurrent theme in many of the experienced officers. Now variation from policy and procedure (not other non-helping officers) shapes their self-definition. In 1986, formal written guidelines designed to structure helping relationships provide the norm against which officers judge their "informal mechanisms" as positive and, in some cases, deviant.

Another point about "policy and procedure" that makes it salient to shaping officer/inmate relationships is the improved record-keeping and communication of directives that it has brought about. No longer are most officers in the dark about how things are "supposed to be run on paper" and no longer is it a safe assumption that "inmates do not know" about regulations, or that inmates are abused or run around by the "system." These themes do not emerge from any of the 1986 interviews. Rather, policy and procedures generally are described as having increased the level of institutional efficiency and accountability. Previously normative "mistakes" and "oversights" are now the exception. Many of the previous motivations for officer helping interventions, thus, are being eliminated.

> There are lots of state directives that cover everything. What they're supposed to have and under what circumstances it can be replaced. There's more accountability on clothing, records are better kept and policy and procedures tell you and the inmate what to do.

Another theme that impinges on officer-inmate human relation is the influx of sergeants and the tendency of many officers to let sergeants handle problems rather than get involved themselves. Some attribute this problem to the influx of younger officers who have not had opportunities to learn how to handle such problems. One officer who is now a sergeant reports:

> What's changed in this regard is the younger officers. Older guys still call around and point inmates in the right direction. They [the younger officers] don't realize that if an inmate works for you, you should handle the problems. Those are the problems they should take care of and now they send the inmate to the sergeant.

Another officer who is now a sergeant, observes something about himself that points to generational differences. He shows that old habits are hard to break (this may be the case for many of the more experienced offices who have become Sergeant).

> That's my downfall. I'll deal with the inmates. I'll call the clothing room. I shouldn't be doing that, but I do it anyway. Then I complain about it. Other Sergeants do it too, and then complain to the state shop people about the inmates not going to the officers.

What we see here is that sergeants and older officers handle problems for inmates much as they used to do. But in doing so they may be creating a set of dependency relationships which may prevent younger officers from developing the skills these older officers developed when they were young officers (recall how they were told to learn how to do things on their own). It may be that future generations of officers may be even more dependent for direction, as these relatively inexperienced officers of today become the experienced officers of tomorrow.

Handling Personal Problems

The development of written policy and procedures, increased efficiency of record-keeping and increase in the availability and number of supervisors have altered the character of officer/inmate relationships with regard to officers handling inmate institutional problems. Other forces, however, are at work affecting the involvement of officers with inmate personal problems. Many officers still feel that talking with inmates about their problems is a job for officers and not just counselors. [60% (N = 28) of questionnaire respondents disagreed with the statement: "Talking with inmates about their problems is a job for counselors, not for correctional officers," and 46% agreed with the statement: "It's important for an officer to go to bat for an inmate when the inmate has a legitimate gripe."] However, many observed that the need for officers to be involved in inmate personal problems has been reduced by increasing inmate access to counselors and by increasing the inmate's ability to handle personal problems on his own.

> *What if an inmate comes to you with a personal problem?*
>
> I listen and tell him the procedures to go through. Have him write a letter to the appropriate people. Now with inmate communications to the outside being better, the phones, better mail procedures, more visits, family reunion program, the inmate isn't so much in the dark. Personal problems are not as big an issue as they used to be, inmates now handle these on their own.
>
> Also, the counselors. They've moved them out of their offices and they hang out in the yard and in the blocks where inmates can get to them.
>
> The chaplains (we now have 4 or 5 instead of 2) handle lots of personal problems. Have an Imam for the Muslims. That's nice to solve their problems. It's a big plus from 10 years ago.

According to one officer such changes are pushing officers out of human services work and into custody and security.

> We're now mandated to tell the inmates to go to counselors. In a general sense, you don't handle personal problems anymore. Now it's security that becomes the officer's main concern. Even as officers used to get involved in lots of areas before, that's not the case any-more.

Finding Out If Inmates Have Problems

Many officers indicated that it was still appropriate to take affirmative steps to discover if inmates they knew well were having problems and to alleviate the problem by removing the inmate from the situation. However, as can be seen in Table 17, Appendix D, fewer of the officers from the original sample thought so and among younger officers, there were fewer still.

This tendency was noticed in many of the early interviews and a new question reflecting concerns with extortion and violence was added to the interview. A hypothetical situation in which the officer became aware that two inmates were extorting and threatening a third inmate was described and the officer was asked how he would handle it. Some officers indicated that they would attempt to intervene by explaining to the threatened inmate the opportunity to go to protective custody.

However, rule enforcement procedures which demand evidence and others which give the inmate responsibility for removing himself from potentially dangerous situations are perceived as limiting correctional officers' ability to intervene. Other officers expressed the opinion that the inmate is responsible for himself and that he must work his way out of the problem or suffer the consequences. This was especially true for younger officers. Officer intervention becomes possible only after the problem manifests itself in an overt rule violation, often a fight.

SUMMARY—1986

Over the course of ten years the increased saliency of "policy and procedures," stricter standards of accountability and narrowed officer discretion, more opportunities for inmates to handle their own problems, the increased availability of counselors and sergeants have all combined to reduce the amount of officer/inmate problem-sharing at Auburn. With these developments, officers have less of a tendency to attend to inmate concerns outside of their formal relationship and inmates reportedly have less of a tendency to seek more "human relationships" with officers. Structure, predictability and accountability are substituting for the support and emotional feedback which characterized the nature of officer/inmate relationships at Auburn in 1976.

NOTES

[1]Bogardus defines social distance as "...the degree of sympathetic understanding that exists between two persons and a person and a group." Bogardus, Emory S. "A Social Distance Scale," *Sociology and Social Research*, Vol. 17 (1933), p. 28. It is the idea of "sympathetic understanding" that this chapter attempts to bring to life as it exists in the prison setting.

[2]There is also the parallel argument (often put forward by some prison inmates) that inmates are "men of the people" and officers are blatantly unrepresentative rural whites and that "never the twain shall meet." In this argument inmates are "normal" and officers are "deviant."

[3]See, for example, Feron, James, "Westchester Executives Oppose More Prisons," *New York Times*, February 13 (1976); also, Kramer, Earl and Kramer, Janet. "Of Tanglewood and a Proposed Prison" (letter to the Editor), *New York Times*, March 3 (1976).

[4]*The Citizen-Advertiser*, Auburn, NY, June 11, 1975.

[5]Thass-Thienemann, Theodore. *The Interpretation of Language*, Volume 1. New York: Jason Aronson, 1973, p. 330.

Guards and Inmates: Authority and the Management of Inmate Misbehavior

5

AUTHORITY AND THE CORRECTION OFFICER

The traditional view of a correction officer's authority attributes his authority to the officer's ability to manipulate a system of rewards and punishments.[1] For the officers at Auburn the ability to manipulate benefits and penalties appears to play a relatively minor part in their view of correction officer authority. When asked what they felt to be the source of a correction officer's ability to get inmates to do what they were supposed to do and not do what they were not supposed to do, only one officer linked his authority to the doing of favors for inmates. This officer explained that "after a while they [inmates] know if you'll give up favors for good work." For over 60% of the officers, however, the officer's authority is derived from their style of presentation of self: from their manner of handling inmates and dealing with inmates, and from the way they conducted themselves with inmates. Others, however, feel that their authority comes from nonpersonal sources. Some perceive their authority is delegated from institutions such as the legislatures that pass the laws and the courts that put inmates in prison or the local prison administration that sets institutional policies. A substantial number link authority to the rules they enforce. A final group expresses the opinion that the mere possession of officer status is enough to give them authority (see Table 10, Appendix D).

Personal Authority

Most officers do not feel that they "have authority" simply because they put on a uniform or because they have rules to fall back on. These officers believe that they must somehow develop and in a sense earn the legitimacy needed to exercise authority effectively. The key to gaining this legitimacy is the individual officer's ability to gain the inmates' recognition that his authority is legitimate, i.e. that he as an officer merits the inmates' obedience to rules and the compliance with his directions.

Some officers find that they gain legitimacy by reacting to individual situations and individual inmates in accord with the way the inmate presents himself to the officer:

> The best way to get along? If a guy's tough, I'm tough, if the guy's a good guy, I'm a good guy. If a guy's squirrelly, I'm squirrelly. But these guys you can't talk tough or easy to. Just kind of listen to him and agree with him.

Though a varied style may work for some officers in some situations, most officers agree that the key to gaining the respect and cooperation of inmates is consistency. If they are consistent, they will gain legitimacy and in the process be able to shift from a reliance on formal authority to more personal types of authority.[2]

The process of acquiring "personalized legitimacy" is generally seen as a long and arduous undertaking. Several of the more experienced officers indicated that it took them from five to ten years to acquire the experience necessary to know how to gain legitimacy with a new group of inmates over a fairly short period of time. When asked what advice they would give a younger officer about how to establish his authority, many enforce the rules to the letter and in doing so "let the inmates know who's boss." The officer could always ease up later, until he reaches a point when reliance on rules is not necessary.

Reliance on rules becomes unnecessary after the officer learns what he can realistically expect of inmates and of himself. Once he establishes these expectations and effectively communicates them to inmates, rules are used only in extreme cases or to set an example. They are no longer a major source of authority:

> You're always tried by people to see how far they can push you. Start off as tough as you can be. If you want to relax later, be relaxed. But you can't back-pedal. Let them see that they can't walk all over you.

* * *

> Any officer, he doesn't have to be new, should run it as strictly as possible to start. Take no guff from the inmates. Unless he does that, he'll have problems. Once he gets to know the situation, he can change it or run it differently. Until then, the best way is straight down the line.

Many of the more experienced officers observed that younger officers, unsure of their authority as officers and unskilled in the exercise of authority, are more likely to have trouble getting inmates to follow their directions than would the more experienced officers.[3] For these less experienced officers, rule enforcement interactions can quickly escalate from a minor to a major confrontation. The officer's self-image seems at stake in the interaction and to lose means that both he and what he feels is his already weak authority are diminished. The following description of a rule enforcement interaction illustrates this self-image defending reaction and the reliance on formal means to gain compliance:

> I gave calls, "20 minutes," "ten minutes," "two minutes," when eight guys were in the showers. I tell the guys to get out, time's up.
>
> One guy says "fuck you." I get an attitude over this and seven or eight other inmates are hearing this. I say "let's go" and I say "if you don't leave you get written up." He says "Okay." I took the guy in the gym office by himself and told him that I was locking him up. I told him that there were about 45 other guys there and if he wanted to apologize in front of them, Okay. But I don't want 45 other guys to think that you can run over me. I told him what would happen if he violated the order and he did it. They don't like to have their pride hurt and neither do I. If pride is involved, even if it's a small thing, either he apologizes or I lock him up.

The importance of establishing shared expectations between officer and inmate and their relationship to authority is underscored by an examination of the locations within the institution where most rule violations that are reported as "refusing a direct order" or "refusal to work" take place. Though "The Daily Journal of Infractions" generally does not indicate the location of a reported infraction, by relating infractions with the job assignment of the officers writing the infractions and the interview data, it is possible to establish some general trends relating job location and infractions.

Those areas where officers have a high tendency to write infractions of the "disobeying an order" type are those where it is most difficult for the officer and the inmate to establish mutual expectations and thereby to establish the legitimacy of the officer's authority. The Media Center—Gym Building, for example, is an area in which the faces of inmates under the officer's supervision change from hour to hour. Different groups of inmates are granted access to the area at different times and on different days of the week. When exceptions are made, the composition of the inmate population is difficult to control. In this area the inmates are more or less on their own, free to choose their activities and locations. Inmate associations are not regulated and the officer's contact with the inmates is negligible, save for his activities as doorman and pass checker.

Though the officer must watch for unusual incidents, his main activity is to stay out of the inmate's way. When he does enter into an interaction with inmates, it is almost always on a formal basis, in his role as officer, and as an anonymous symbol of authority. The intrusion of such an outside force as a guard into the relatively free environment of the Media Center—Gym area is likely to be viewed by inmates as more intrusive than a similar action taken by a block officer, whose interventions into inmate activities are expected. Without "personalized legitimacy" to fall back on, officers in public areas are more likely to enter into confrontations that lead to the issuance of a formal report.

Another area where officers have difficulties establishing "personalized legitimacy" is the kitchen and mess hall area. Again, a high number of "disobeying order" reports come from officers working this assignment. Though the officers in the area are working with "gangs" of inmates, all officers admit that the area suffers from a high inmate turnover rate and a great deal of confusion.[4] It is generally agreed that inmates assigned to the mess hall have trouble working anywhere else and that mess hall duty is considered a form of punishment. Under these conditions it is often difficult, even for an experienced officer, to establish "personalized legitimacy." Constant turnover in his workers means that the officer is consistently trying to establish his reputation. Failing this, a reliance on formal reports is much more frequent than in other areas of the institution where inmate turnover is much less rapid.

Our findings, when placed next to Glaser's findings concerning inmate expectations, appear to indicate that correction officers are correctly *reading* the messages concerning appropriate officer behavior that are communicated to officers by inmates. According to Glaser:

> For custodial officers, what seems to have been a trait of fairness and predictability was the major influence upon inmate preference and prejudice, with manner of expression, whether friendly or hostile, next in importance.[5]

In addition, Glaser found that "permissiveness" (granting requests and favors, flexibility) was the characteristic least often mentioned as a reason for liking correction officers. If we assume that the inmates at Auburn were similar to those in the institution studied by Glaser, the failure of our officers to associate granting favors with authority is not surprising and would either reflect the officer's reading of inmate expectations or a congruence of views between prisoners and guards.

Legalistic Authority

Though most officers believed they had "authority" only when they had established their own personalized legitimacy, others failed to hold this view. A substantial number (23) of the officers expressed the belief that their authority rests on legal foundations and that it is not necessary for them to earn the right to exercise it. Although legitimacy is also a concern of these officers, the grantors of legitimacy are not seen as the inmates, but rather as elements of society's legal machinery.

For six officers the fact that society has chosen to deal with lawbreakers as it has is enough for officers to deal with lawbreakers as they do, and is enough for them to have legitimate authority. The men they supervise have, after all, broken the law and have been judged guilty by the courts. As criminals, these men have what rights the legislatures and the courts choose to give them. Therefore, as part of society's criminal justice process and as its embodied representatives, correction officers have a lawfully defined authority over those who have chosen to break society's laws.

Nine officers held a narrow view of their legally based authority. They thought that correction officers have the right to direct the behavior of inmates because such power is vested in the correction officer's role. These officers viewed themselves less as society's representatives and more as people who hold jobs in correctional institutions whose job description happens to include having authority. Authority is not something they have to earn, but something they have because their uniform is a different color than that of the inmates.

A third group of 12 officers holding a legalistic view of authority believed that the correction officer's authority derives from the rules and regulations of the institution and the strength of the administration of the institution. Without rules to fall back on, without support from the administration, these officers felt there was little they could do to get inmates to follow their instructions.

These "legalistic" officers are most apt to criticize court decisions as being too liberal and as favoring inmates. They have a tendency to express reservations about departmental policies that expand the freedom of inmates. The perceived failure of local administrators to back officers in disciplinary matters is frequently a concern. Rather than relating slippages of authority to individual inadequacies, such men view authority deficits as symptomatic of an overall societal, departmental or institutional trend toward lessened discipline and diluted responsibility of officers.

RULE ENFORCEMENT

Defining Inmate Misbehaviors

When a correctional officer begins his career at Auburn, he is issued two documents that provide him with formal statements of departmental policy concerning the regulation of inmate behavior and the enforcement of inmate violations:

1. "General Rules of Inmate Behavior" and
2. "Employees' Rule Book."

The first of these documents defines for both officer and inmate the behaviors that are officially regulated, the procedures for handling offenses and the alternative penalties attached to each offense. This document is patterned after the State Penal Law. It lists and numbers each rule and classifies offenses into categories (A,

B and C) according to seriousness and attaches a variety of penalties to each class of offense. Some offenses, such as "the possession of contraband," "interference with an employee in the performance of his duty" and "refusing to obey a district order," may be classified as A, B and C offenses, depending on the circumstances surrounding the offense. Generally, however, Class A offenses include all penal law and other offenses, including the "danger to life, health, security or property"; Class B offenses include all behaviors considered crimes under the State Penal Law, but not involving such danger; and Class C offenses, considered "less serious," include violations of institutional rules and procedures, some forms of contraband and a multitude of regulations pertaining to specific areas of the institution such as the school, industrial shops or gymnasium.

Though a few officers deny ever having read the inmate rule book and some admit having discarded it, most are generally pleased with its classification system and its provisions for procedural regularity in dealing with reported offenses. Generally, however, officers accept the truism that full enforcement of institutional regulations would bring the institution to a halt. They feel this would result not from a reduction in inmate cooperation, but because all inmates would be locked in their cells for violating rules. In admitting this, officers are indicating that they exercise a great deal of discretion in deciding when and how to intervene in rule violation situations. For the correction officers at Auburn the fact that a particular inmate action is officially restricted is of little importance. What triggers an officer's intervention in a rule violation situation is the officer's perception of the actual or potential impact the regulated behavior has on themselves, on other inmates or on the overall atmosphere of the institution. If an inmate's behavior passes beyond acceptable limits, the officers feel that it is always possible to find a rule to fit the inmate's actions.

In judging inmate behavior by its impact rather than by its definition as "officially deviant," officers often rely on their individual assessment of the future impact of a violation, as well as on their perception of its effect at the time the behavior occurs. For example, an inmate's showing disrespect to an officer is a Class C offense and a violation of Rule 4.1 which states: "Disrespectful communication or conduct in any form to facility employees or other inmates will lead to disciplinary action." If an interaction between an officer and an inmate involving a show of disrespect to an officer takes place in an isolated location away from other inmates or officers, the decision on how to deal with the disrespect may be made solely on the officer's perception of how offensive the incident was to him personally. However, should the same disrespectful behavior take place in the presence of other inmates in a shop area or mess hall, it takes on added significance. Though the potential for escalation is a consideration, the officer may consider the effects of his handling of disrespect on his future ability to handle other inmates who observe the situation. Failure to intervene may cause the officer to have problems in the future. Inmates may interpret his nonintervention as a weakness and an invitation to future violations.

The decision to intervene is also made when an inmate's behavior is felt to be infringing on the "rights of other inmates," even though the restricted behavior in itself appears minor. Loud talking in the cell blocks after the evening quiet bell provides an illustration. As defined by the inmate rule books, loud talking after the 7 p.m. quiet bell is considered a nonserious matter. For the officers, however, it is quite serious. Loud talking in the block, like disrespect to an officer in front of other inmates, might have a potentially contagious effect on other inmates and could lead to disruption throughout the block. However, officers also view "loud talking" as behavior signifying the offender's lack of respect for other inmates. Recognizing that some inmates wish to retire early, study, read or write letters and to do so in peace, officers strongly resent the inmate who seemingly thinks only of himself.

Officers also interpret minor violations in terms of the potential effects the violation might have on the overall running of the institution. If an inmate is late for a count, he is violating a rule. However, the importance of that violation to the officer often depends on when the inmate is late. If the offense takes place in the evening, it may not be considered serious because the inmate is not causing anyone, except the officer involved, to be delayed. However, should inmate tardiness occur at noon, the seriousness of the offense in the officer's eyes is magnified. Other officers will be thrown off their schedules and the feeding of inmates can be delayed. Chances of the officer intervening in the latter case are reported to be much greater than in the former.

In holding unofficial beliefs about the seriousness of inmate misbehaviors, the officers at Auburn feel that they generally have the support of the inmates. The officers believe that most inmates recognize the need for rules and that most rules are for the inmates' own protection and comfort, although officers admit there are some inmates for whom rules represent authority and for whom authority is instantly interpreted as a personal challenge.[6]

There is a consensus among officers that many problems associated with rule enforcement are created not by the rules themselves, but by the inconsistent manner in which they are enforced by the officers. In dealing with the *how* of enforcement, correction officers face the classical question facing all who must exercise discretion: How can an individual retain flexibility in decision-making without the overall system appearing inconsistent? One officer describes this dilemma:

> If the rules were applied evenly and fairly, we wouldn't have the problems we do. Some officers are more lax than others, they overlook trivial things. The inmates don't know which end is up. But you've still got to be a little bit flexible. I don't mean look the other way on everything, but you still have to enforce the rules.

Although this officer recognizes the dilemma, his solution is but a restatement of the original problem: "Be fair but flexible," enforce rules "evenly and fairly." The questions of how and when officers actually enforce rules remains for them to solve.

Strategies for Dealing with Minor Offenses

From my preliminary examination of literature related to correction officer work styles I expected to find three rather distinct strategies of rule enforcement: issuing formal written reports, giving informal warnings and ignoring. During initial interviews, however, it became very apparent that an officer's decision on how best to enforce minor rules rested not simply on an individually preferred style, but it depended on a number of situational factors and alternative perceptions of the meaning of rule violation interactions.

While the inmate rule book provides general definitions for inmate misbehavior, the "Employee's Rule Book" provides the officer with a statement of departmental policy concerning the *hows* of rule enforcement. Two employee rules dealing with the "Discipline of Inmates" offer the officer guidance on how he should handle minor infractions:

> 8.1 Minor matters of discipline, where no danger to life, security or property exists, shall be handled quietly and routinely.
>
> 8.3 When the conduct of an inmate is disorderly or not in conformity with the rules relating to the conduct of inmates, it shall be the duty of any employee ascertaining the facts to report the matter on a prescribed form to the deputy warden or the designated disciplinary officer.

As interpreted by officers, these two rules are mutually contradictory: The first rule tells staff to handle minor matters themselves without recourse to formal written reports, while the second implies a written report of all observed violations. Faced with this seeming contradiction, most officers feel they are on their own in deciding when and how to deal with inmate misbehaviors.

Although formal means are available for dealing with minor infractions of institutional rules by inmates, officers generally handle such violations informally by following one of two general strategies. Most indicated that their primary intervention strategy was to bring the violation to the inmate's attention by "telling" or "warning" him. The remaining 20% expressed a preference for "ignoring" minor violations or "letting things slide." In no case did an officer indicate that his primary strategy was to write a formal report of the minor violation.

In addition to submitting formal reports or giving warnings, a few officers indicated that officers sometimes resort to means outside of established procedure to make a particularly aggravating inmate "pay" for his offenses. When the officer believes that established procedures will prove ineffective in preventing future inmate violations or in providing "just" punishments for past offenses, he is able to exert control over goods and privileges to the inmate's detriment. For example, knowing that no action will be taken on weekend violations until Monday, an officer may submit a report of a violation on Friday and effectively place the inmate in "keep lock" for two days in instances where the actual penalty would probably have been less. Other devices include locking a man out of his cell for a period of time while others are locked in, so the inmate begins to fear that he may have done something wrong. Turning off the inmate's water supply or electricity are also devices resorted to. Leaving a "keep lock" tag on a cell door lever will effectively keep a man "locked up" for a couple days until someone discovers that the tag was an error. Not notifying the inmate when he has an appointment scheduled is another way of "getting back" at persistent, aggravating rule violators. Making an inmate stand and wait for a sergeant while he is holding three pints of ice cream from the commissary is an example of ingenious retribution.

The key to each of these extralegal approaches to rule enforcement is that the officer must let the inmate know that his (the officer's) action is purposeful and not accidental. In doing so, the officer is letting the inmate understand that the officer can and will find ways to make the inmate's life uncomfortable. He is creating more problems for the inmate, but is doing so in a way that makes it impossible for the inmate to prove a case of harassment. Lights do go off, water pipes do sometimes break down and it may be legitimate, though unnecessary, for the officer to detain an inmate with ice cream. In acting this way the officer feels he is meeting and beating the inmate on the inmate's own terms. Often the officers feel that respect, rather than resentment, develops from such encounters.

Data gathered from "The Daily Journal of Infractions" tends to support the officers' description of their strategies for dealing with what they consider minor rule violations. An examination of Table 5.1 indicates that there is a tendency for officers not to write reports on what they consider minor violations. For example, 20 officers mentioned that they considered violation of haircut and shave regulations to be minor and ten officers actually wrote reports citing inmates for violations of this regulation. However, only five officers both mentioned the regulation as minor and wrote reports. This same pattern holds true for each of the minor violation categories mentioned.

Table 5.1. Minor Offense Categories as Defined by Officers[a] and Officers Actually Writing Reports for Each Offense[b]

Minor Offense Category	Number Mentioning Category	Number Writing Reports	Number Mentioning as Minor and Writing Report
Haircuts, shave	20	10	5
Cleanliness (cell and personal)	13	5	2
Hats on in restricted area	8	0	0
Smoking in restricted area	8	0	0
Late for count (loitering)	7	8	2
Loud talking after quiet bell	4	5	2
Obstruction of view	6	2	0
Sarcasm in talk	5	6	2
Taking food from mess hall	5	6	1
Gambling	2	3	0
Feeding pigeons	1	0	0

[a] Summary of responses to interview question "What things do you consider to be minor rule violations?"

[b] Data gathered from the institution's "The Daily Journal: A Daily Report of Every Infraction of the Rules and Regulations of the Facility by Officers or Inmates and Actions Taken in Each Case and Memorandum of Any Complaint by Inmates of Bad or Insufficient Food, Want of Clothing or Cruel or Unjust Treatment by an Officer" (1976).

Despite the general agreement that it is best to bring a violation to the inmate's attention, the meaning that officers attached to this intervention varied considerably. For some, what is on the surface an informal strategy is actually an alternative "formal" method of handling violations. By giving the inmate a warning, these officers believe that they are carrying out administrative policy and properly "doing their job." They feel that the administration wants all rules enforced and that "telling the inmate" is the appropriate first step in the rule enforcement process:

> The administration would like you to handle things without writing the man up. When you write a man up [for a minor violation] you're telling the administration that you're doing all you can with the man and now he has to be handled by somebody other than you.
>
> * * *
>
> [On minor things] it's like a cop could arrest someone for D.W.I., or not arrest him. [In the institution] whether it's a name tag or personal hygiene, [the rule's] there for a reason. If you can enforce it without a write-up and you enforced it without discipline, then you did your job.

But where some officers readily bring rule infractions to an inmate's attention, others do so only grudgingly. Unsure of the administration's policy toward preferred rule enforcement strategies and unable to discern the rationale behind minor rules and regulations, some officers tell inmates about violations only because they believe that ignoring inmate violations represents a dereliction of duty.

Another meaning of the "telling the inmate" strategy derives from the officer's characterization of the officer-inmate rule violation encounter as a "test." Officers often suggest that it is not the violation itself that is important. What is significant is that the violation may represent an attempt on the part of the inmate to see how far he can push the officer before the officer reacts. For his part, the officer is waiting to see how far the inmate "will really go." Through the interplay of rule violator and rule enforcer, the officer's tolerance limit for unacceptable behavior becomes established.

> I locked a guy up once for not cleaning his area. He was either playing dumb or is dumb. He refused to clean up his section. Some officers go along with such things for a long period of time. I saw hope for the guy and went along for a while. The guy thought that I was just playing a game and that I would just talk and tell him about it, so I took the next step and locked him up.
>
> * * *
>
> You try to be diplomatic, tell the guy [his hair] is kind of shaggy. Usually I don't tell him about the rules, he knows, I give him a way out, I don't give him a straight order. Then if I get feedback and he says he's not going to do it, then I'll lay it down. Tell him to shave by such and such or I'll lock him up. I try to let him make his own decision. Not to order him, but to make him feel that it's his judgment.

In letting the inmate know that they are aware of his violation, these officers are taking the second in a series of steps that may eventually lead to formal intervention and a written report. Prior to telling the inmate, the officer may have indicated his knowledge of the violation by making certain that the inmate was aware that the officer observed the behavior in question. Since the officer believes the violation is part of a testing process, he assumes that the inmate is violating the rule in a way that ensures that the officer is aware of it.

Should the behavior persist, the interaction reaches the second stage. The officer acknowledges the escalation by verbally telling the inmate that he is aware of the violation and that the officer would like him to stop. At this point the officer believes that both he and the inmate are aware that the next encounter will probably result in the issuance of a formal written report.

Some officers bring rule violations to the inmate's attention not because they desire to enforce the rule in a specific violation encounter, but rather because they feel that inmates do not always know what the rules are.

> I tell them, "No loitering on the gallery," if a guy hangs out too long. I tell the guy the rule so he'll try to remember. He might not know the rule. I just bring it to his attention, just let him know.
>
> * * *
>
> Lots of times, the way infractions are, I'm not going to say the guys don't know. It slips their minds, like ours. They say, "I forgot." Well, maybe he didn't shave and I'll just kiddingly make a remark where some might get out and write an infraction.

These officers are providing the inmates with information, letting them know that the rule exists and specifying what is expected of them. As with the officer who feels tested in minor encounters, officers for whom telling the inmate means providing information are also engaging in a rule enforcement process that extends beyond the immediate situation. By providing an inmate with information about rules, the officer assures himself that the inmate is "willfully" violating the rules should he spot the same inmate violating the same rule in the future. Should a second violation occur, the officer is more likely to resort to a formal written report as an enforcement strategy.

Twenty percent of these officers indicated that they occasionally ignore minor misbehaviors or let such violations slide. Many officers who claim that they ignore minor violations feel that the rules they consider to be minor are not really necessary. Where this is the case, the officer's sense of fairness dictates that he not even bother confronting the inmate about his violation.

Some officers perceive inconsistency on the part of the administration when it comes to both general rule enforcement policy and the enforcement of specific rules. Rules governing length of hair and facial hair were often cited in this regard and the history of the "hair regulations" from 1975 through 1976 provides an illustration. Prior to October 1976, institutional policy on haircuts and shaves as stated in the inmate rule book was as follows:

> Rule 4.17 Hair length will be no higher than three inches from the head or shall not extend below the eyebrows or the collar. Face will be clean shaven with the following exceptions:
> a. Mustache—no portion of the mustache will go below the corners of the mouth.
> b. No beards, goatees or facial hair will be allowed.
> c. Sideburns are to be extended no further than the lowest part of the ear and shall be cut on a horizontal line.

In October of 1976 the rule was rewritten to read as follows:

> Rule 4.17 Hair must be neat, washed and the length cannot exceed the bottom of the shirt collar. (Verified native American Indians may wear long hair.)
> a. Mustache—must be neat and cannot extend beyond the lower lip.
> b. No beards, goatees or other facial hair will be allowed. (Verified Sunni Muslims may wear a one-inch beard.)
> c. Sideburns may extend to one inch below the ear lobes.[7]

Uncertainty concerning the rule, coupled with a skepticism concerning the validity of the rule, prompted many officers to ignore violations of the hair length rule, even when it was operative.

In addition to administrative inconsistency, the possibility of bringing another officer's mistakes to the attention of the administration also makes some officers reluctant to act when they observe rule violations. This argument is one of the common justifications officers employ to support their ignoring of minor misbehaviors:

> If a guy's out of place, I generally shrug because I could get another officer jammed up. Swag? [Personal work done by an inmate for another inmate in return for payment in cigarettes or other favors.] It's an iffy thing with the administration, so it's iffy with me. It's probably the worst thing to let go because of the contraband.
>
> *Why do you handle things in that way?*
>
> I let things slide because that's the tone of the institution. Haircuts, shaves. Other officers come up to me and say to write the guy up. I say, "If you want to, go ahead." There's a rule on hair trimming, I got on it for a while, but as time goes by it's back to the way it was. If the sergeant told me to tell the guy to shave, I'd do it, but there's a lack of administrative follow-up on cases like this, and an officer won't put himself out on a limb to make enemies. If the administration doesn't care, why should you?

Rationales for Enforcing Strategies

Much of the literature dealing with the rule enforcement function of correction officers views the officer's lax behavior as part of a process of corruption of authority that results from the interaction of the officer's authority and the necessity to gain the cooperation of inmates in the maintenance of the institution. From the officer's perspective, the matter is much more complex. Although the cooperation of the inmates is certainly a factor, other more personal interpretations of the officers' and the inmates' relationship to institutional rules play a part in determining how minor rules are handled.

While most officers preferred to bring observed minor rule violations to the inmate's attention and a few chose to ignore such violations, their reasons include a number of themes interacting within the individual when confronted with a rule enforcement situation (see Table 11, Appendix D). Significant because of its absence is the theme of punishment. No officer mentioned the need for penalties to be imposed.

Rule Enforcement Strategy as Functional

Over 40% of the officers indicated that they felt their strategy of enforcement was functional (i.e. that telling the inmate or ignoring misbehavior helps the officer obtain some end he deems important). Though it includes gaining cooperation from inmates, this theme also includes obtaining objectives that relate to the functioning of the institution as a whole.

Inmate-Oriented Functions

For some officers their particular strategy is seen as useful because it prevents the inmate from developing a hostile, rebellious attitude. The officers feel that writing a formal infraction report for a minor piece of misbehavior may be interpreted by the inmate as an arbitrary exercise in authority, an indication that the officer is unable to handle things "man to man." Although some officers believe that their strategy will help them gain inmate cooperation, the predominant direction of this rationale is not to lose the cooperation they had already experienced by evoking hostilities over trivial matters:

> *What do you consider minor rule violations?*
>
> Things that irritate them and probably shouldn't exist. Like shaves, haircuts, usually it's just one guy trying to get away with it. It's not big enough to cause an uproar over. You let the guy go and talk to him later on. You'll find that other inmates get after him too, a rebellious type. There was one, he was colored, he was the only guy who hadn't shaved. If I go after him he might cause a disturbance. So I let it go and I heard the other inmates telling him to shave. He came around, he changed his attitude.

Why did you handle things in that way?
I figured if I pounced on him, he'll be rebellious right away. I look at all of them differently. They are. So you take it day by day. You can't say, "Do this," and expect that to be the end of it. Years ago you could, but not today. They don't know discipline, they've never worked, they have no sense of values. They think you're trying to pull your authority on them.

* * *

What do you consider minor rule violations?

Haircuts, sideburns, mustaches are the main things to be handled by the officers. Things they violate quite often.

What do you do when you see an inmate violating one of these rules?

I just say, "Your mustache is a little long, rules say the upper lip." Or I just say "Shave." Nine out of ten guys will say, "You've got it," and they will get it done. But if you use force right away and tell him among other inmates, he'll resent it and not do it. There's a way you tell a man. First you do it in a way like you're asking. Then tell him. Most will comply later.

Why do you handle it that way?

If you order him, the man becomes belligerent. Disobeys a direct order. Curses and screams in front of other inmates. He's forced your hand, you have to show authority then.

Officer-Oriented Functions

Strategies of dealing with minor offenses are also seen as functional in terms of concerns that relate directly to officers. For example, a report indicating that an inmate is "out of place" could be interpreted by someone else as an admission by the officer that another officer was negligent in his duty in allowing the inmate to get from point A, where he was scheduled to be, to point B. In addition to protecting other officers, there is a desire to protect oneself from administration reprisals for neglecting one's duty. The following interview excerpts illustrate these points:

What do you consider minor rule violations?

When they can get [hot] water [in their cells]. Maybe haircuts would be. The administration says it's part of personal hygiene.

What do you do when you see an inmate violating one of these rules?

That's where you run into problems. Say the guy totally refuses to get a haircut. You lock him up. But I usually tell them verbally and give them a day or two to straighten out. I get their name, number and cell location, and I check up on it later.

Why do you handle it in that way?

Basically you're protecting yourself. If there's a fighting on the gallery and a guy's out of his cell, they come back on you. So if you write him up, you've got it on paper. You protect yourself by putting it on paper.

* * *

What do you consider minor rule violations?

The neatness-of-the-cell rules. Unless the cell is really sloppy I don't enforce it much. They're supposed to play their tape players only with an earphone, but if the volume is real low, I'll leave him alone.

What do you do if you see a violation?

I warn him the first time, write an infraction the second time. The third time, the adjustment committee takes it, it's out of our hands.

Why do you handle it in that way?

I don't have time to push minor infractions. If I push it with one, I'll have to push it with all and I don't have time.

There are 200 in the block probably violating something, so I kind of look the other way because there's not enough manpower. It's like enforcing firecrackers on the outside on the 4th of July. There's not enough police to go around.

Unnecessary Rules

Over 25% of the officers believe that many of the minor rules they are asked to enforce are unnecessary or out of date. In reaching this conclusion, officers often compare values they hold outside the institution with those they believe should be applicable inside. Observing that hairstyles in the 1970s are longer than in the past, many officers believe that restrictions on hair length are anachronistic, a remnant of prison regulations of 50 years ago. Some officers, recognizing that wearing hats "is part of black cultural expression," believe that rules governing the wearing of hats in restricted areas should be ignored. Smoking regulations are equally held in disregard since "almost everyone nowadays smokes." Even regulations governing gambling are occasionally questioned. Although gambling is often associated with violence, some officers still feel that gambling is natural. "As long as you have two people on earth, you'll have gambling." The conflict involved in maintaining a double standard of morality, one for those outside and one for those inside, leads many officers to disregard some rules.

The conflict inherent in the double standard is shown for correction officers not only in reference to beliefs they hold about general social values, but also in reference to their own behavior and that of other correction officers inside the institution. "Why," they ask, "can't inmates have their hair longer when officers can wear longer hair?" or "How can an officer tell an inmate to stop smoking when he's standing there with a cigarette in his hand?" Such comments indicate that at least some officers judge the rules that govern inmate behavior by rules governing their own institutional behavior.[8]

Officers also conclude that some rules are unnecessary after observing inconsistencies in the rule enforcement practices of supervisory staff and of other officers. "After all, how important can a rule be if a supervisor or most officers pass right by an inmate violating it, ignoring him?" This comment illustrates the failure of many correction officers to view the behavior of other officers in the light of their own. Where most officers indicate that they approach rule violations from a situational perspective (that is, they react to rule violating behavior not merely because it is proscribed, but rather because of the context within which the behavior occurs), they often interpret the apparent nonenforcement behavior of other officers as laxity. Where they may see themselves as "fair or flexible" in handling similar situations, they may judge equivalent behavior by another officer as an example of overall institutional inconsistency.

Personal Involvement in Enforcement Decision

Another enforcement rationale finds the officer becoming personally involved in the decision as to *how* to enforce rules. Rather than weighing the functional qualities of an enforcement decision or judging the rules themselves, 20% of the officers said that they reacted as they do to violations of minor institutional rules because the inmate action or the enforcement decision had meaningful implications for *their sense of self as an officer*. For others, personal involvement means involvement in the interpersonal "testing" process, and the enforcement decision is viewed as a decision to intervene in a negative way as far as the particular inmate is concerned. Rather than being an exercise in leniency, the decision to "tell" the inmate becomes an exercise in strength; the officer indicates to the inmate that he is personally in charge of the situation and that the inmate had better acknowledge the fact lest more drastic action be taken:

> *Why do you handle things in that way?* [telling inmates about violations]
>
> Because I take it personally. I feel he's scraping me, so I take it personally. If it's not serious and he did it to me and I don't like it, I tell him. I say, "What do you think, I'm dumb or something?" He's insulting my intelligence. Maybe it's wrong, but that's how I handle it.

For others, telling the inmate about a violation was seen as an *authority reinforcing* alternative to issuing a formal written complaint. For these officers writing formal complaints in minor cases degraded the officer and demonstrated that he was incapable of handling such offenses without resorting to "authority." The officers make such comments as "You get a sense of failing if you can't get a guy to do it without locking him up," or "As an officer, if you don't enforce things, you're degrading yourself."

Fairness

For a substantial number of officers their strategy of handling minor rule violations was a reflection of their sense of fairness. Fairness to these officers means recognizing that everyone, even an inmate, has bad days, forgets things or may not be aware of a rule. It means telling the inmate about a transgression to give him a chance to correct the situation without inviting formal interventions. These officers are not reluctant to place themselves in the inmate's position and are willing to interpret inmate actions in light of their own feelings:

> I'm human. I forget things. Maybe he had a problem the night before.
>
> * * *
>
> Not that it's the easiest way out to sit and counsel. But you have to realize that we're all human and we all make mistakes.

The Escalation Process: Minor Rule Violations Become Major

Just as a policeman's actions are often influenced by factors other than the nature of an observed law violation, so too are the correction officer's. As an initial intervention strategy, an officer may ignore or informally deal with a minor rule violation situation. However, those misbehaviors that the officer usually considers minor occasionally develop into situations he believes merit filing a formal written report.

In general terms there are two sets of considerations that can lead an officer to handle a minor rule infraction by writing a formal report: decisions determined by the environment in which the event occurs and those deriving from the interaction occurring between the officer and the inmate involved.

Environmental concerns include the location of the incident and the visibility of the incident to either supervisory personnel, inmates or to other officers. Incidents occurring in the mess hall area or in the auditorium where large groups of inmates are congregated are usually interpreted as being particularly dangerous, although minor. The officers' belief that inmates in a group are most apt to display hostility toward officers when confronted with rule violations leads officers to treat incidents in these areas as serious. Even a seemingly minor event, such as moving from one seat to another, can be viewed with suspicion by the officer and can be reported because of the perceived potential for danger.

The presence of supervisory personnel at the site of a rule violation sometimes inspires an officer to write a formal report of an incident, although he might otherwise prefer to handle the matter informally. Here the officer is acting to protect himself. In the event the incident is reported by the supervisor and the officer has failed to report it, he is subject to administrative sanctions.

An officer may issue a formal report of an infraction where he might otherwise prefer to handle the matter informally when other officers are present. Though only 50% of our officers indicated that they would handle infractions differently if other officers were present, some indicated that their reaction to peer presence would communicate that they "were tough" and that they did not let inmates "run all over them." Other officers indicated that they might formally intervene in the rule violation situation out of self-protection. Fear of being reported to the administration by another officer may be involved in the decision. Rather than risk administrative disciplinary action, a formal report is filed as a precaution.

More often, however, it is the character of the interaction between the inmate and the officer that leads to the issuance of a formal report for a minor infraction. The data in Table 5.2 that summarizes the infractions reported by these officers highlight the importance of inmate-officer interactions in the decision to write a formal report. The violations "refusing an order," "threatening an officer" and "disrespect to officer," all of which reflect a negative officer-inmate interaction, account for 231, or 43%, of the total reports written by the group of officers.

Table 5.2. Rule Violations Reported by Sample of 50 Officers During 1976[a]

Violation	Number of Incidents N=541	Percent	Number of Officers Writing Reports[b] N=50	Percent
Fighting	47	8.7	18	36
Contraband	74	13.7	23	46
Stealing	16	3.0	9	18
Late from furlough	8	1.5	1	2
Destroying state property	6	1.1	4	8
In another man's cell	3	<1	2	4
Gambling	3	<1	3	6
Refusing an order	182	33.6	24	48
(a) a direct order	93	17.2	15	30
(b) to work	49	9.1	9	18
(c) loitering on gallery	40	7.4	8	16
Loud talking after quiet bell	46	8.5	5	10
Out of place	40	7.4	12	24
No shave or hair cut	25	4.6	10	20
Threatening an officer	18	3.3	6	12
Disrespect to officer	13	2.4	3	6
Lying to officer	8	1.5	4	8
Arguing with inmate	8	1.5	6	12
Cleanliness	7	1.3	5	10
Late for work	6	1.1	1	2
Swag work	5	<1	3	6
Mental problems[c]	13	2.4	4	8
Locked in at own request[c]	13	2.4	6	12

[a] Data gathered from institution's "The Daily Journal of Infractions" (1976).

[b] 12 officers wrote no reports. Eleven of these worked in job locations giving them no contact with inmates: towers, administration building and front gate.

[c] These behaviors appear as offenses in the 1976 "Inmate Rule Book."

Interactions with inmates may be interpreted by officers primarily as informal person-to-person interactions rather than as formal officer-inmate confrontations. When the officer is challenged by an inmate, he may step out of his role as officer and interpret the inmate's behavior as a personal challenge. Here the officer acknowledges his acceptance of the inmate's demand to be "treated like a man." Officers generally feel that they are personally treating inmates like "men" when they inform them that they are breaking a rule, or when they request that the inmate perform his assigned duties. As "men," officers feel that they themselves would react positively to such moves and that "men" in general should willingly do what they are told if they are approached in the proper way. This "individualistic" approach to officer-inmate interactions is underscored by the nearly total absence of officer statements attributing inmate actions to a dislike or a disrespect of officers in general. Officers recognize that certain inmates react to certain officers in negative ways, and they attribute the inmates' negative reaction to the fatal flaw in an officer's "tough guy" approach, the officer's individual style.

By far the most important factor in determining an officer's response in a minor rule violation situation is the officer's perception of the inmate's attitude when the offense is brought to the inmate's attention. Many officers indicate that attitude is more important than actual behavior. In addition to reporting an offense, they frequently report their perception of the inmate's attitude as one "showing disrespect to an employee." Such phrases as "used vile language" and "displayed contempt for reporting officer" are used on reports to heighten the apparent seriousness of the offense or to provide an additional offense. Some officers indicate that they sometimes reported the attitude and ignored the behavior that initiated the rule enforcement interaction when submitting their written report:

> I told the guy he was getting out of line. The guy still said, "No. Fuck you." I told him that he was completely out of line. So I put in a report. I would have torn it up, but when he started foul mouthing me in front of other inmates, you can't let that go.
>
> * * *
>
> Let's say, if I said to take his hat off and he says, "Why?" I'll write him up from what he says, "Mother fucker, etc." Whatever he says, you put in the report. He's not written up on the rule, but on the manner he reacted with when he was informed about the rule.
>
> * * *
>
> It depends on the guy's attitude. If he's got a snotty attitude, I might write him up sooner than a guy that says, "Okay, I won't do it again," even though you know he probably will do it again. The guy might get written up for his attitude even if it's his haircut that led to it. He's disobeying a direct order. The guy's attitude plays a big part, more than the rule.

Experienced officers report that they can often manipulate an inmate whom they know is particularly apt to react strongly by verbally antagonizing the inmate. (I have observed such incidents.) When the inmate then predictably reacts, he becomes subject to disciplinary proceedings. Even if a trivial matter ostensibly triggered the incident, the evoked "disrespect" defines the seriousness of the offense.

The officers at Auburn tend to believe that, in general, institutional rules, even minor ones, serve to maintain order. As the officers see it, every society needs rules and regulations to function smoothly, and prison society is no exception. With this assumption in mind, officers tend to react strongly to inmates whose attitude and behavior they believe tend to disrupt the institution's social order. The officer feels justified in reacting with formal interventions against such inmates because he believes that these inmates disrupt ongoing programs for the vast majority of inmates who wish to take advantage of them. But even here the officer's first strategy may be to "give the guy a break":

> You go by the guy's attitude. If he's consistently against the order of things, doesn't want to go along with the program, you have to write him up. He'll disrupt it for everybody else if you don't. You can't do it the first time, usually you give the guy a break. In the basement there was a guy who was supposed to make sandwiches for supper. I told him to go to his job and he didn't. I told him twice. He didn't want to go, so I wrote him up. He didn't seem to care. He didn't belong in the mess hall anyway; he didn't want to help the other guys out.

SUMMARY—1976

From the guard's experience, authority is not a unitary concept. For many correction officers, authority is not something one has simply by virtue of his title: It is something that is earned through a legitimizing process. Authority resides in the person, not in the uniform. For others the opposite is true and authority is seen as coming with the territory.

As applied to the management of inmate behavior, "legalistic authority" is something one applies only when "legitimate authority" is not available, and the rule enforcement process often reflects the personal situational concerns that are part of the correction officer's human services rule. From the guard's perspective, decisions concerning when and how to enforce rules involve a variety of meanings and strategies. These decisions are made for a variety of reasons with situational and contextual cues rather than stereotypical "good guy-bad guy" personality traits evoking guard responses.

RULES AND AUTHORITY 1986

Changes in Inmate Life

If there is one thing that all of the officers interviewed agree on it is that the years between 1976 and 1986 saw a dramatic change in the nature of inmate life. Key components of the change involved drugs replacing "booze" as the prison's main contraband item; a move from individual (one-on-one self-image-related) violence to organized group violence; and a move from individual coercive and exploitive relationships to group extortion rackets. The seemingly survival oriented atomized inmate society of the 1950s, 1960s and 1970s has become the group and power oriented inmate society of the 1980s.

How do inmates behave?

> Seventy to seventy-five percent there's no problems with. Tell them to do things and they do it. They look at the CO as doing a job. But fifteen to thirty percent you have problems with regardless. They hate the world and the CO's because they deal with the CO's most frequently and the CO's represent the state. Those guys give you lots of problems with drugs, extortion and verbal abuse. They're constantly into something.
>
> Extortion works in groups. I've seen a guy 5′6″ go to a guy 6′5″ and threaten him. Tell him not to walk the yard. He knows the guy's not by himself. They don't do nothing by themselves. When they're after a guy, it's two or three guys on one. Then they leave and get rid of the weapon. The guys tell him to pay for protection from them. Maybe they'll firebomb his cell when he's away. It happens.
>
> * * *
>
> The inmates are better educated now. More organized too. More in groups rather than as individuals. The Muslims, the different groups have converged. They're involved in drugs too, and extortion. They're more negative towards other groups of inmates controlling power and drugs. Homosexuality is not as prevalent because of AIDS. But extortion is prevalent.
>
> There used to be the old-timers to control the kids. Now it's the younger inmates with macho attitudes and gangs. It's popular in the streets and in prison, too. Neighborhood gangs, white bikers, Muslims. They get jobs in the same areas, are in the same blocks. Extortion is like block to block, not throughout the facility. The full population is not together. Three or four guys in A block, three or four in D and they control their side of the prison: drugs, money, hypodermic needles. With trailer visits, visiting room, lawn picnics there are lots of females around and some passive sex so the sexual stress is not as much as ten years ago. So it's positive from a sex point of view.
>
> Protective custody is being used constantly and it's constantly filled. You can have an inmate in a housing block who can extort the whole

> block. It's hard to prove—lots of times you go to investigate and interview an inmate and he lets you know he's being threatened by Joe Blow. What the guard would like to do is lock up Joe Blow; but often you have to put the other guy in protection when you can't prove it. You can't take the other inmate's word to lock someone up.

These perceptions of increased violence and drugs are supported by data gathered from the institutions "Daily Journal of Infractions" (see Table 18, Appendix D). These data show that the number of offense reports for Inmate-Directed Violence and Self-directed violence have increased substantially over the years. In addition, sex and drug-related offenses also increased. Only officer directed violence seems to have remained relatively stable over the years. Surely the inmate society in 1986 is different from what it was in 1976 with the focus of inmate attention shifting from inmate/officer-institutional confrontations to inmate/inmate conflict.

Besides being concerned with drugs, violence and sex, officers also note a difference in the inmates' awareness and use a variety of legal remedies to solve conflicts.

> The inmates know they have more rights now. Plenty of access to legal things. Before they couldn't talk to a visitor and ask them to go to a reporter. Now they can call reporters on the phone. They can call anybody. That was unheard of. I remember when a reporter first came to the institution and he was swamped in the yard. Now, nobody cares. And the grievance procedures. Mostly it's minor problems but it gives the inmates access to the grievance officer and the rules. Lots of problems can be worked out confidentially, but at least it gives the inmates the right. It happened to me recently. An inmate can write a letter to the warden with accusations about an officer or a sergeant and it gets passed through channels to be investigated. You have to prove it didn't happen that way.

The implementation of these various due process features may have contributed to reducing inmate focus on the fairness and equity concerns represented in the person of the correctional officer. This may have helped to maintain the stability of the amount of direct inmate/officer conflict in spite of an increasingly violent intra-inmate world.

Officer Authority in the 1980s

In an atmosphere more laden with conflict and violence, more governed by prescriptive "policy and procedures," more concerned with protecting inmate rights and more populated by younger inmates and officers, interviews with both the experienced and younger officers discovered changes in the perceptions and application of correctional officer authority. The "personal" and "legalistic" approaches to authority still remain, and many officers still refer to the "firm, fair and consistent" principles which helped them gain "personal legitimacy." In describing the advice they would give to younger officers, the importance of establishing a reputation and gaining experience still dominates.

> It's hard to establish your authority. You have to gain a reputation. If you're on the same company or shop, they'll get to know you and where you'll go. The word spreads. It probably takes about five years before you really have it. The more experience you have the less authority you have to use. You have to flaunt it early, then lay back and it runs itself.

From the officers hired since 1980, some of the necessary strategies for developing that reputation emerge. These strategies reflect a growing connection between legalistic and personal authority. As the officer gains experience it is expected that "legalistic" authority becomes more "personal" and coupled with the application of informal sanctioning processes.

> I'd ask the new officer where he was having difficulties. Say he's the last guy to get his inmates back in their cells. You have to tell some guy four or five times to lock in. They're playing with you and you play with them. You go up to the individual and say, "what's your name? Whether you get locked or not doesn't matter to me. But I can let you out late, have some problem opening your door." Maybe you let him out last or if you get a call that he has a visit, don't let him know for an hour or so. Once the inmate doesn't want to be fooled with he'll come and ask you why you're doing this. Then you're in control.
>
> * * *
>
> I'd tell a new guy not to take any crap from these guys. Don't let them get it over. Just lock them up. Your authority comes from them knowing that you'll lock them up for a while.
>
> * * *
>
> I'd say write like a son-of-a-gun. Give an explanation of why you're writing. Later you just explain and don't need to write.

For the older officers three new authority-related themes are merging with the "personal" and "legalistic" themes emphasized ten years earlier. First, *a knowledge* of state and institutional directives, institutional policy and procedures and, second, *an ability to explain things* to inmates become new components of the "firm, fair and consistent" triad.

> If you do the job correctly, you'll establish your authority. You've got to know how to explain things now. If you have a good knowledge of the rules and regulations and keep up with policy and procedure the inmates will know that you know what you're talking about. It's gone from a personal thing to your skill and knowledge. We abused authority so much in the past that now it's different.

Another theme that emerges is the dilution of officer authority by the *increase in the number of sergeants* and superiors. Now younger officers reportedly have a tendency to call on supervisors when they cannot handle a problem and inmates tend to ask to see sergeants when the officer attempts to enforce a rule or get an inmate to behave in a certain way.

> Your authority is not as great as before. You still tell them what they're supposed to do but you can't have officers yelling at inmates. Some of the older officers might be able to get away with it but they know how to do it without getting resistance. Often the younger officers will call a sergeant if the inmate doesn't go in his cell. Sometimes the inmate will say, "I want to see a sergeant."

One of the original officers who is now a sergeant reinforces this observation and compares it with the Attica he experienced when he initially received his promotion.

> At Attica you're just kind of there as a sergeant. They (the officers) tell you, we'll come to you and get you if we have a problem. I was standing watch in the mess hall and an inmate broke line and shook my hand. Fifteen officers grabbed the guy and reprimanded him. I was shocked because here at Auburn, sergeants are more involved with the officers and how they deal with the inmates. At Auburn inmates tend to bypass the officers and go to the sergeant. That's not good, bypassing the officers, I'd just as soon go back to the Attica way.

CHANGING DEFINITIONS OF INMATE MISBEHAVIOR

With the increase in violence and drugs and in legal restrictions on officer decision-making many officers noted that what were minor rule violations in the past were now not even problems. Some of the things that were problematic and handled with infraction reports in 1976 are now not violations or are commonplace and handled informally in 1986. Hair length, "droppers" and sexually explicit material much focused on in the 1970s are now generally not subject to restriction. Even the smell of marijuana "two joints could get you thirty days in segregation" in 1976—is now handled by some officers by telling the inmate, "Don't smoke on my shift."

Still, however, misbehaviors related to disobeying direct orders, disturbing the block, late for count, creating problems in the mess hall, place order maintenance activities as the major function of officer rule enforcement practices. Keeping the institution running smoothly still provides the dominant rule enforcement theme for all officers (see Table 18, Appendix D). For some (especially younger officers) orderly rule enforcement practice also has a sense of self-image investment.

> Rules are just to keep order. They are vague and you have to figure out ways to apply the situation to the rule. Which rule and how many? Many don't write good reports. They charge but they don't back it up. But I try to do a good job.

New Rule Enforcement Practices

As all of the above changes were taking place rule enforcement procedures were also altered. State Directive #4932 (1983) established a tier system which categorized offenses according to seriousness levels. It also tied tier level to who in the hierarchy had to review and make a decision concerning the violation and the appropriate penalty. An officer with 13 years' experience explains this procedure in detail.

> You can't write up on local rules anymore. We used to have them. Now it's only statewide rules. But this means that there are certain things that don't get covered given the way each institution runs differently. Now we have the Tier System. If an officer writes an inmate up on a Tier 1 offense [violation hearing], the sergeant can handle it. He might take an inmate's recreation away for a certain number of days. If it's more serious, a Tier 2 [Disciplinary hearing], a lieutenant can handle it and the inmate can lose commissary, packages or be "keep locked" for a number of days. If it's Tier 3 [Superintendent's Hearing], then it goes to a lieutenant or above and then it's possible that they can lose good time.
>
> If it's Tier 2 and you want to keeplock the inmate you have to show the misbehavior report to the sergeant in the area and he has to

> approve it. If he doesn't think it merits a KL you can't send it in because the sergeant won't sign it.
>
> The 11-7 lieutenant reviews all of the reports that come in on a particular day. Those he feels shouldn't be keeplocked he releases and those he feels should stay in, he keeps in. The inmate has to receive a copy of the report within 24 hours and the inmate is asked if he needs assistance in preparing for the hearing. If he says, "Yes," then they will show him a list of officers he can pick from to help out. The chosen officer then interviews the inmate and other witnesses if they want to be. He then puts the information in a report and turns it in. It may be necessary later for the officer to be present at a disciplinary or Superintendent's hearing. [This procedure is defined in Directive #4932 Chapter V Standards—Behavior and Allowances, Subchapter A, Procedures for Implementing Standards of Inmate Behavior (8/2/83).]

Most officers still report issuing warnings before writing reports and considering inmate demeanor as an escalating factor making a written report more likely. With the above changes, however, officers report a number of subtle alterations to the basic process of decision-making related to rule enforcement.

First, they report that there has been a reduction in "bullshit" (trivial) reports written by officers. Now, with the necessity of having the reports reviewed and questioned by sergeants, officers have to pay a great deal more attention to "how" they write their report and the evidence they have that substantive violations have occurred.

> It's a lot more formal now. Before you could get away with a weekend lockup and nobody would cut the inmate loose. Now you can't do that because of the paperwork and you have to cover yourself because you might be brought up on charges. Some officers still embellish their reports but not as many. Many officers (experienced and young) don't know how to write reports, they think you've got to be a lawyer. I've also heard some officers say they now write reports better.
>
> The process has gotten more like on the street. Inmates can challenge reports, bring witnesses, plus there's a greater variety of penalties all spelled out in advance. The inmates like it if the officer's report isn't any good because they can bring witnesses. The old kangaroo court is out now. Before if I wrote you up, you were guilty. Now one good thing is where officers used to blow up reports, now they don't do it.

> The reports are more honest now. This helps get officers in shape. Because the officer can be challenged the officer has to be more professional and do a better job.

General acceptance of these new procedures is often coupled with an admission that charges were needed to correct the correctional officers' past abuse of rule enforcement authority. In addition, there seems to be a general recognition that implementation of these reforms has upgraded the quality of correctional officer behavior. Where the "professional" identity of correctional officers was being informally found in "human services" activities in 1976, in 1986, correctional officers are finding professional status in their ability to adhere to and to utilize formal policy and procedures. This change takes on added significance when one realizes that nearly 50% of the officers now working at Auburn have known only this system. This then becomes a significant characteristic of correctional officer generational change.

SUMMARY—1986

The nature of the inmate world officers are asked to control in 1986 is drastically different from that of 1976. Though officers still devote most of their authority application (rule enforcement) activity to order maintenance, violence and drugs occupy much more of their attention than they did in 1976. Officers are now asked to control this new inmate environment less with individual discretion and more with knowledge, explanation and formal procedures which structure their behavior and make them more accountable. Knowledge of regulations and accountability aspects of authority are beginning to form the basis of a "professional" identity among the changing officer corps at Auburn.

NOTES

[1]Sykes, Gresham. *The Society of Captives*. New York: Atheneum, 1970, p. 50.

[2]See Glaser, Daniel. *The Effectiveness of a Prison and Parole System*. Indianapolis, IN: Bobbs-Merrill, 1969, p. 84 for a similar finding.

[3]This observation is supported by data on infraction reports gathered from the institution's "The Daily Journal of Infractions." Of the 182 reports citing refusal of a direct order as the infraction, 118 or 65% were written by six officers, all of whom had less than five years' experience. In addition, seven of the ten officers who indicated that they took minor infractions personally were also from this less-experienced group.

[4]For these reasons 70% of the officers mentioned the kitchen area as the place they would least like to work. The mess hall is also the work area least desirable to most inmates.

[5]Glaser, Daniel. *The Effectiveness of a Prison and Parole System*. Indianapolis, IN: Bobbs-Merrill, 1969, p. 87.

[6]Both of these assumptions prove to be correct. Many inmates, particularly older and long-term inmates, prize predictability and value-consistent rules. Some young inmates, on the other hand, react oversensitively to discipline. (See Toch, *Living in Prison*, Chapters 6 and 7.)

[7]On January 1, 1977, Departmental Directive #4914 concerning inmate grooming standards set down new regulations: (Only relevant portions of this directive are cited here.)

A. Beards and Mustaches

1. All inmates may grow a beard and/or mustache not to exceed one (1) inch in length.

B. Hair

1. Hair may be permitted to grow over the ears to any length desired by inmates. The corn row style is allowed. The hair must be neatly groomed and kept clean at all times.

[8]This represents the guard counterpart of inmate attitudes toward the "principle of equality" described by Mathiesen in *The Defences of the Weak*. London: Tavistock Publications, 1965, pp. 154-156.

The Corruption of Authority Revisited

6

Literature that discusses correction officer social distance from inmates usually does so by relating social distance to the officer's authority and his rule enforcement behavior. In this view, an officer who places little social distance between himself and inmates is an officer whose authority has been corrupted by pressures from inmates. To the extent that corruption occurs, it follows that the guard lacks the ability to enforce institutional rules and regulations.[1] Here an officer's inability to enforce rules or to offer favors for compliance (low social distance) indicates corrupted authority: Corrupted authority means low social distance (to gain compliance) and an inability to enforce rules. Each concept is both an indicator and cause of the others. These relationships among social distance (an attitude), authority (a status) and rule enforcement (a behavior) are assumed to exist, but these implicit relationships have yet to be explored systematically.

While interviewing the Auburn officers, these three areas (social distance, authority and rule enforcement) were examined as independent concerns. By correlating interview material concerning social distance and authority with the data on the number of rule violations formally reported by officers, this chapter sheds new light on guard-inmate relationships and the corruption of authority premise.

DEFINING THE CONCEPTS

To examine the corruption of authority premise more closely, the three related concepts had to be operationally defined independently of one another.

Social Distance

Borgadus' definition of social distance (sympathetic understanding) was operationalized using five questions each officer was asked concerning his tendency to help inmates with their institutional and personal problems and his willingness to share his life, both institutional and personal, with inmates.

1. What do you do when an inmate comes to you with an institutional problem?
2. How about if an inmate comes to you with a personal problem?

3. Do you ever find yourself discussing with inmates institutional problems you're having?
4. Do you ever find yourself discussing your personal outside problems with inmates?
5. Do you ever try to find out if particular inmates are having problems?

Individually, responses to these questions provided information about personal and helping relationships that develop between officers and inmates discussed in Chapter 4. Taken together, however, they serve as a rough indicator of social distance needed to make distinctions among individual officers. An officer whose responses suggest that he takes *affirmative steps* to solve inmate problems and that he shares his problems with inmates presumably places *less* social distance between himself and inmates than an officer who employs passive techniques such as referring inmates to "proper channels" or who fails to share his own problems with inmates.

Following this categorization principle, a rough social distance (SD) scale was developed by dividing responses to the questions into two categories: generally positive responses showing that the officer took an *active* part in problem-solving or sharing (e.g. setting up an appointment with the chaplain) were scored 0, indicating low social distance; generally negative or passive responses (telling the inmate to see the chaplain) were scored 1, indicating higher social distance. By applying these criteria to all five questions each officer was placed on a scale ranging from 0 (lowest social distance) to 5 (highest social distance) (see Table 6.1 for distribution).

Table 6.1. Social Distance and Rule Enforcement

Social Distance Score	N	$\bar{x}$ Number Reports[a]	Range	SD	N of Group Above Grand Mean[b]	% of Group Above Grand Mean
0	5	8.4	1-17	5.49	2	40
1	8	11.6	0-38	11.94	4	50
2	14	13.8	0-36	13.22	5	36
3	13	12.8	0-58	17.81	5	38
4	8	6.9	0-29	9.18	1	13
5	2	10.5	6-15	4.50	1	50
Total	50	11.0	0-58	13.4	18	36

[a] Data gathered from the institution's "The Daily Journal of Infractions" (1976).

[b] Mean number of reports for total sample $\bar{x} = 11$.

Authority

In Chapter 5 it was shown that not all correction officers view their authority in a simple legalistic fashion. Many experience authority as the result of an interaction process in which the ability to gain compliance derives from the "personal legitimacy" of one's claims to authority. For purposes of the analysis presented here, each officer was placed into one of two groups according to his perceived source of authority: "personal" or "legalistic."

Rule Enforcement Behavior

The number of formal rule violation reports filed by each officer served as an indicator of the extent of an officer's rule enforcement behavior. If the description of officer rule enforcement procedures (Chapter 5) is accurate, the adequacy of this indicator is questionable. A more accurate measure would include both formal and informal interactions and the character of the officer's response to each interaction (e.g. was the violation handled satisfactorily or ignored). However, gathering such information on each of the officers was beyond the scope of this study.

Social Distance and Rule Enforcement

When the rule enforcement behavior of the officers in each social distance category is examined, no clear pattern emerges, as the mean number of violations for each social distance category indicates (see Table 6.1). Looking at the range and percentage of officers in each category writing more than the average number of reports, there is a great deal of variability within each social distance category as well.

When social distance categories are combined, one finds that 46% of those officers with lower SD scores (0, 1) wrote more than the average number of reports, while only 32% of those with higher SD scores (2, 3, 4, 5) did so. Though not statistically significant, this relationship is in the opposite direction from that suggested by the corruption of authority premise. That is, these data seem to indicate that officers who place less social distance between themselves and inmates write more reports than officers who maintain greater social distance.

Source of Authority and Rule Enforcement

To determine if officers who perceive their authority "legalistically" differ from those who experience authority "personally," the mean number of reports written by officers in each category was calculated. Table 6.2 shows that, on the average, officers who view authority in personal terms write more reports than the legalistic authority officers. This table also shows that there are twice as many officers in the personal authority group who wrote more than the average number of reports than in the legalistic authority group. The practical significance of this difference prompts an explanation, though the difference itself is not statistically significant.

Table 6.2. Rule Violations Reported by Source of Authority

Source of Authority	N	$\bar{x}$ Reports[a]	SD	N of Group Above Grand Mean[b]	% of Group Above Grand Mean
Personal[c]	22	11.1	14.4	9	41
Legalistic[c]	18	7.9	11.2	4	22
Total	40[d]	9.2	13.1	13	33

[a] Mean number of rule violations reported by each officer during 1976. Data gathered from institution's "The Daily Journal of Infractions" (1976).

[b] The grand mean is the mean number of reports filed by total sample = 11.

[c] Personal authority means that the officer feels he derives his authority from the way he does his job; legalistic authority means he feels he derives his authority from rules, administration or his uniform.

[d] The number of officers is less than the 50 in the interview sample because officers with multiple responses to the questions concerning the source of their authority were eliminated from these computations so that the two groups would be mutually exclusive.

For the "legalistic" officer a rule violation may present an opportunity to do nothing more or less than handle a rule violation. If the officer is able to obtain compliance without writing a report, the incident is promptly forgotten. For the officer who views his authority in "personal" terms, however, the rule enforcement situation may present an opportunity to do more than just stop the violation, and the violation interaction is placed within the context of the officer's pattern of relationships with inmates. In deciding whether or not to write a report, the "personal authority" officer receives cues from and interprets the probable results of his decision within the context of his relationship pattern. Simply telling an inmate about a violation may curb the violation, but it might not be action enough to satisfy broader concerns.

Since the officer views his authority as a personal matter, he may also have a greater tendency to interpret a rule violation as a breach of relationships and may therefore more readily perceive the existence of the factor most frequently cited by officers as leading to a formal written report of the rule violation: a negative attitude on the part of the inmate.

Filing a written report might also provide the "personal authority" officer with an opportunity to demonstrate the "firm, fair and consistent" attitude he believes necessary to gain the inmate's respect. In writing a report these officers may be telling inmates that they are "men of their word" and "not people to be fooled with."

Social Distance, Rule Enforcement and Situational Factors

The above discussion of rule enforcement, social distance and authority has focused upon the expressed attitude of correction officers toward authority, the manner in which they report dealing with and sharing problems with inmates (social distance) and one measure of officer behavior (number of rule violations reported). In examining the rule enforcement process, however, it was learned that situational factors appear to have an extensive influence in determining how correction officers behave in these interactions. To determine the effect of situational factors I looked for differences in rule violation reporting among officers working in different institutional job assignments.

Though the number of officers in each job category in Table 6.3 is relatively small, it is apparent that the tendency of an officer to formally report rule violations is closely related to the opportunities provided by his job assignment. Officers in those job assignments having high contact with inmates (block, work gang, shop, yard), where they presumably have more opportunities to observe inmate behavior and to interact with inmates, wrote substantially more reports than those officers who have little or no contact with inmates (wall and administration building assignments).

Table 6.3. Job Location, Social Distance and Rule Enforcement

Present Job Location[a]	N	$\bar{X}$ SD[b]	$\bar{X}$ RE[c]	Low SD[d] N	Low SD[d] %	Above Mean[e] Enforcement N	Above Mean[e] Enforcement %
Block	10	2.20	15.3	6	60	5	50
Gang	7	2.00	12.3	4	57	3	43
Shop	2	1.00	20.5	2	100	1	50
Yard	8	2.75	23.4	4	50	6	75
Administration building	6	2.17	1.8	4	67	0	0
Wall	7	3.00	0.9	2	29	0	0
Relief	10	2.30	7.5	5	50	3	30
Totals	50	2.34	11.0	27	54	18	36

[a] Job location means the job assignment the officer was assigned to at the time of his interview. Job location may have changed during the year for which I obtained rule enforcement data; I did not determine whether this occurred. However, since 42 of the officers in my sample had had their assignments for two or more years prior to our interview and only four indicated that they planned on changing assignments soon after our interviews, it seems safe to assume that these assignments were stable. Also, officers working overtime on assignments different from their regular assignments adds another complication to interpreting those data. However, for my purposes I will assume that the officers worked their assignments throughout 1976.

[b] Mean social distance score on the social distance scale.

[c] Mean number of rule violations formally reported during 1976.

[d] Low SD = Scores of 0, 1 or 2 on the social distance scale.

[e] Above $\bar{X}$ enforcement means officer wrote more reports than the mean number written by all officers in the sample $\bar{X} = 11.0$

In addition, there exists a great deal of variation in the number of rule violations reported by officers within the high inmate contact group: yard officers averaged 23.4 reports; block officers, 15.3 reports; and work gang supervisors, 12.3 reports. Since each of these assignments involves a high degree of contact with inmates, an explanation for these differences might involve the varying quality of the inmate-officer relationships likely to develop on these different assignments and in the varying situational contexts presented by each assignment within which the officer interprets both his and the inmate's behavior.

Officers assigned to each of these high inmate contact job assignments also vary in the amount of social distance they report maintaining from inmates: those officers assigned to yard duty having the highest mean social distance score (2.75); those assigned to block work averaging 2.20; and those supervising work gangs having the lowest mean social distance score (2.00) for the three groups. Since the social distance measure was based on reported officer problem-solving and problem-sharing behavior, this might indicate that social distance, as well as rule enforcement, is related to situational factors inherent in the officer's work location and the extent that job assignments are a reflection of the officer's personal needs (see Chapter 2); this finding may reflect relationship preferences of individual officers.

General comments made by officers during their interviews and observations made by the author over the years shed light on the relevant situational characteristics of these three job assignments.

Supervising Inmate Work Gangs

When an officer supervises a work gang, he usually has high contact with a relatively small group of inmates (usually ten or less). Both the officer and the inmates are charged with accomplishing specific tasks, managing a store house, working on institutional maintenance or handling clothing or commissary inventory. The officer and the inmate are in comparatively intimate contact throughout most of their working day. The pace of the work varies, but there is usually time for officer-inmate discussions. As my discussion of officer work concerns shows, the assignment of work gang supervisor is most often associated with the ability to *control* one's work environment. Within this work situation it may be that the relatively low violation reporting rate (low for the high inmate contact assignments) reflects the work gang supervisor's ability to establish shared expectations with the inmates within his charge. It might also be a reflection of the low threat value of violations occurring in work locations relatively isolated from the main body of inmates. In such situations more options may be available to the officer for dealing with violations. He might exercise his authority to increase the amount of work the inmate is assigned, or the officer may feel his relationships with a particular inmate allows him to express his disappointment at the inmate's failure.

In doing so he may be seeking to control inmate behaviors by exploiting his one-to-one relationship with his inmates.

Relatively low social distance between officer and inmate might develop more easily in this work situation than in others. Usually the officer has more time to deal with inmate problems and therefore more opportunities to help.

Yard Officers

Those officers assigned to yard duty wrote more reports, on the average, than either of the other high inmate contact groups. The social distance scores for yard officers (2.75) were also substantially higher than for either the work gang supervisors or block officers (2.00 and 2.20, respectively). With regard to rule violations, three of the eight yard officers interviewed described yard duty as "being a policeman" and "looking to make a good bust." These three officers were the only officers to indicate that they became actively involved in investigating rumors of potential violations, especially those involving the possession of contraband. In addition, rule violation reports by yard officers may be higher because the options available to an officer working in the yard for dealing with inmate-officer interactions resulting from rule violations appear to be limited. The yard officer may not have an opportunity to talk to the inmate in the more controlled environments available to block and work gang officers. In the yard, officer-inmate discussions are apt to take place within view and hearing of a number of other inmates. Within this context the stakes in the conduct and outcome of a violation interaction for the officer and for the inmate in terms of self-image promotion and protection may be much higher than for either the inmate and officer alone in the work gang, or the inmate and officer in the block. On a work gang the officer can deliver stern lectures or engage the inmate in an understanding conversation with no threat to either his or the inmate's position, since usually no one else is around. In the yard, however, displays of anger on the officer's part are apt to lead to an excited inmate and other excited inmates, while displays of understanding are apt to be interpreted as weaknesses by those observing. With this in mind, the filing of a formal report of the violation incident without a great deal of discussion reduces the chances for confrontation, since both officer and inmate play the role expected in the yard environment.

In terms of social distance and helping inmates with problems, the yard officer again may have few opportunities and options available to him. In the yard the officer does not have time to discuss personal problems with inmates. Discussions initiated by inmates may be viewed as a means of distracting the officer from his security concerns. In addition, the yard officer does not have access to a telephone, a main institutional problem-solving device and therefore inmates would be less likely to bring their problems to the officer who works this job. In addition, the authority of the yard officer would appear to be more formal than that of either the block or work gang officer. While in the yard, he has less opportunity to develop a set of mutually agreed upon expectations between himself and the inmates, since the inmates in the yard are relatively free from the officer's immediate control except in the case of rule violating behavior.

Cell Block Officers

The cell block officer falls in an intermediate position among the high inmate contact groups, both in terms of rule violations reported and social distance. Again an examination of the context within which block officers perform their work can help explain this finding.

In the cell block the officer must deal with a great many more inmates than the work gang supervisor and fewer than the yard officer. Though the cell block provides a more structured environment for both inmates and officers than does the yard, it is in some respects less structured than the work gang situation. On a work detail, inmates have specific tasks to perform and the officer's job is to supervise and assist his inmate workers; expectations and accepted work behaviors are clear. In the cell block, however, inmates have no specific tasks. Though confined to their cells a good deal of the time, inmates are often moved from place to place within the cell block and between the cell block and other parts of the institution. Whereas work detail officer-inmate interactions are structured around task requirements determined by the officer, in the cell block, officer-inmate interactions may be structured around "need requirements" as determined by the inmates. In the cell block the inmate is "at home," in the place "where he lives." Within this context the inmate may find it easier to make requests of officers to satisfy his (the inmate's) personal needs, and freer than in a work situation to engage in individually expressive behaviors such as singing, loud talking and "verbal horseplay." It is the kind of behavior interpreted by officers as "loud talking after the quiet bell" that results in many violations reported in the cell block area.

Though less structured than the work situation, the cell block offers more structure than the yard. Here the inmates in their cells offer less of a threat to an officer willing to deal with violations on a personal level. Here understanding, rather than being viewed as a sign of weakness as in the yard, might be interpreted as a sign of "caring" and "humaneness." In his cell the inmate has few options, there is little threat of immediate violence or escalation. Writing a formal report in such circumstances may be viewed as an exercise in power over a helpless individual, except in extreme cases where both officer and inmate implicitly agree that some formal action should be taken. Such cases often occur when inmates complain to an officer about the disruptive behavior of another inmate.

Social distance between the officer and inmate in the cell block might also be interpreted as a reflection of opportunity and options. Clothing, medical needs and cleanliness receive constant attention. It is in the cell block that the inmate concentrates most on his own needs, since there is little else to occupy his time. Officers also have more opportunity to deal with inmate needs in the cell block, having ready access to all parts of the institution by telephone. However, due to the number of inmates the cell block officer must serve, there may be little opportunity for cell block officers to discuss their own problems with inmates.

We can thus see that an officer's work behavior may be shaped more by his work environment than by his individual attitudes. The opportunities and options available to the officer as he enforces rules and helps inmates with problems in the variety of work locations would appear to be of major importance.

SUMMARY—1976

This chapter offers tentative evidence that when social distance between guards and inmates, authority and rule enforcement behavior are defined independently, the relationships among them are in the direction opposite to that predicted by the "corruption of authority" premise. Personal perception of authority and low social distance seem to be related to the issuance of formal reports by an officer. This finding can be understood in terms of the guards' perceptions of their role and the rule enforcement process.

Rule enforcement practices and social distance also seem to be related to the situational opportunities provided by varying work assignments, rather than to corruptive pressures exerted by inmates and the lack of rewards for inmates provided by the prison administration.

ORDER MAINTENANCE AND PRISON ENVIRONMENTS: 1976-1986

A combination of interview and rule enforcement data coupled with officer job assignments led me to suggest that understanding of correctional officer rule enforcement practices could best be understood by focusing on the interaction of correctional officer perceptions of authority, social distance (problem-solving and sharing behavior) and situational factors inherent in the subenvironment (officer job assignments) in which officers and inmates interact. This analysis added complexity and called into question the "corruption of authority" formulation described by Sykes. From this more complex analysis one would expect that specific institutional locations are more likely to produce specific officer-inmate interactions than others. Interpreted from Toch's perspective of person-environment transactions[2] one would expect the different resources available in different subenvironments to shape the interactions that take place within them.

Order maintenance rule violations written by officers can be used as an indicator of specific inmate behaviors which might vary across environments. From the description of rule enforcement practices related to "minor" violations (see Chapter 5) and job location (see Chapter 6) one can see that such interactions permit officers to exercise the greatest amount of discretion. Infraction reports resulting from inmate challenges to legalistic authority (violate rules designed to regulate inmate activities in specific areas such as cell blocks and shop areas), and challenges to personal authority (e.g., insolence, disobeying a direct order) are certainly the most frequently written reports as well (see Table 18, Appendix D). It should be clear, however, that formal infraction reports certainly do not represent all of the order maintenance interactions that take place. Many are frequently overlooked by officers, others result in informal counseling or "talking to." However, formal reports may serve as an indicator of the combination of the relative limits of permissible inmate behavior and officer tolerance for such behavior.

In order to determine if characteristics of institutional location influence the distribution of certain types of officer/inmate interactions, order maintenance rule violation reports written by all officers at Auburn from 1976 to 1985 were analyzed. Table 19, Appendix D, summarizes these reports.

While over 30,400 order maintenance reports were written during this ten-year period, only 50% (16,000) contained information regarding the location of the infraction. The percentage with location varied widely from year to year. In examining the production of order maintenance violation reports *with location*, however, it is clear that relative proportion of order maintenance reports produced in various institutional locations maintained stability over time.

In looking at the mean percentage of total reports written, the cell blocks (27%), the kitchen/mess hall area (7.7%) and the school (6%) are the only areas that consistently have more than 5% of the reports. Special Housing Unit (SHU) averages about 4.8% of all reports each year, and frequently accounts for 5% or more. On the other hand, the shops, yard, gym/library building and visiting area consistently produce less than 4% of the total number of reports.

When looking at the substantive content of the violations occurring in the different areas and other subenvironment characteristics, it appears that four "resources" might provide environmental contexts which shape the officer/inmate interaction process described above and help explain the stability of across-location while officers working in these locations and inmates moving through these locations vary. These resources are: (1) the existence and number of specific regulations governing inmate behavior; (2) the number of inmates and the amount of time inmates spend in a specific area; (3) the nature of the activities inmates engage in while in a specific area; and (4) the visibility (ease with which officers can observe the violations) of inmate behavior.

Content analysis of the substantive descriptions of the violations found in the "Daily Journal" demonstrates that the areas vary in the *type and number of "legalistic authority" regulations* that apply to each area (see Note 2, Table 19, Appendix D). The blocks have, by far, the greatest number of substantive regulations to provide opportunities for violations. Regulations governing inmate movement, cell cleanliness and orderliness, count regulations, provide many opportunities for challenges. The kitchen and mess hall area also is well regulated: food quantities, serving procedures, work habits (important because of their impact on the entire population if not up to par). In the school, inmate attendance (or lack of it) and unauthorized movement within the school (out of place) provide opportunities for order to be breached.

Another reason which certainly makes it more likely that the cell blocks, mess hall/kitchen and school are more likely to produce rule enforcement interactions is the *presence of inmates*. *All* inmates live in the cell blocks and spend between eight and fourteen hours in these areas. Nearly *all* inmates pass through the kitchen/mess hall area three times each day. Over eight hundred inmates participate in school programs on a daily basis. The shops, visiting room, library/gymnasium and SHU each service much smaller numbers of inmates. In addition, inmates in these areas are deployed in characteristically different ways than these inmates in the blocks, school and kitchen/mess hall area. While inmates are congregated in the blocks, school and kitchen/mess hall, they are relatively dispersed (e.g., separated by work locations in the shops, in separated recreation/study areas in the gym/library).

The yard, which traditionally holds large numbers of inmates in concentrated fashion (similar to the blocks) suggests the importance of the type of inmate activity occurring in an area and offense visibility in order maintenance reports. Though the yard is traditionally a location with many inmates, the behaviors of the inmates in this area are less subject to the legalistic regulations of the blocks, and the school. In the yard inmates are relatively free to set their own agenda of activities. In addition, order maintenance offenses occurring in the yard are more likely to be of the kind that focus on the challenges to personal authority rather than legalistic. For the challenge to occur, it is most likely that it will be officers who initiate the interaction: giving an order, or requesting information. When the inmate fails or refuses to comply, it is then that formal processes are invoked.

Given the low number of violations reported from the yard it appears that this happens infrequently. However, it should be noted that a high percentage of the reports *without specified location* are for personal authority challenges. It is possible (there is no way to know) that many of these confrontations occurred in the yard.

In the gymnasium/library, shops and visiting room, inmate *activities* would seem to occupy the inmates' time in ways which make regulation violation and challenges to personal authority unlikely. Involved in study, work and visits, inmates in these areas have a greater stake in compliance than in rule violation.

Finally, the *visibility* of legalistic order maintenance violations in the blocks increases the likelihood that a high proportion of such violations will occur there. Noise, clothes hanging on bars, dirty and smelly cells, inmates loitering on galleries when they should be in their cells are relatively easy to spot. Since such behaviors provide inmates with opportunities to exercise autonomy it is not surprising that they are likely to run afoul of the officers' desire for structure and order.

SUMMARY—1986

Data on order maintenance activities of officers demonstrate that our understanding of the rule violation behavior of inmates and the rule infraction behavior of officers can be enhanced by studying the environments in which officer/inmate interactions take place. The stability in the proportion of infraction reports from various subenvironments over time might indicate that "environmental opportunity structures" are important factors in explaining officer/inmate rule violation interactions at the institutional level of analysis.

NOTES

[1]See Sykes, Gresham. "The Corruption of Authority and Rehabilitation," *Social Forces*, Vol. XXXIV (1956), pp. 257-262; McCorkle, Lloyd W. Guard-Inmate Relationships," in *The Sociology of Punishment and Correction*, edited by N. Johnston, L. Savitz and M. Wolfgang. New York: John Wiley and Sons, 1970, pp. 419-422.

[2]Hans Toch. *Living in Prison*. New York: The Free Press, 1977.

GUARDS REACT TO THEIR WORK

III

Recently the subjects of work and people's reactions to their work have received increased popular, political and scholarly attention. Studs Terkel's *Working,*[1] *Work in America*[2] (a 1973 Department of Health and Welfare Task Force report), and Daniel T. Rodgers' historical study *The Work Ethic in Industrial America*[3] are concerned with the meaning of work for those who perform it. They explore the relationship that flourishes in the meeting of tasks, work environments and people. What emerges from these studies is a portrait of workers alienated from and dissatisfied with their work, but workers still capable of adapting to an increasingly negative environment. More recently, the study of work has begun to focus upon *stress* in the workplace and its impact on the individual workers.[4]

But what about prison guards? How do they experience their work and work environment? How do they cope with its pressures? Where do they find satisfaction? To date, there have been no answers to these questions; indeed, the questions have rarely been asked. Consequently, guards have had few opportunities to express themselves on the personal meaning of guarding prisoners as an occupation and of the prison as a workplace. When guards react publicly it is usually during times of prison crisis. Thus accounts of prison riots often cite unrest among the custodial staff among the conditions existing prior to riots.

In Chapters 7 and 8 the focus is not upon guard reactions to exceptional circumstances, rather, emphasis is placed upon the guard's reactions to his everyday occupational situation. Chapter 7 explores what guards perceive as the most salient negative features of their workplace. While they describe the techniques employed to cope with these features, long-submerged perspectives on the guard's role in the informal daily life of the prison community come to the surface. In Chapter 8 sources of correction officer job satisfaction are explored. Here the guard is seen searching for those incentives which keep him on the job and realizing that these satisfactions are what his work is all about.

NOTES

[1]Terkel, Studs. *Working*. New York: Pantheon Books, 1972.

[2]Special Task Force Report to the Secretary of Health, Education and Welfare. *Work in America*. Cambridge, MA: Massachusetts Institute of Technology Press, 1973.

[3]Rodgers, Daniel T. *The Work Ethic in Industrial America*. Chicago: University of Chicago Press, 1978.

[4]Cooper, C.L. and Marshall, J. "Occupational Sources of Stress: A Review of the Literature Relating to Coronary Heart Disease and Mental Health," *Journal of Occupational Psychology*, Vol. 49 (1976), pp. 11-28.

The Pressures of the Work and Ways of Coping

7

Living in prison is not easy. Prison inmates must find ways of coping successfully with a wide variety of external and internal stress-producing conditions if they are to survive psychologically.[1] Though the subject has received little attention, it is apparent that those working in prisons also face diverse pressures[2] and guards, like inmates, must also learn to deal with the stress-laden prison environment if they are to pursue their careers successfully.

This chapter focuses upon what prison guards perceive as the most salient negative factors in their work and work environment. Although its subject matter is essentially negative, the men whose experiences provide the raw material for discussion here are in reality "success stories." They took jobs in prison under conditions of great uncertainty, and with little preparation they have managed to pursue their careers. Special attention is thus given to the mechanisms these guards employ to cope with demands of their work. It is here, in the processes of adapting to prison life, that the guard becomes part of and affects the everyday life of the prison community.

I begin by concentrating on those negative conditions officers identify as the most salient to them. Later I will turn to officer experience with eight specific aspects of their work previously identified as having a relationship to job dissatisfaction and the techniques employed by officers to cope with these conditions.

GENERAL ATMOSPHERE AT AUBURN

To give perspective to the discussion that follows, it is important to get some feeling for the general atmosphere of Auburn Prison as a workplace. In this respect, Auburn Prison appears to offer a rather positive environment. This conclusion is reached when one examines two indices of the degree of job dissatisfaction associated with the conditions in a specific workplace: the turnover rate among its employees and the rate of worker absenteeism. As measured by these indicators, there does not appear to be an abnormally high degree of job dissatisfaction among the correction officers at Auburn. A comparison of the January 1, 1976 and January 1, 1977 correction officer seniority lists found only 15 additions and 12 terminations occurring during this period, a turnover rate of 7.5%.[3] This turnover rate is extremely low when compared to that found by Jacobs and Grear[4] at Stateville Correctional Center in Illinois. They found that 60% of the officers hired between July 1, 1973 and June 30, 1974 no longer worked at Stateville on September 19, 1974. The Auburn turnover rate is also very low when compared to the average staff turnover rate of 24.8% (using my formula, 51.4%) found by Luden in a national sample of over 63 correctional institutions.[5]

The low turnover rate at Auburn may reflect low levels of job dissatisfaction, but it may also reflect other factors. As Argyle explains:

> Labor turnover depends on other factors besides job satisfaction. In particular, it depends on the availability of other jobs, and it is found to be less during periods of high unemployment, and in small towns where there are no other firms offering similar work.[6]

With many of the officers at Auburn reporting that they became correction officers after dissatisfying experiences in the local labor market, the conditions associated with the small town economy described by Argyle appear to be operating here. When guards complain about their working conditions, administrators often say, "If the officers don't like it here, they can always leave." In theory those administrators are correct, but in practice the perceived lack of viable alternatives binds the guards to the prison as much as the inmates are bound to it by the law.

A second frequently used index of job dissatisfaction is the rate of voluntary absenteeism among the work force. Once again, as measured by this indicator, Auburn does not appear to be an abnormally negative place to work. Over one-half of the sample used sick leave at a rate of one-half day per month or less (see Table 12, Appendix D). Over 80% used one day or less per month, with the mean sick time used being 0.68 days per month. This is less than the absentee rate for the officers at Stateville, where Jacobs and Grear found that 27 white officers who were discharged or resigned averaged 0.80 days absent per month, while nine officers still employed averaged 0.90 days absent per month.[7]

JOB DISSATISFACTION THEMES

To discover conditions correction officers perceive as the most salient in shaping the negative side of their work situation, each officer was asked the following questions:

1. If you had to tell someone who was thinking about becoming a correction officer what the worst thing about the job was, what would you tell him?
2. What's the biggest problem you have doing your job?
3. What's the most difficult thing about being an officer?

Analysis of the responses identified three central themes (see Table 7.1). The first focuses upon the officer's *relationships with inmates*. Many officers express a concern with danger and talked of the mental strain that is brought about by the uncertainty of violent occurrences. Many officers also refer to abusive treatment often directed at them by inmates. Difficulties encountered in attempting to exercise discretion with impartiality are also cited.

A second set of concerns revolves around the theme of *powerlessness*.[8] In perceiving himself as lacking responsibilities and decision-making power, the officer sees himself as unable to participate meaningfully in the functioning of the institution. The officers feel they are unable to enforce what decisions they do make because they lack support from all sectors of the institution. A feeling of individual isolation surrounds the correction officer. A lack of opportunities to provide effective input into the decisions affecting management policy and his immediate work process further separates the individual officer from his work. In short, the officer experiences the classic symptoms of alienation: He feels divorced from his workplace and those with whom he works.

Table 7.1. Sources of Job Dissatisfaction in Correction Officers

Job Dissatisfaction Theme	Number of Officers Mentioning			% Mentioning[a] N=50
	Worst Thing About Job	Biggest Problem	Most Difficult	
Inmate related				
Physical danger and mental strain	17	1	11	50
Trying to treat inmates fairly	2	4	6	22
Treatment by inmates	7	9	3	28
Powerlessness				
Lack of responsibility and/or decision-making power	3	6	4	18
Lack of support from administration, supervisors, officers	6	15	10	54
Lack of opportunities for input	3	2	2	12
Inconsistencies and communication				
Overall policies	4	8	4	28
Rules and regulations	3	3	4	20
Supervision	—	4	1	10
Work schedules	6	—	2	14
Nothing	—	4	4	—
Others	9	3	2	—

[a] The percentage of the total sample of officers referring to the job dissatisfaction theme at least once.

A third set of concerns is *inconsistency and poor communication*. Here officers are concerned not with the specific content of institutional policies, rules and supervision, but with their inability to reconcile seemingly contradictory statements and behaviors, and with the inability of the administration and supervisors to communicate effectively the content of their policies and directions to the officers.

INMATE-RELATED JOB DISSATISFACTION THEMES

Sources of correction officer job dissatisfaction that have to do with inmates fall into three categories: a belief in the ever-present possibility of physical danger and tension that is related to apprehensiveness; the way officers are treated by inmates; and the difficulty of maintaining impartiality in dealings with inmates.

Physical Danger and Mental Strain

Roughly one-third of the officers referred to danger and mental tension as the "worst thing about the job" and approximately one-fifth viewed this aspect of the custodial role as the "most difficult" part of their work. This perception of danger by the officers is not related to a high probability of violent occurrences in prison. It relates, rather, to the unpredictability of prison violence:

> [The worst thing about the job] is the fear there might be a riot. That you might be dead, that you might not come out. It's there every day, but you just wonder if it will happen today.
>
> * * *
>
> [The most difficult thing] is the mental strain. It's more mental than anything else. Your mind's working all the time. You can go in there every day for 20 years and never break up a fight, never get assaulted. But the thought's there that it can always happen. This is more taxing than having to tussle with anybody.

Most officers express the opinion that large-scale prison violence is a constant possibility and can be precipitated by seemingly random events. Many believe they could "sense" the onset of a large-scale confrontation in changes in both inmate and officer behavior patterns. Such changes are gradual and begin to appear months in advance of an actual incident. Inmates who are usually quiet become boisterous, while outgoing inmates withdraw. Officers who have few problems with inmates begin to encounter an increasing number of challenges, while those who normally have difficulties are avoided by inmates. As this process progresses, the introduction of an "incident" provides a focus and large-scale violence erupts.[9]

Many of these officers were involved in a large-scale disturbance at Auburn in 1970 (some as hostages) and others were at Attica in 1971. Though the officers' involvement in these violent occurrences was not pursued during the interviews, there was information volunteered by these men that is relevant to an understanding of the officers' attitude toward large-scale prison violence and the difficulties it poses.

In evaluating the incidents, officers are more critical of the correctional administrators' handling of events leading up to and following violent confrontations than they are of the inmates whose violence they have to confront. Officers feel frustrated by many of the same conditions complained about by inmates. To the extent that they believe this comparison is valid, the officers' fear of large-scale violence is more a reflection of a lack of faith in correctional administrators than it is proof for the officers that inmates and/or the prison environment are inherently violent.

In addition to large-scale violence, officers are also concerned with being injured in isolated violent incidents stemming from physical confrontations between individual inmates or in those involving inmate violence directed at officers. Officers generally view inter-inmate violence to be the result of inmate involvement in homosexual activities, "booze," gambling or other illicit inmate activities. Violent outbursts by mentally disturbed inmates are also seen as a source of potential danger. Fights arising from disagreements over such trivial matters as "the location of a building in New York City" reinforce the officers' belief that violence in prison is unpredictable.

According to these officers, incidents of inter-inmate violence are most often "self-image" related. Recognizing the inmate's need to "save face" and "preserve or establish his reputation among his peers," officers observe that inter-inmate confrontations rarely occur when two inmates are alone or when an officer and a small number of inmates are involved. The presence of a "group" of inmates, however, rapidly increases the potential for violence. The following incident illustrates how an officer utilized this observation to prevent an incident:

> I had two guys working for me who got to where it looked like they were going to have a fight. So I set them to work by themselves, away from the other guys. They came back and there wasn't any fight. They had the pressures on them all day long. Most are willing to go along, they have respect for themselves. You only get grief when they're in groups.

There is also a negative side to the observation that inmate violence is "self-image" related. Knowing this not only allows the officer to prevent violence, but it also provides a tool to incite violence. By planting stories or spreading rumors, officers are able to set troublesome inmates against one another. When a fight occurs the troublesome inmates are often removed form the general population, thus removing the officer's problem.

Officers also point out that fights between inmates often occur where there is an officer nearby. This happens, they believe, so that the encounter can be stopped before either party becomes seriously injured and that it is the "ritual" of violence, rather than its outcome, that is significant.

Many officers readily admit that their "lives are in the hands of inmates." They depend on inmates to "tip" them off to impending trouble and often hope that their fair treatment of inmates will merit fair treatment by inmates should violence erupt:

> If I tell a guy I'll do something either for or against the inmate, I do it. And I always feel that if trouble happens, I'll do my best to get out of the way. But by doing my job like a professional, checking on things and having pride in my job, I feel a guy will tip me off to any trouble before it happens. But I don't really think about it that much. They outnumber us four to one and if they want hostages, there's nothing you can do.

Other officers are less sure that they can depend on help from inmates in times of violence, believing that existing relationships mean little once battle lines are drawn:

> I don't think about [violence]. I try to blot it out of my mind. But you know it could happen. If you go in and you're fair, you don't have to worry too much. But if you're in a place where it jumps off, it doesn't matter who you are. Some of the officers hurt during the riot here, they were nice guys, but they were in the wrong place.[10]

Inmate Behavior Toward Officers

A second source of correction officer dissatisfaction that is related to inmates involves the treatment that officers receive from inmates. Officer dissatisfaction in this area has to do with the officers' perception of the way inmates feel about officers in general and difficulties in obtaining inmate compliance with orders.

These officers express concern about what they perceive as a "double standard" employed by inmates in their judgment of officer and inmate behavior. They voice disappointment and resentment at inmates' failure to "understand" the lot of the officers while they (the inmates) desire to be understood by officers:

> [There is] a lack of understanding between the officers and the inmates. They don't understand what your job is, but they want you to understand their problems in doing their time. They want officers to take them as individuals, but they take officers as a group.

For others, inmate-related job dissatisfaction stems from the "hostile" manner some inmates exhibit in their interactions with officers. The repetitiveness of seemingly hostile interactions enhances the negative impact such sequences have on the officer:

> *What's the most difficult thing about being an officer?*
>
> Being able to take a little guff, sarcasm and insults from inmates. No matter who the inmate is, you're difficult to accept. Even if a guy asks you to do something for him, he says it in a sarcastic manner. I ask him to go away and come back later and he goes away cursing. A few days, he comes back and he's okay. After that I might see him in the hall or out of place and tell him to get where he belongs and he mumbles under his breath. To put up with this kind of stuff every day is tough.

It is interesting to note that correction officer complaints about the treatment they receive from inmates are often coupled with negative feelings about the treatment they receive from supervisory and administrative personnel. This tendency to couple prison administrators and inmates highlights the isolation many officers experience. They see themselves as working against everyone and not with anyone:

> *What's the most difficult thing about your job?*
>
> Just biting your lip and taking the bullshit you have to take from the inmates and the brass we've got.
>
> * * *
>
> Keeping your cool. Not letting them work you up to blow your stack, both the inmates and the brass. If the inmates know they can work you up, your ass is grass. If it's the brass and you trip up, they're trying to get you for something anyway.

Occasionally officers also encounter difficulties in getting inmates to follow orders. Whether it involves the inmate's job assignment or obedience to specific regulations, officers may face inmate resistance and they see this as frustrating. But as with large-scale violence, officers often relate difficulties in obtaining inmate compliance to the perceived mishandling of grievances by administrative personnel, thus relieving both themselves and inmates of responsibility for the problem:

> Just getting these characters to shower and keep their cells clean and do what they're supposed to do is a problem.

> *How do you deal with this?*
>
> Put in reports. Then it's up to the inmate to decide where it goes from there. The adjustment committee handles it and not always very well. Lots of times the inmate comes back more aggravated. Because of the way they treat him he's more belligerent and disrespectful.

While most officers suffer abuse from inmates as "part of the job," a few have developed techniques for coping with such problems. One officer employs an unusual strategy that he believes reduces the number of abusive encounters he experiences, though it increases the potential severity of those in which he does become involved:

> When I get [inmate abuse] I act a little crazy. If they act crazy and you act crazy, they won't bug you. One time a guy comes and wants to get into the [building]. I went through the whole rap and told him the schedule. He says, "I'm comin' in." I say, "No." And he says he'll punch me in the face. I go over to the phone and he says, "Calling the Sergeant, baby?" I told him I was calling the hospital to reserve a room for him when I beat the shit out of him. If he challenged me, I don't know what I would have done.

Maintaining Impartiality

Correction officers also experience job dissatisfaction from difficulties in keeping favoritism and prejudice toward inmates from entering their work. While acknowledging "partiality" as a general "human failing," some officers nevertheless experience dissatisfaction with their own inability to exercise discretion without showing impartiality:

> It's difficult to maintain order and abide by the rules. If you do it to one guy, you've got to do it to all. You can't let anybody slide by. I've done it, but you can't make it too obvious. You get a feeling when you let somebody slide by. But you catch yourself letting it slide and you get the next guy. That bothers me.

Officers know that they will be rebuked by inmates should an inmate happen to observe seemingly prejudiced behavior. To avoid this officers sometimes behave in ways they believe to be "unfair" considering all the circumstances of a particular situation in order to give the "appearance of fairness" to an inmate who observes only the culmination of a particular officer-inmate interaction.

The following "fairness incident" illustrates both the potential for prejudiced behavior on the part of the officer and the potential for misinterpretation on the part of inmates. It also underscores the frustration experienced by officers in their handling of such situations:

> Right now I work on a yard post. There's a bench where I am and I let inmates come up and sit with me sometimes. This one time there were four inmates there and they were all white and I told a black guy he couldn't come up. This guy says it's because he's black and I'm white. Another guy comes up and he's white. I tell him that he can't come up. The first reaction of the black inmate is that I'm running a prejudiced thing. I should have let the white guy come up just to spite the black guy. But I couldn't and I didn't.

POWERLESSNESS

A second set of correction officer job dissatisfaction concerns revolve around the central theme of powerlessness—the officer's inability to influence his work environment in an effective manner. About one-fourth of all responses to the questions designed to elicit general job dissatisfaction themes centered on this issue, and over 60% of the officers referred to this theme at least once.

Powerlessness is experienced by officers primarily as lack of support and cooperation from both departmental and institutional administrators, from both supervisors and other officers. Officers are also concerned that they lack the responsibility and decision-making power necessary to contribute effectively to their work environment. A third concern that is related to powerlessness is the officer's perception that opportunities to provide effective input into decisions that affect their specific duties and the general lot of officers are unavailable.

Lack of Support

The most frequently mentioned manifestation of powerlessness stems from the officer's belief that administrators, supervisors and, at times, other officers not only fail to assist them in performing their jobs, but that those for whom and with whom they work actually operate against them. Whether the issue involves working conditions of his specific assignment or the general working conditions of all officers, the individual officer experiences isolation and the feeling that he is in a continuous battle with just about everyone working in the institution. In some work areas, lack of support affects the officer's ability to maintain effective security:

> The lack of cooperation is the most difficult thing. Lately they [the administration] have decided to use the second officer [from my location] on different jobs. I've told a couple of Sergeants that it was

> bad because it leaves us shorthanded there. If there's a big fight and there's only one officer there, they wonder why. They just don't care. If the 6:30 a.m. officer calls in sick, my job is chaotic. The phone's ringing and I can't answer it because I've got to take time to get [supplies]. If I answer the phone, it irritates the inmates because it holds them up from finishing their jobs and they're late for recreation. The Sergeants know, but they do nothing. There's no cooperation from anyone.

The correction officer sees his work as chaotic. He believes that those in authority will avoid making decisions. When decisions are made, the officer readily interprets them as short-term solutions to what the officer sees as long-term problems. From the officer's perspective, administrative decisions are usually designed to lessen immediate conflict while doing nothing to solve deep-seated difficulties. When supervisors or administrators leave, the officer sees himself left behind to face recurring problem situations alone:

> Nobody wants to make a decision. The honor housing group makes noise and disturbs the rest of the block. The head brass comes down and the honor housing men say there's no noise and the brass leaves. You have to deal with it. They won't put the weight on their shoulders. Nobody ever puts anything in writing because then it's there for all to see and it's their responsibility.

Officers are also critical of what they perceive as a lack of support in the handling of inmate discipline. If an officer warns an inmate about being out of place, the inmate often complains and frequently goes to a supervisor. As a result, the officer ends up being warned by the supervisor to attend to his own business:

> [The administration] gives you rules to enforce and when you go to enforce them and write a guy up and send them to the adjustment committee, nine out of ten, they counsel and release. If you continue to write them up for minor things, the administration comes down on you and says you're not doing your job.

The feeling that officers will not receive support is also experienced in potential violence-producing situations. Changes in intervention policy leave the officer uncertain about both the limits of his authority and appropriate responses:

> With our job today we really don't have authority like we used to. You're restricted. The state doesn't back you if something happens. They don't want to know right from wrong. Now when there's a mob situation, you just stand and observe. Years ago you would disperse

> them, persuade them to move. Today they're hesitant. We just let things boil longer and let things develop into confrontations.

On occasion, the behavior of other officers is perceived as lax and noncooperative, and even disruptive. Disagreement over proper procedure and competition for job assignments sometimes generates ill will among officers:

> I worked with a guy who bid on the same job I did. I got the job and the guy didn't help me one iota. Since I was new, he was able to undermine what I tried to do. I was fighting him constantly. The inmates saw this and took advantage of it. Some even came up to me and said, "You don't have to take that."

Lack of Responsibility

Although in practice officers exercise wide discretion in solving inmate problems and in dealing with inmate misbehaviors, many officers express dissatisfaction with the scope of their responsibility. From their experience they draw the conclusion that the administration looks upon officers as incompetent and incapable of performing more than routine custodial functions:

> You feel downgraded by the administration. Like in the mess hall. I'd take a line. But I want something more to do than being stuck against the wall. For example, I'm on the food service line and one guy [inmate] asks to give his meat to the guy in back of him. Before the rules said he couldn't do it, and if I let him, I'd get chewed out. I should be able to make that decision. That's what I'm hired for. They've taken away the officer's responsibility. They treat you like an incompetent.

Inherent in this officer's observation is the perception that the correction officer's opportunities to make a contribution to his work are minimal. Whether the issue is helping inmates or increasing the efficiency of institutional procedures, many officers feel left out. Recent increases in correction officer salaries coupled with a change of job title from "prison guard" to "correction officer" heighten the perceived contradiction between their nominal role and the lack of responsibility:

> They pay [the officer] adequate money and they don't trust him to make adequate decisions. In industry you get $15,000 per year and you get more control over decision-making, you're expected to do it. You're left alone. Because of the chain of command, there's very little decision-making at the officer level. You can't do anything new, you can't innovate, even if your ideas are better, even if it's common sense. It's frustrating.

> You get the feeling that you could help more people. Not with the study, education or work part of it, but by contact with them. We should set an example. There are guards in there that have the ability to be their counselors, better than the guys they have.

Lack of Opportunities for Effective Input

Officers also express dissatisfaction with the extent to which they are able to influence decisions that affect the working conditions and procedures of specific institutional assignments and of correction officers in general. They feel that decisions made by the administration rarely take problems of implementation into account, although there are exceptions to this attitude:

> I didn't think little people could suggest anything, but I suggested that instead of bringing the head clerk in to notarize inmate papers, they make an officer a notary. They did it. It showed me that somebody upstairs was listening and took my suggestion as a constructive one.

This positive reception is not what officers typically perceive as the administration's response to officer suggestions. For most officers it is difficult to believe that any suggestions they make will be taken seriously. Thus many officers refrain from making suggestions, believing that their efforts will be futile. When their advice is sought, officers often interpret such solicitation as "asking for asking's sake," not as a "real" attempt to solicit an officer's suggestions. The long length of time that often passes between officer input and administrative response detracts from the officer's ability to see his input as effective:

> After the riot they wanted to know what they could change to help [my area]. We said to get rid of two antiquated [machines] that would continuously break down. The inmates working there had a tough job and got little pay. It took nearly six years to get the machines. They also asked about security measures for my area. I wrote a statement, it's probably in the waste basket, but six years later it's still the same.

When changes in institutional procedures are made, many officers feel that the problems involved in actually implementing a decision are rarely considered. They feel that the person actually performing a given task is seldom asked how the task might be done better:

> When they make policy they don't realize [what's involved]. They should compile information from the people actually working the jobs. We catch all the flak and baloney if policies don't work and we

> have no say in it. I'm not saying we're always right, but we should at least have a say.

When asked what they could do about their lack of input, many officers responded as they did with regard to feelings of danger, that they had no alternative but to go along:

> It's a frustrating experience and there's not much you can do. We're the small man on the bottom of the totem pole and you know the top man won't ever come to us for suggestions.
>
> *How does this affect your job?*
>
> It often leads to low morale and that definitely affects the job. It's one of the biggest deterrents to a properly run institution. When a decision comes down, morale sinks low. In comes the typical "Albany doesn't care" syndrome.

Others, however, translate their frustration at being left out of the decision-making process into independent action, altering the letter of directives to meet the realities of their day-to-day work, sometimes doing so with supervisor approval and at other times on their own:

> It's easy to sit up front and say this and that. It's cut and dry. They [administrators] make changes in people's lives, without even asking them about it. They'll send a notice and you try to implement it and it almost causes a riot.
>
> *How do you deal with this?*
>
> I often ignore what they say. I do what should be done. What I know. If I come to the job and there's a change in the rules and it seems to cause more harm than good, then I'll go to the sergeant and tell him about it and see if I can change it. Most of the time the sergeant will say to do it your way because you're working the job. Sometimes they'll shut the door on you, but most of the time you have an opening to do it your way; 90% of the officers make things work by doing things their own way and making things look good.

INCONSISTENCY AND INADEQUATE COMMUNICATION

Many correction officers also experience dissatisfaction with what they perceive as inconsistencies in institutional procedures and supervisory direction. While recognizing that differences in physical plant, staffing capabilities and inmate populations necessitate variations in institutional procedure among the state's maximum security institutions, many officers nevertheless find such variations to be a source of discontent:

> The nonstandardization is bad. Attica is completely different from Auburn. At Attica they march two by two, at Auburn you open the doors and off they go.
>
> * * *
>
> Take the aerosol spray cans. Why are they okay in one institution and not in another? These inmates spend their money on these things at one place and when they come here we've got to tell them we've got to throw them away.

Though such variations in procedure and policy may occasionally offend an officer's "sense of fairness," officers experience these "inconsistencies" as providing inmates with opportunities to engage in what Mathiesen calls "censoriousness" behavior.[11] When inmates bring such "inconsistencies," as those described above, to the officer's attention, the officer is put in the position of trying to defend a policy he does not understand. Forced to respond to the inmate's challenge with such unsatisfactory replies as "a rule is a rule," the officer begins to develop feelings of inadequacy.

While he perceives himself as powerless to alter his situation, an officer may urge inmates to invoke what he perceives to be their "power." When confronted by an inmate's criticism of departmental or institutional policy, an officer may advise the inmate to "file a grievance." While this sort of remark is occasionally uttered sarcastically, it is often a serious attempt by the officer to improve his own working conditions by having an inmate bring a problem area to the administration's attention. Some officers report having helped inmates present their grievances in a proper manner.

Officers also experience what they consider inconsistencies in supervisory interpretations of administrative directives. "One supervisor tells you one thing and another tells you something different" is a typical expression of such discontent:

> A directive came down about allowing inmates to wear blue T-shirts. I asked four different supervisors about it and got four different answers. Now what am I supposed to tell the inmate?

Again the officer can provide only an inadequate response to an inmate's question.

The correction officer's perception of "inconsistency" is closely aligned with his experience of inadequate communication between departmental and institutional administration and the correction officers. Preshift briefings are the vehicle through which officers learn about changes in rules, procedures and daily schedules. Some officers see these briefings as extremely beneficial:

> The preshift briefing is mandatory and excellent. The supervisors read directives from the superintendent and deputies. At least you're informed. If you're well informed, it cuts down on conflict.

Such evaluations of the briefings are not typical, however. Many officers described briefings as "a farce" or "a joke," expressing the belief that the administration "tells you only what they want you to know, not what you need to know." Officers on vacation or on day off when changes are made report experiencing great difficulty in discovering new procedures. Unaware of changes, an officer may insist on following "old" procedures and immediately encounter resistance from inmates who are prepared to proceed with the "new." At times the mistrust created by inconsistent or incomplete information that is received through regular channels, and even from other officers, creates confusing or dangerous situations:

> This new guy was supposed to work on the wall post way in the back and asked another officer how to get there. The guy told him the truth, but with all the rumors around here he didn't believe him. So he went another way. He gets to what he believes is Wall Post 3 and it's really Wall Post 4. Now there's another officer on Wall Post 4 from an earlier shift. There had been rumors going around that some of the Black Panthers were talking about taking over the towers, so the officer on the tower hears the noise and wonders what's going on. The new officer goes to push up the trap door in the floor and there's an officer with a loaded .38 pointed at his head.

When he receives what he considers "inconsistent" or untrustworthy information from the prison administration, the correction officer turns to inmates as a source of information. Inmates not only provide officers with information concerning illicit behavior of their fellow inmates, but on occasion they also help officers keep abreast of past and impending changes in institutional regulations and procedures.

According to Johnson, inmate "rats" serve "the prison's formal organization as a communication link with the inmate informal groups."[12] From the guard's perspective, inmates also serve as a vital communication link between the prison administration and the correction officers. When asked how they obtained information concerning "goings-on" in the prison, over half of the officers gave "inmates" as a first response. The "inmate-grapevine" is generally perceived as more prompt and accurate than regular administrative channels. "Inmates know before it happens," "they tell the inmates before they tell the officers" are expressions indicating the officers' lack of confidence in the prison administration as a source of information.

Many officers confirmed the existence of an inmate "rat" system in Auburn. Some saw inmate "rats" as the correctional analog to the "police informer." Such rats are sometimes cultivated by officers who provide inmates with favors or ignore minor inmate rule violations in exchange for information.

All rats are not sought by officers, however. In fact, many officers deny having rats, saying they feel uncomfortable about putting an inmate in a position where he informs on his fellow inmates. However, inmates sometimes utilize officer uncertainty concerning institutional communication as a lever in establishing an officer-rat relationship based on the exchange of information for privilege. One officer provided a striking description of this process and the relationship between officer and rat as experienced by the officer:

> There was a time when I could ask an inmate what you were doing, what you did, what you ate for lunch or smoked. I could find out anything about anyone through rats. To get one they've got to respect and like you. There's not a man alive who's not looking for personal gains. It's more so in jail. A rat's a treacherous man. He's after personal needs or the needs of others and he's looking for a payoff. That's where you can get in trouble. I'll help him get things the state provides, but nothing from me, nothing from the outside. When you're dealing with a rat, you can put yourself in a bind, one mistake and you can get a man killed. You had better know what you're doing. Do you have any rats?
>
> *No. I've never felt the need for or wanted any.*
>
> You don't have to want them; a man can force himself on you.
>
> *How can he do that if you don't want him?*
>
> Don't kid yourself. A guy might come up to you and give you some information you've got to take to the [administration]. Now what are you going to do? You go to the administration and here he comes back later asking you for something, a favor or information. He says, "Either you give me the information or I'll let it slip that I ratted." It can be done, you don't know who else he's ratted to and you know that if the inmate whom he ratted on finds out what he did, he might get killed. And by you not giving him what he wants, his life might be in your hands. You're in trouble if you do and if you don't [do what the inmate wants].

According to some officers, inmates obtain information by becoming "invisible." Working as porters in areas of the administration building or in areas near supervisors over a period of time, inmates tend to be ignored by staff working in these areas. Administrators, secretaries and other staff readily discuss institutional problems, policy and procedures while the inmates are present, perceiving the inmates as part of the general office atmosphere. Such information as inmates obtain is readily transmitted to cell blocks from inmate to inmate. Officers often obtain such information from inmates by themselves becoming "invisible" to the inmates with whom they have daily contact.[13] Some officers believe that inmates purposely keep officers informed in order to reduce the possibilities for inmate-officer conflict. Officers also observe a tendency of inmates passing information to officers to demonstrate the "power" that the inmate has to obtain such information.

One further aspect of institutional communication that officers often cite as a negative characteristic of their work is "the rumor."[14] Rumors pervade the institutional atmosphere: rumors started by inmates, officers or civilians. Rumors are a device through which some officers seek to exert influence on their work environment. Taking advantage of the uncertainty with which officers must work, some officers admit starting rumors to influence the behavior of inmates, supervisors or other officers. Often rumors will be directed at "officer rats" (officers who carry information about other officers to the administration) in the hope that the false information will be transmitted to higher-ups in the prison administration. If the information is investigated and proven false, the officer rat will lose face, giving the officer who initiated the rumor a sense of satisfaction. In the event that the rumor is not investigated, the rapidity with which rumors move through the institution is a constant source of amazement for the officer who utilized rumors as a form of "play." Officers may even start a rumor at the beginning of their shift and wait to see how much time will pass before it returns to them.

OTHER FACTORS FREQUENTLY ASSOCIATED WITH JOB DISSATISFACTION

A number of factors associated with worker dissatisfaction are common to both the literature relevant to correction officers and that concerned with "work" as a general subject. In order to discover the extent to which such factors produced job dissatisfaction in correction officers and to explore the methods employed by officers to cope with such dissatisfaction, each officer was asked to discuss his feelings about

1. general department policy;
2. the local administration's policies towards inmates;
3. administration policies toward officers;

4. what others expect of officers;
5. supervision;
6. conflict between counseling and rule enforcement aspects of their work;
7. boredom; and
8. routine.

For the officers, the more removed a particular factor is from the immediate control of the officer, the more likely dissatisfaction is associated with that factor (see Table 7.2). Over half of the officers we interviewed indicated dissatisfaction with departmental policy, the administration's policies toward both officers and inmates and the expectations others have of them. Each of these areas is characteristically perceived as being beyond the officer's power to influence. However, those factors that relate to the officer's immediate duties (as opposed to general policy considerations) have less of a tendency to be associated with dissatisfaction. Boredom, routine and counseling–rule enforcement role conflict all fail to be associated with job dissatisfaction by a majority of these officers. Supervision, which serves as a link between policy and officer work performance, is associated with job dissatisfaction by less than one-third of the officers. The officer's ability to "pick" his supervisors that is furnished by the "bidding" system provides an officer with some measure of control over his supervisor. The correction officer's experience with each factor is discussed below.

Table 7.2. Distribution of Officers Expressing Dissatisfaction With Specified Areas of Worker Concern

Worker Concern	Number Expressing Dissatisfaction[a]	Percent N=50
Departmental policy	45	90
Administrative policy toward inmates	36	72
Administrative policy toward officers	34	68
Expectations others have of officers	25	50
Supervisors	15	30
Counseling–rule enforcement role conflict	15	30
Boredom	18	36
Routine	17	34

[a] Expressing dissatisfaction means the officer gave positive response to questions such as "Do the policies of the Department of Corrections as a whole *bother you?* (See Appendix C for specific questions.) The factor under consideration not only had to be experienced by the officer, but also had to be felt as a problem ("bothered") to be categorized as a response indicating dissatisfaction.

Departmental Policies

When asked, "Do departmental policies ever bother you?" 90% of the officers in our sample indicated that they were concerned about and bothered by such policies. In addition to the feelings of powerlessness and problems of inconsistency discussed above, two other dissatisfaction themes emerged from responses to this question. One relates to the manner in which inmates are treated by the State Department of Corrections, the other relates to the officers' perception of their own position within the Department of Corrections.

Officers are concerned with what many of them consider to be the Department's overextension of programs and "fringe benefits" to inmates. To the officer, work release, education release and general education programs represent benefits that the inmate receives from the state as a result of the inmate's participation in criminal activity. Many officers resent "criminals" obtaining work while "law-abiding citizens" are unemployed. Officers often take exception to an inmate receiving a college education at the state's expense while officers and citizens in general "struggle to send their children to school":

> I can't condone why they give inmates so much for nothing. We've got a welfare state. Now you get rewarded if you're a bad ass. Inmate X, a rapist, inmate Y a murderer, a cop killer. So they take him out to play football. What makes him so good? You read in the paper about an inmate giving somebody a painting. How about those outside who struggle without the state to help them? Maybe I'd get a master's degree if I killed somebody. I'd get my picture in the paper.[15]

This image of prison as a bestower of benefits on the criminal is difficult for the correction officer to reconcile with the traditional conception of prison as a dispenser of society's punishment.

Correction officer dissatisfaction with departmental policy is also expressed in the cynical attitude many officers have toward the leadership qualities of correctional administrators and the lack of perceived purposefulness with which programs designed to help inmates are implemented:

> I think it's just a big, phoney organization. They're always afraid to do something. They always leave you in the dark. They act like they're the bad guys. They never really explain things even though they say they will.

The officer's commitment to the organization for which he works is reduced by what he perceives as administrative indifference to effective program implementation. Even such symbols of group solidarity as the uniform fail to inspire officer feelings of belongingness to the Department of Corrections and serve to further alienate the man from his position:

> A lot of stuff is just for show. Like the night school program. I'd keep track of how many inmates actually showed up. It's less than 50%. It's just a paperwork farce. They were talking about dropping guys if they missed three classes, but it was never enforced. And the Uniforms they pick out for you. You might have to break up a fight and you're wearing a sport coat. It looks too much like a bus driver's uniform. A lot of officers degrade themselves and the department because of the uniform they're wearing. They don't even give everybody the same uniform. They talk professionalism but it's mostly talk.
>
> *Does this affect the way you do your job?*
>
> Yes. If you take a state trooper, he's got pride in his uniform, his job and his department as a whole. But here, you're not all given the same equipment. Not all treated the same. It makes you lax in your job. You don't have a good attitude. A lot don't even polish their shoes. They come in looking like clowns. They don't care. The administration can enforce codes, but there's no pride, not of your own accord.

The Administration's Treatment of Inmates

About 75% of the officers found fault with the manner in which the Auburn administration deals with inmates. Those satisfied with the administration's policies, however, found the policies to be fair and the inmate opportunities and programs beneficial, contributing to the prison's generally relaxed atmosphere:

> I think that with a few flaws they do as good a job here as anywhere else. And we've got a more difficult inmate population. But I think they do a good job with the population: Education, food and work programs are pretty well run.

Such positive evaluations of administrative performance as it relates to inmates were not typical, however. Most officers characterized the administration's behavior toward inmates as "weak," "indecisive," and "inconsistent," reflecting the general job dissatisfaction concerns discussed earlier. Though a few officers interpreted administrative actions as a general tendency to be "too liberal" and "to coddle criminals," most were more concerned with the effects that administrative decisions had on their ability to "do their jobs" effectively:

> They seem to give the inmates anything they ask for without thinking what it means to the staff to try to implement it.

Though the responsibility for actually implementing administrative decisions affecting inmates often rests with the officer in charge of a particular area, the officer is often less concerned with carrying out policy than with ensuring that problems developing from such policy can be traced back to the prison administration. The officer copes with this problem by *divesting himself of responsibility* for the effects of his actions:

> You know something is wrong. You come back [to the block] and there are four companies, 60 to 70 inmates on two floors standing there for 15 to 20 minutes, grab-assing, hitting each other, windows being broken. But they [the administration] don't change. They don't even look into it. So I take an attitude. I don't give a shit what happens. *They can't blame me*. I've turned in reports and that's it.

Feeling powerless to influence institutional policy, some officers follow administrative directives and make no attempt to overcome the difficulties a particular policy creates. Officers perceive problems as *purposely caused* by the administration. If a specific policy incites inmates, it seems to the officer to be a willful attempt by the administration to create discontent:

> You just have to go along with [their policies towards inmates]. You can gripe, bring it up at union meetings, but you can't actually do anything about it. You become more lax for a time and hope it straightens out. If *they* [the administration] *want* something to happen, you let it happen that way.

Even though a policy increases inmate frustration, the officer does nothing to remedy the situation, because it is, as he sees it, not his responsibility:

> You might end up ruffling the inmates' feathers because you don't do your other duties, and you're slow or late and the inmates get upset. Inmates are used to officers being on time, now they're upset. It doesn't bother me. It's the inmate's time, it affects him directly. It frustrates them and that's not good. But that seems to be the way the administration *wants it*.

Besides placing responsibility for difficulties on the administration, officers cope with perceived difficulties by reducing their problems to jokes:

> You start off talking about it to other officers to get it off your chest. You make jokes about it, make it funny and laugh at it. First a bull session, then a joke, then you get rid of it.

THE ADMINISTRATION'S TREATMENT OF OFFICERS

Given the correction officer's general feelings of powerlessness, isolation and estrangement from his workplace, it is not surprising that many officers express dissatisfaction with the prison administration's treatment of officers. Officer descriptions of their treatment by the prison administration are strikingly similar to those of inmates. "Infantilization" and "dehumanization" are two themes central to the officers' perception of administrative attitudes toward officers:

> We are professionals, not children. We're men, not complete idiots. Sometimes we're treated like children or mental defectives.

* * *

> I don't think they have any regard for the officers. They use you like a number. Like Attica, they sent us there and they're ready to hang us later. If you complain, they say, "There's the door."

Some experienced officers trace the administration's behavior to the introduction of the correction officers' union. Prior to the union's existence the administration was perceived as more amenable to suggestions from officers and as more communicative. With the union's introduction, however, some officers observed the development of an "adversary" relationship between the administration and the correction officers:

> They seem to operate on the basis of fear that the officers and the union have too much control and they're reluctant to give up control on policy even where it's beneficial. The union could go and show them a better idea and they'd get a hassle just because it's from the union.

Just as they view certain administrative actions toward inmates as purposeful attempts to anger inmates, officers often interpret administration actions affecting officers in a similar way, reacting to perceived administrative agitation with behavior designed to create more work for the administration:

> The way they deal with our shift, it's the peon shift. *They try* to agitate us by always changing our routine.
>
> *How do you deal with this?*
>
> We stick it to the administration. It's a needle to the administration and we stick it in. We'll get even, but they always get back at you one way or another. They read a directive at our shift only about inmates

> with shabby mustaches. We told the inmates they had three days to shape up, then we wrote more reports than the administration could handle.

Even though this officer feels his behavior violates his own personal code of fairness, he allows the frustration that is caused by perceived administration provocations to affect his treatment of inmates. I asked if such treatment by the administration affected the way he does his job.

> It does and it's not right. You drift away from the firm, fair and consistent. Like the haircut thing. The superintendent is saying to us, "Do your job," and so we put in reports. Lots of times you give a warning first, the next time a misbehavior report. But if the administration jumps on your tail, you won't give a guy a break.

Other officers react to what they perceive as administrative indifference to officer concerns by performing their duties at less than peak efficiency, believing that the efficient officer only creates problems for himself:

> You could check things out and do more than you do, but who's going to find out? So you relax on the job and slack off. Just do the job enough not to make waves. If an officer wants to do a 100% job, he gets flak from everybody. He has to step on toes. Most go the 60% to 70% route. Those guys that do the job as they're supposed to, they're the ones that everybody hates.

Supervision

Although inconsistency and poor communication characterize the correction officer's view of administrative behavior, and supervisors are sometimes used to illustrate such behaviors, the majority of our sample do not admit to experiencing difficulties with their immediate supervisors. Officers who have satisfactory relationships with their supervisors consider themselves "fortunate" or "lucky," indicating their belief that relations between officers and supervisors are generally poor. These officers feel they can "talk" with their own supervisors and criticize their supervisors' actions without offending them. Although they believe their supervisor is open to criticism, these officers most often simply "do what they are told," believing that sergeants are as powerless as officers to effect change and that sergeants only "do what they are told" by the administration.

While most officers do not experience dissatisfaction with their supervisors, slightly under one-third do. These officers are dissatisfied not with the quality of the direction they receive, but rather with the *attitude* of their supervisor towards officers. Many feel that some sergeants are "power hungry" and on "ego trips," ordering officers to perform unnecessary tasks only to satisfy their need to command. Officers who complain about supervisors also feel that sergeants were more interested in seeing to it that officers "had their shoes shined" and their "ties on straight" than in controlling the behavior of inmates. These officers also feel that their supervisors respond personally to negative criticism and that most problems could not be discussed with them since the "supervisor was always right." Officers cope with such supervisors by avoiding them or, where avoidance is impossible, by doing what they are told. As with the administration, however, officers often translate negative feelings about supervisors into the avoidance of responsibility:

> If I've got to go someplace and a sergeant says, "Do this and that," I just do what he says. I've tried to communicate and couldn't. If you give a suggestion and he thinks it makes him look bad, he ignores it, even if it's good. So if there's trouble, even if I know about it, I say to hell with it. Everything falls back on the sergeant, not me.

Expectations Others Have of Officers

Fifty percent of the officers indicated that they are bothered by the experience of having different staff members expect them to perform different and often conflicting behaviors. Conflicting role expectations occur most frequently when an officer's supervisors change and when the officer perceives differences in administrative approaches to security.

In the first situation, supervisors make changes in the methods devised by individual officers to perform their assigned tasks. Sergeant X, for example, may permit an officer to allow an inmate to handle a certain record-keeping chore. When Sergeant Y is in charge, he may feel this delegation of responsibility to an inmate to be inappropriate and require the officer to perform that function. However, officers do not see such conflicting expectations as a characteristic peculiar to correction officers:

> It's just like on the street, like anyplace else. Some people expect you to be Superman, others are reasonable and others don't care.
>
> *Does this bother you?*
>
> I suppose it does. It makes it hard to do the job well. If somebody expects too much, it bothers me. I like to do the job the way it was set up.
>
> *How do you deal with this?*

> I try to do the best I can and complain as I do it. It doesn't do much good to squawk, but I do it anyway. I'd rather take it out on supervisors or other officers than on inmates. I have my way of doing things. I set my standards as to where I stand. I get less trouble and it's smoother this way, rather than change with whoever happens to be the sergeant on duty.

Officers not experiencing conflicting role expectations perceive the expectations others have of them in very general terms. "Do the job as best you can," "handle all the situations you can on your own level," and "keep things running smooth" are phrases typically used to describe what these officers feel others expect of them. Within these general guidelines, officers approach their duties situationally. They handle inmate problems, rule violations, violent incidents and everyday duties by using "common sense," relying on their personal evaluation of the appropriate action in a given situation:

> I know what they expect of me, to keep everything running smooth. But that's what I like about the job. I can run it as orderly and as best as I can and never have a sergeant or a supervisor come in. It's up to the officer to keep the block running smooth.

Role Conflict

There are many references in the literature on corrections to the role conflict experienced by correction officers as they attempt to reconcile the counseling and security aspects of their jobs. In Chapter 6 there was the discussion of social distance and rule enforcement explaining that the custody (rule enforcement) and counseling (low social distance) roles of the correction officer are not mutually exclusive, but rather may often go hand in hand.

To focus more directly upon this issue, the officers in my sample were asked if they experienced any difficulties reconciling the counseling and security aspects of their work. Slightly less than one-third indicated that they experienced and were bothered by difficulties in reconciling these two roles.

Role conflict as experienced by the correction officer, however, stems not from an inability to reconcile the contradictory demands of his position, rather it derives from experiences during which the officer was restricted in doing what he felt necessary by virtue of rules to the contrary or by adverse supervisory decisions. One officer provided the following experience of role conflict in an extreme situation:

> There's been times I could have done something for a guy but I couldn't because of the rules. In one situation where they'd gassed a

> whole section, the guys [inmates] were vicious. They [other officers and supervisors] wouldn't help them. I opened the windows and turned on the water. One guy was vomiting. I called the medical authorities. The guy wanted air, and I wanted to give him a cup of milk. The medical personnel says no. So there was nothing I could do.

Officers also experience conflicts in trying to blend security with the duties of their individual assignments. At times officers find it necessary to ignore proper security practices in order to ensure a smoothly running work area.

> If I'd adhere to security in [my area], I couldn't leave to call to see if a guy's commissary account was straight. Lots of times in my job I breach security. I have to get supplies; if I don't do it the supplies won't be there and the job won't get done. I have to break security, they [the administration] won't allow me to do otherwise.

Experiences of role conflict relating to the officer's security and "helping" roles do not relate to any formal expectation that both roles will be performed. Rather they result from the officer's perception that the administration desires only "proper security," while the officer desires to perform "helping" functions as well:

> The inmates and the administration know we're there for security to contain them, lock them in, count and make rounds. But I'd rather have a guy come up to me with a problem where you can help a guy out.

When it comes to reconciling administrative and individual conceptions of the proper correction officer roles, officers generally take one of two approaches. Some do what they believe is right in spite of their perception of the administration's position. Believing that the administration wants them to "do nothing" reinforces their belief that "helping" actions are appropriate:

> The administration expects you to sit on a platform like a stick and don't move. They expect you to have no mind at all. I feel they hired me and if I wasn't competent they should fire me. Everything I do has a reason; if it didn't, I wouldn't do it. If it's on the edge [between security and counseling], I'm trying to accomplish something. You've got to be on your own to use your ability.

Other officers justify their inaction in certain cases by relying on their perception of "administrative expectations" rather than on their individual judgments:

> Lots of times I have to enforce things I don't think are right. There is no leeway in the framework of the correction officer's job that allows me to deal with problems. Most problems I send to the sergeant on the service unit and that's not right; but that's the job and that's what we're expected to do.

BOREDOM AND ROUTINE

When asked if they experienced difficulties with the boredom and routine often associated with the correction officer's work, slightly more than one-third of the officers responded that they did. Boredom is most frequently associated with tours of duty on the solitary wall post or on yard duty. However, some officers noted boredom as a general characteristic of the correction officer's job. As the officer adapts to boredom, he falls victim to what one of the more experienced officers called "the prison stupor," an ability to turn oneself off to the need for outside stimuli at the beginning of the work day and maintain the "stupor" for the duration of the eight-hour tour of duty.

Officers cope with their boredom in a number of characteristic ways. Some find relief in outside interests and second jobs, feeling they need such outside interests to stay mentally healthy:

> Can you stand boredom, idleness? If you can't don't take the job. I've gone backwards since I started. The job's made me lazy. Before I started to work two jobs, I found myself having trouble spelling simple words. We just sit and watch.

* * *

> Boredom is one of the greatest killers on the job. It stifles mental growth, it really does. It's not healthy for officers or inmates. It's one of the worst hazards of prison. It leads to laziness and every other bad thing. You lose track of time. You mark time by what you do outside, not what you do in there. If my job was all I had to do, I wouldn't know what day it was.

A second characteristic way officers cope with boredom is by establishing a *routine*. Rather than being a cause of boredom, the correction officer's "exaggerated routine"[16] may often be a reaction to boredom. A regular schedule of activities provides the officer with landmarks that help him "make it through the day" and "pass the time."

From the correction officer's perspective, his routine may be less an attempt to impose order on inmates than it is an exercise designed to provide the officer with feelings of certainty and structure in what he perceives as an otherwise chaotic environment. A fixed routine also may give an officer a sense of control over his immediate work environment, a control which he often views as lacking in dealing with departmental, institutional and supervisory policy.

Faithfulness to a routine may also serve as an excuse for *not* engaging in an activity requested by an inmate or a supervisor. Desiring not to be bothered by inmates or supervisors, the officer can always say, "I've got to check the count," "I've got to fill out this form first."

I observed some typical correction officer behaviors that illustrate varying techniques officers employ to reduce the effects of boredom. Some officers, for example, are known to create elaborately color-coded record-keeping systems, systems which demand their constant attention to keep them up to date. These officers create such systems not because they are required (which they are not) or because they are functional (which they are), and not because they will receive some degree of recognition for them (which they generally do not). Officers create systems that need revision simply because it gives them something to do and helps them manage their boredom.

Another boredom management technique is the "break." Coffee breaks or cigarette breaks provide opportunities for group interaction and conversation that give content to the officer's activity and move the day along. Officers who report difficulties with boredom often "walk around," "talk with inmates" and "make coffee." Such activities keep them "mentally active" and are also found to be characteristic of inmates and factory workers.[17]

SUMMARY—1976

As prison guards perform their tasks, they do so in an environment that they perceive as both chaotic and boring. Faced with the threat of danger, a sense of powerlessness and inconsistent communications, the guard is a classic example of an alienated worker. To cope with these frustrations he resigns himself to the inevitability of forces beyond his control and finds alternatives to or strikes out against situations within his grasp.

From the guard's perspective, inmates in prison are a relatively minor problem. For the guard it is the prison administration that commits a multitude of sins and has the responsibility for the negative character of his work environment. For the guard, his work is simple, if only his superiors would let him perform it.

THE REDUCTION OF STRESS: 1976-1986

The pressures of correctional work at Auburn have exhibited both stability and change. However, the general level of concern with negative features of the work environment has been reduced. As negative aspects of the environment relate to inmates these officers still express concern over the physical danger and mental strain that accompanies their work. However, concerns related to direct officer/inmate interactions (i.e., trying to treat inmates fairly, treatment of officers by inmates, and rules and regulations) seem to have decreased in saliency. This decrease seems to have occurred in spite of the general perception that the inmate population has become more "hard core" and that inmate violence has increased. As discussed earlier, *it appears that the increase in structure provided by new rule enforcement procedures, redeployment and the development of policy and procedure has reduced concern with an area that had previously been laden with officer discretion, i.e., officer/inmate relationships.*

With regard to powerlessness themes, some officers still complained about lack of support in rule enforcement practices, increased liberalization and lack of opportunities for input. However, the sense that the institution was chaotic and that administrators and supervisors would avoid making decisions seems to have diminished greatly. In addition, the experiences of officers with opportunities to be involved in developing policy and procedures, developing job descriptions associated with redeployment and the strengthening of practices associated with increased communication appear to have lessened the amount of dissatisfaction associated with the sate DOC and the local administration.

Physical Danger and Mental Strain

Though still identified as a primary negative characteristic of correctional officer work by about one-half of the officers, the unpredictability of violence and the association of danger and mental strain with potential collective violence appears in 1986 to be connected with a much more *immediate* potential for inmate violence and the "law enforcement strategies" necessary to prevent it. One officer who initially responded, "I don't have many problems" ended his response as follows:

> You have informers. Inmates tell officers things if they've been working with them for a while. You check stuff out. Maybe you find stuff in a guy's cell. A guy's smoking (marijuana) in the yard and you spot it and you know they get rid of it. You wait 'til they are leaving the yard, grab them and frisk them. You find a lot of stuff that way. Twenty-two straight razors were found last year. A civilian lost a box and didn't report it. Being observant. You can't get it all, but it keeps them on their toes. At Auburn, they had lots of shanks coming from the shops, guys were mass producing them. Now they frisk in and out of the shop areas everyday. There's a lot to the job. We hit the cells everyday, randomly, so many a shift so they don't know when or where it's coming.

* * *

> The inmates are more aggressive now. Not like before when we had the older inmates and they wanted to do their bit and get out. They used to look after the officers in the old days. Now you have to be more observant. Watch how they do things.

For some officers, tension is created by increased numbers of mentally ill inmates in the general population. These inmates pose special problems and require special handling. One officer who identifies this problem, practices a "disconfirming expectations" strategy to get responses:

> The worst thing about the job nowadays is that there are so many mentally unstable. You can't talk to them. They don't even realize you're there. When they closed Marcy [an institution for the "criminally insane"] they just put them in prison. They're tough.
>
> *How do you deal with this?*
>
> Sometimes you just act as crazy as they do. Make faces or statements. A guy asked me for some sugar once. I got him a whole bunch. Gave him more than he needed. He got thrown off. He thought I'd be like everybody else. I at least got a smile out of him, even though he could stare all day long.

In 1976, officers attributed interpersonal inmate violence to homosexuality, gambling or to "self-image"-related situations. During the past ten years, however, inmate violence has taken on a more instrumental character and has become more threatening to the inmates and officers involved.

> It's changed a lot. It's more violent. The drugs, the extortion. They steal and take from other guys. It will go on 'til the guy fights back or goes to protective custody. Ten years ago if you had a fight, they'd duke it out and then step back. Now with the peer pressure they'll fight and try to kill each other. Ten years ago a guy might go bughouse. Today he might get a knife. With the availability of drugs and other things they get used to it on the street and with the money around they turn to violence. Fights aren't just personal conflicts any more. They're conflicts over extortion, power conflicts, drugs and other things like that.
>
> * * *
>
> Now if there's a fight out in the yard, getting inmates back into their cells is tough. Years ago it was easier, they were more alone. You take some of the big brutes, they had their fight and it didn't amount

> to much. Now they all gather around and you don't know what's coming off.

Among the "new officers" interviewed, there appears to be a greater tendency to apply negative stereotypes to inmates and threatening inmate behavior than there was ten years ago.

> The worst thing about the job is a possible riot. It's always hanging over your head. You hear stories from old timers. You know they're not exaggerating. And knowing that collectively they're animals and that they'll do hideous things to you and to themselves if they get the chance. Like taking the 55 gallon drums of gas, having matches and making officers sit in the middle of them [an incident from the 1970 riot]. They will rape you, humiliate you, beat the shit out of you. You always have a chance of this.

For another officer with two years' experience, simply being around inmates is a problem because of who the inmates "are":

> The worst thing is always working around people who've done lots of degrading things in their lives. The environment isn't always pleasant. They put people in there that look normal, but even in a normal environment they'd be scary.
>
> *How do you deal with this?*
>
> You have to be constantly knowing who you're dealing with. You have to expect inmate problems. Inmates who can't read or write. What's natural to you, might not be natural to them. I can't go in there and sell dreams, talk over their heads. You have to understand their level without lowering yourself.

Some officers, who ten years ago had two to three years of experience and were now veterans of 12 to 13 years, describe a relationship between these sources of stress and their personal life and non-prison-related behavior.

> I find that the worst thing about the job is the constant fear that something will happen. What will develop, will I come out alive?
>
> *How do you cope with this?*
>
> It's just like when I was in Nam. You just accept it. Some days it's eating. Some days it's drinking. You really can't deal with it, that's the most disheartening thing.

* * *

> The situation you put yourself in every day. You're always outnumbered six or seven to one and if they want you they can get you. Just the mental anguish to deal with each day. The overall tension is the hard part, ongoing and leaving all your personal problems at the front gate and leaving the institution inside. The inmates don't want to hear my problems and my wife doesn't want to hear the inmates' problems.
>
> *How do you cope with this?*
>
> It took a long time to learn to cope with it. I took it out on my wife and kids but I finally realized that it was just a job and that I've got to leave the problems inside. To deal with these things now they have the Employee's Assistance Program, but I never got to the point where I had to use them. I got to the point where I can do my eight hours and then when I come out there's a different way to act.

Inmate Behavior Toward Officers

Though officers perceive the inmate population as having gotten worse, more demanding, and more hard core, only two of the 22 officers interviewed and eight of the 28 officers responding to the questionnaire indicated that the way officers were treated by inmates was the worst thing, biggest problem or most difficult thing about the job. However, rather than seeing personal conflict resulting from the repetitive demands of inmates for services, inmate hostility toward officers and lack of understanding of officers, inmate behavior toward officers is translated through the now well-established *filters of inmate rights and institutional rule enforcement practices*. As one officer who is now a sergeant observes:

> Inmates do stand up more for their rights. There are more confrontations between officers and inmates that you have to resolve. You have to side with the officers more, but if the officer's out and out wrong, then you favor the inmate. Trying to balance that is tough. Especially because years ago the officer was always right. Now you have to listen more because of the rights and grievances.

A 25-year veteran officer who worked for 15 years in segregation and only changed job assignments in 1984, finds problematic inmate treatment officers occurring in the context of institutional rules:

> The biggest problem is explaining set rules to inmates. You have to have a good approach. You can't just say this is the rule and that's it.

> The Department of Corrections sets them and the judiciary in the jail makes sure that you comply with them. The inmates have lost some freedom but they still have more than they had in the past. If they ask about something, I have to tell them yes or no. If I say no then they have to cope with it.

This shift from the personal character of officer inmate interactions as described in 1976 to the absence of saliency of this aspect of correctional officer work, and the transformation of personal relationships to bureaucratic ones reinforces the perceived changing nature of correctional officer tasks and the substitution of policy and procedure for officer discretion.

Administration's Treatment of Officers and Inmates

Many officers still expressed displeasure with the Department of Corrections' and the local administration's tendency to grant benefits to inmates. However, increased involvement in policy development and improved communication have made the context within which they placed this displeasure more sophisticated. No longer is it "officer as citizen"-oriented, comparing the inmate benefits with those of free members of the community. In 1986, officers see administrative tendency to increase inmate benefits and privilege as part of the state bargaining strategy and as a reflection of court intervention.

> *Do you have any problems with what the Department of Corrections is doing?*
>
> What I see, the latest thing is that they make deals with the inmates. Right now the package room is a source of contraband. The commissioner with the liaison committee will give the inmates TV in their cells if they let them do away with the package room. Since Attica, they've bartered. Visits, they give stuff. Trailers within the institution. Prior to that it was we told you and that's how it will be.
>
> * * *
>
> To me, it's backing the inmates or letting the courts direct them in how to run the prison. They should see that they are tough on crime and not getting a free vacation. Things like the trailer visits, inmate grievance committee, inmate assistants on Tier III hearings.

There is also a greater awareness that the "politics of corrections" lies behind much administrative and departmental action. This officer's comments reflect the observations of many who saw departmental actions linked to state budgetary concerns:

> I don't feel a prison is a prison anymore. It's more than walls and cells. The privileges, the little things. There was an uproar when they started with radios, now they're talking TV's. Appease the inmates, get more money from the state.
>
> * * *
>
> It's give, give now. Everything is involved in politics.

When it comes to evaluating the administration at Auburn, officers in 1986 were more positive. The comments of one 20-year veteran actually express admiration for the superintendent and link this to satisfaction in the fact that Auburn "seems to work." This observation that "Auburn seems to work" was made by several officers and something no one seemed to understand (see Chapter 9).

> *How do you feel about the way the administration at Auburn handles inmates? Any problems there?*
>
> I admire the guy. It's a wonder he can keep the lid on. Doing a good job. Henderson is one of the best-liked superintendents on an overall basis. He's walking a tightrope between the officers, the brass and the inmates. To keep the lid on and have few serious problems. This is with more violent inmates. People say it will blow up, and yet the top stays on. People complain that this place is so screwed up, but people don't know why it still works. It seems like everyone is just doing their job, just doing enough. The high brass, the civilians, the officers, we're not as bad as we think we are. We're doing a good job. How do we do it? Everyone takes care of problems on a small scale so we don't have the big ones.

Finally, most officers, both the more experienced and the newer officers, observed that as far as the local administration is concerned "power has shifted to Albany," and that administrative power within the institution had been dispersed, through the various deputy wardens and the more numerous sergeants.

> The power is centered in Albany, they've got directives and they've got to go with that.
>
> * * *
>
> First the Administration won't make decisions concerning anything unless it calls Albany. If the warden knew what was going on, he'd care. The Deputy Superintendent knows the procedures and it's his job to filter it to Henderson. But if I were Henderson, I'd know the answers.

* * *

> *Has it changed over the years?*
>
> The biggest change is the deputies. Three and the super deputy. The old P.K. is gone. In those days, he ran the jail. The Deputy of Security now doesn't do it the way the old P.K. did. Authority is more spread out. Things are much more diluted.

To cope with problems created by displeasure with administrative actions and decisions, the comments of many officers now reflect more active and "potent" strategies than before. Rather than expressions of fatalism and feelings of "infantilization" and "dehumanization," rather than "divesting themselves of responsibility" formal channels for addressing problems have been found. Where, previously dissatisfaction was linked to the perceived "purposelessness" of weak, indecisive and inconsistent administration, officers can now identify "purposeful" state and local administrative goals. Even though they are often troubled by the direction of change, officers are much more likely to indicate that they "take responsibility" for the work that they do.

> *How do you deal with this?*
>
> I do it through the Union. I bitch and complain to other guys. Get officers to approach the administration to change things. You don't always get what you want, but at least it helps to relieve the frustration.

Though some still feel that the administration does not care much for officers, others noted an increase in avenues of communication between the administration and officers and a tendency for decisions to be less arbitrary.

> Recently, they've gotten lax toward officers. There are a lot who are doing stupid things. You don't know if the person is dealing with inmates or just handling things laxly. It's good that the administration now has an open-door policy. Just make an appointment and talk to them concerning the institution's image.

* * *

> When I first started here, the Sergeant says one thing and the superintendent says something different. Now the deputy doesn't answer until he checks with supervisors and there's no decisions without going to the supervisors and getting input on how the job is done.

Among the younger officers and some of the senior officers a great deal of attention is paid to the threat of being investigated and disciplined. For one new officer (three years' experience) this new concern generates "survival strategies" and reinforces the impact of "accountability" in corrections.

> *Do you have any problems with the way the administration here treats officers?*
>
> You watch out for your own ass because they're after you. On our shift, our captain and lieutenant are the best in New York. They take care of us, never hurt us. They go out of their way to see that we're covered. But if you do something wrong and the IG [Inspector General's office] comes in, you're on your own. Once you're in the upper echelons, the way for advancement is to find officers doing something wrong.
>
> *How do you deal with this?*
>
> As much as you can you go out of your way to cover yourself. May not do part of your job so you're not going to make a mistake. You look out for yourself and other officers.
>
> If you have to lie your way out of it, it's better to lie and get out than to tell the truth. The survival of the fittest. If they weren't so intent on getting you in trouble, they might get a lot of things done.

Communication with Officers

Where positive evaluations of institutional communications channels were rare in 1976, and inconsistency and untrustworthy information forced officers to turn to inmates, by 1986 much improvement was noted. Where previously officers felt that the administration did not want them to know about problems lest it alter their dealings with inmates, officers now point to the pre-shift briefing as a useful activity.

> They do give you more information now. The roll call is 15 minutes and they give you a briefing. They tell you about the problems of the day before. Bulletins from Albany. This stuff should have been there years ago. Before, along with everyone else you never thought about it. You'd just go in blind and hope that nothing happens. Years ago, I'd be working in the kitchen before I knew there was a riot the day before.

* * *

> It's a lot better now. Years ago, they [the Administration] would tell you a little bit. Now at roll call, they read unusual incident reports. The sergeant will say such and such happened if there was a fight in the yard. So you watch the block the inmates are in. That's better. In in-service training they tell you about inmates' friends in other places, drugs. The officers are more informed now. Some officers know these things and check them out.

Where rumors fed institutional paranoia ten years ago, officers point to new rumor control strategies:

> Before when I was an officer, people didn't know when problems existed. You would find out when inmates would tell you a story. Third- or fourth-hand and they would embellish it. They made a big thing about the Muslims getting together, but it turned out to be nothing to worry about. The rumor mill still goes on. Before they didn't do anything to quell rumors, now with so many sergeants, they send them to see what is going on and get a true picture.

Though the inmate "rat" system is still acknowledged to exist, the changing nature of institutional violence and inter-inmate relations has, according to some officers, brought inmate sources of information to the officer, often for self-protection. The following officer describes how he uses such information:

> I probably have a large number of individuals who give me information. No snitches or rats. I don't believe in asking for it or giving favors. I won't participate in that. People come to me and tell me about shanks, marijuana, or thefts. That's because they know if they come to me who told won't come out and I'll investigate. If it's a shank or marijuana I'll call a frisk officer and give them a tip and they'll check it out. Extortion or something like that, I talk to the officers where the inmate works or to the officer on his gallery or watch him [the aggressor] without directly letting him know. If it looks like a legitimate problem, I'll approach the aggressor and let him know I know what's going on and I will let the administration know.

Here we see how human service aspects of correctional officer work that previously helped prisoners psychologically cope with the pains of imprisonment have become transformed into law enforcement-related protection strategies related to physical, not psychological, survival.

SUMMARY—1986

In spite of working in a more violent environment, it is evident that changes in patterns of involvement and communication, increased regularity of procedures have reduced the amount of dissatisfaction correctional officers experience with their work. Though in 1976 officers were aware and critical of the "increasing liberalization" of the early 1970s, by 1986, their dissatisfaction has turned to acceptance as more and more changes (especially those relating to court and DOC mandated procedures) become institutionalized parts of their environment.

NOTES

[1]Toch, Hans. *Living in Prison: The Ecology of Survival*. New York: Free Press, 1977; Cohen, Stanley and Taylor, Laurie. *Psychological Survival: The Experiences of Long Term Imprisonment*. New York: Vintage Press, 1973; Irwin, John. *The Felon*. Englewood Cliffs, NJ: Prentice-Hall, 1970; Mathiesen, Thomas. *The Defences of the Weak*. London: Tavistock Publications, 1965; and Sykes, Gresham. *The Society of Captives*. New York: Atheneum, 1970.

[2]See Thomas, J.E. *The English Prison Officer Since 1850: A Study in Conflict*. London: Routledge and Kegan Paul, 1972; Jacobs, J. and Retsky, H. "The Prison Guard," *Urban Life*, Vol. 1 (1975), pp. 5-29; Kronstadt, S. "Prison Guards: An Unhappy Lot," *New York Affairs*, Fall (1974), pp. 60-77; May, E. "Prison Guards in America: The Inside Story," *Corrections Magazine*, Vol. 2 (1976), pp. 3-12.

[3]This turnover rate was calculated by the following formula:

$$\frac{\text{(number of additions + number of terminations)}}{\text{total on January 1, 1976}} \times 100$$

[4]Jacobs, James B. and Grear, Mary P. "Drop-Outs and Rejects: An Analysis of the Prison Guard's Revolving Door," *Criminal Justice Review*, Vol. 2, No. 2 (1977), pp. 57-70.

[5]Luden, Walter A. *The Prison Warden and the Custodial Staff*. Springfield, IL: Charles C. Thomas, 1965, p. 87.

[6]Argyle, Michael. *The Social Psychology of Work*. New York: Taplinger Publishing Company, 1972, p. 24.

[7]Jacobs, James B. and Grear, Mary P. op. cit.

[8]See Jacobs and Retsky, op. cit., p. 23.

[9]This experience is identical to that reported by C. H. S. Jayewardene, H. B. McKay and B. E. A. Krug McKay, for Canadian prisons, see "In Search of a Sixth Sense: Predictors of Disruptive Behaviors in Canadian Institutions," *Crime and/et Justice*, Vol. 4, No. 1 (May 1976), pp. 34, 35.

[10]Such fatalism concerning their ability to control factors related to their physical well-being is similar to the inmates' situation described by Sykes. See *The Society of Captives*, pp. 76, 77.

[11]See Mathiesen, Thomas. *The Defences of the Weak*. Pp. 150-165.

[12]Johnson, Elmer H. "Sociology of Confinement: Assimilation and the Prison Riot," *Journal of Criminal Law, Criminology and Police Science*, Vol. 51 (1961), p. 529.

[13]In a sense, both correction officers and inmates become "familiars" in the living and work space of the other. Werthman and Piliavin describe how "familiars" may walk through the territory of gangs without causing disruption in on-going activities. See Werthman, Carl and Piliavin, Irving. "Gang Members and Ecological Conflict," in *Juvenile Delinquency*, third edition, edited by Rose Giallombardo. New York: John Wiley and Sons, 1977, pp. 305-326.

[14]The prison environment in which the correction officer works would appear to be highly conducive to the development of rumors. As Allport and Postman observe about the conditions facilitating the development of rumors:

> First, the theme of the story must have some *importance* [emphasis in original] to speaker and listener; second, the true facts must be shrouded in some kind of *ambiguity* [emphasis in original]. This ambiguity may be induced by the absence or sketchiness of news (for correction officer, information), by conflicting nature of the news, by the distrust of the news, or by some emotional tensions that made the individual unable or unwilling to accept the facts set forth in the news.

Allport, Gordon W. and Postman, Leo. *The Psychology of Rumor*. Russell and Russell, 1947, p. 33.

[15]These comments represent the officer talking as "citizen"—not as "correction officer." When officers discuss inmates *within* an exclusively institutional framework, they generally speak of inmates as individuals and in relatively positive terms. However, the inclusion of a noninstitutional reference point usually invites more derogatory remarks:

> Some people say the inmates have nothing, and yet they constantly throw things away. They have a lack of respect for property, for themselves, for one another. They break things. They say it's not theirs, so it doesn't matter. It costs money to keep a guy in there. It's a better life than he's ever seen. He sees a doctor every day if he wants. Gets new teeth, cosmetic surgery. Why should I pay for some asshole's surgery and then he thinks he doesn't look pretty.

[16]Motivans, Joseph. "Occupational Socialization and Personality: A Case Study of the Prison Guard," *Proceedings of the 93rd Congress of the American Correctional Association* (1963), p. 140.

[17]See Cohen, Stanley and Taylor, Laurie. *Psychological Survival: The Experience of Long Term Imprisonment*. New York: Vintage Books, 1972, pp. 48-49.

The Rewards of Being a Guard

8

While the conditions that breed dissatisfaction among correction officers force them to develop techniques for coping with their day-to-day problems, the search for rewards represents the guard's attempt to find meaning in what he does—a meaning capable of sustaining his long-term commitment to his chosen occupation. To discover the rewards of being a guard, each officer was asked to identify both the best and the most satisfying thing about his work. These responses were categorized according to Maslow's hierarchy of needs.[1] In addition, eight predetermined areas (again representative of Maslow's hierarchy) were explored to generate impressions concerning the potential satisfactions of the work (Table 8.1 summarizes these responses). In adjusting to their work environment, correction officers learn to adapt their expectations to the realities of their workplace. Most gladly take what it has to offer and seemingly learn not to expect what it is "unable" to provide. That guards perceive limited possibilities for satisfaction in the work is also suggested by the fact that about 25% of the officers said that there was "nothing" about their work they could characterize as "most satisfying."

Table 8.1. Sources of Correction Officer Job Satisfaction (N=50)

Maslow's Hierarchy of Needs	Indicator	Best[a]	Most Satisfying[b]	Satisfied with[c]
Physiological	Pay	60%	8%	86%
Safety	Job security	60%	2%	94%
Belongingness and affection	Relations with co-workers	2%	8%	72%
Esteem and self-respect	Personal pride	—	8%[d]	72%
	Advancement	8%	16%	16%
	Recognition	—	12%[e]	16%
Self-actualization	Accomplishment	6%	30%	34%
	Utilization of capabilities	16%	6%	28%
Nothing		8%	22%	NA

[a] Question: If you had to tell someone who was thinking about becoming a correction officer what the best thing about the job was, what would you tell him?

[b] Question: If you had to tell someone who was thinking about becoming a correction officer what the most satisfying thing about the job was, what would you tell him?

[c] Question: For specific questions see Appendix C.

[d] For three of these four officers the people they enjoyed working with were inmates.

[e] For five of these six officers recognition was received from inmates, not members of the prison staff.

SECURITY AND PAY

Drawn into their correctional careers by promises of "job security" and "good pay," most officers appear to be satisfied with their work to the extent that it fulfills the needs they had when they accepted their positions. Pay and security were mentioned by 60% of these officers as the "best" things about their work and about 90% said they were satisfied with them. Most felt that the prison business is one of the most stable fields in the American economy, and that as long as there is crime, there will be prisons and jobs for the guards. Rising crime rates and burgeoning prison populations are viewed by guards as insurance against the possibility of layoff.

Correction officers at Auburn earn basic annual salaries of $12,000 to $15,000. They are able to supplement this base pay by working nearly as many hours of voluntary overtime as they desire. (See Table 13, Appendix D for the distribution of the yearly incomes including overtime.) An individual's satisfaction with his earnings is most often a reflection of his relative position rather than of the absolute amount of dollars he takes home, and correction officers often refer to their salary in such relativistic terms. They viewed their income as adequate "for the work we have to do," "for the education" (a high school or equivalency diploma is the educational requirement for the position) or "for the area" in which they live, and generally feel they are well off. A noncontributory pension plan, health insurance, liberal sick leave, personal leave and vacation benefits also contribute to satisfying the officer's most basic needs. Sometimes money and security serve as substitutes for other satisfactions not found in the job, indicating a lowering of expectations:

> Probably the most common answer is the money and the benefits. Though I don't like to think it's that, it is.
>
> *Did you expect it would be that when you started?*
>
> Not really. I expected I would actually be dealing with guys on an individual basis. I had the idea I'd be rehabilitating these people. We deal with them, but don't rehabilitate. There are certain things we can do for an individual, but the system doesn't allow the officer to really do things for the inmate. In fact, it's frowned upon.

* * *

> It's tough to say what the best thing is right now. It used to be personal satisfaction from small accomplishments. But I've got a lot of outside interests now and I'm getting the attitude to put in eight hours and get out. Now I don't give a shit. I'm still pissed about that deal [where I didn't get training]. I did all that work and didn't get

> the benefits. But the best thing is the money. At least compared to a factory. It's not a physical job and it's an easy way to make a good living. You work day to day and all of a sudden you've got five years in. Then the best thing is job security.

BELONGINGNESS AND AFFECTION (INTERPERSONAL CONCERNS)

The ability of a particular job to fulfill social needs is determined by the character of the relationships formed between the individual worker and other members of his work group. Responses to my questions concerning this need present contradictory perceptions. While over 70% of the officers indicate that their relations with their fellow workers are satisfactory, only one officer indicated that such relationships were the "best" or "most satisfying" part of his job. To say that a correction officer finds his relationships with his fellow workers to be satisfactory does not mean that officers "derive satisfaction" from such relationships. To better understand this distinction, the nature of the correction officer individual—group relationship merits further attention.

In the process of becoming a correction officer described above, there was a tendency for officers not to perceive their "work group" as their "reference group." Officers also tended to see themselves as "individuals," not as "correction officers," thus betraying the lack of a strong group identity. Further evidence for this tendency comes from the officers' evaluation of their group relationships.

When an officer indicates that his relationships with his fellow officers are satisfactory, he usually qualifies his reply by placing it within the context of his "work relationships." Satisfactory relationships result not because officers enjoy working with one another, rather cooperation is perceived to be a *necessity* in the correction officer's work:

> There's a good bunch of guys down there, really. Everybody's either got as much or more education than you. That's good so you can learn from one another. I've never seen anybody there who wouldn't help another officer. It's like you're all brothers together. This is your job. *You've got to work together*.

Even when the existence of "personal friction" among officers is acknowledged, work relations are still perceived to be satisfactory:

> We have some minor friction with each other, but you try to get along together at work. Together things are better. It's not the kind of place where you can go in opposite directions. You try not to let personal convictions get into your feelings at work. Most often it's better to turn and walk away if there's a problem.

Officers who tend to separate themselves from the group in their outside activities still manage to maintain effective work relations:

> There aren't many officers down there I'd give you two cents for. There's very few I'd socialize with. I don't see many outside, but you've still got to work with them inside.

Though the work situation would appear to force officers to work together even where personal relations are strained, many officers note the existence of *cliques* that serve to emphasize divisions among officers and to isolate "outside" individuals. Though cliques are generally acknowledged to be present, there is little consensus concerning the basis for such cliques. Age, shift, work area, ethnic background, religion, sports, are all mentioned as possible alternatives:

> There are shift and job cliques. If you're not a part of the group, they won't tell you about different details of a certain job if you're a relief man filling in. Say, if you're in a shop and you're filling in for somebody, there may be little things you're supposed to do, like a certain time to take the count or a certain inmate has been a problem, and the other guys on the shift or in the shop won't tell you these things. Or they'll give you misinformation. Then you get chewed out by the brass for screwing up. And these guys get their jollies off just by getting you in trouble.

The strength of the relationships between the individual officer and the group can also be examined in relation to the correction officer's normative behavior.[2] The existence of generally accepted norms and of characteristic sanctions for norm-violating behavior might support the existence of correction officer group identification. In attempting to discover group "norms" of correction officers, each officer was asked to specify those forms of officer behavior that other correction officers *generally* found unacceptable. (Table 14 on page 192 presents a summary of responses.)

There is a lack of consensus among correction officers concerning the definition of norm-violating behaviors. Together, the 50 officers in our sample list 17 different behaviors and only one behavior ("dealing in contraband") was mentioned by more than one-quarter of the men. In addition, seven of the officers said that they did not know of any officer behaviors that would generally be considered offensive by officers. In answering, most of these officers appear to be responding as individuals, focusing upon behaviors *they* consider inappropriate, without regard to what other officers think. Indeed, most officers are not aware of the feelings of their fellow officers, or if they are aware of such feelings, they ignore these "group" opinions in favor of emphasizing their "individuality."

Even though there appears to be no consensus among officers concerning the definition of "deviant" officer behaviors, there is a measure of agreement on the sanctions imposed for whatever individuals consider inappropriate officer actions. Officers generally "avoid" deviant officers both at work and in social activities outside. They also raise the offending issue with the offending officer in an attempt to eliminate the problem. Even in sanctioning "deviant" officer behavior, the necessity of "working together" is emphasized:

> There are instances of hatred between officers, but it's right out in the open. A guy tells me I'm on his shit list, but if I see something he needs to know, I'll tell him just what he needs to know for his job, for his safety and mine. I may not like him, but I'll still talk to him. I've got to know and he's got to know.

Others take the enforcement of what they perceive to be norm-violating behavior to the extreme of physical encounters:

> In the last year there have been several fights in the parking lot. I've never heard of such a thing. It's getting so that the officers and the inmates are just as bad. Most fights are over personal things, not job related. One, however, was a case where an officer "ratted" another officer out. Some officers watch other officers more closely than they do inmates.

If correction officers were a close-knit group, it might be expected that exposing an officer's indiscretions to administrative personnel would be frowned upon—that the "code of silence" enforced by the officers would prevail. This, however, does not appear to be the case. Only 12% of these officers indicated that being a "rat" was against the "code" of officers, and even here the definition of a "rat" was often qualified. Merely informing the administration about another officer's "offenses" is not enough to define the officer in question as a rat. It is acceptable to "inform" on an officer if his behavior violates security, and even if it creates problems for other officers, in addition to the informer and the offender. If the behavior affects only the two officers involved, they are expected to resolve the conflict themselves:

> Sometimes an officer will talk to him, tell him "straighten out or I'll take it higher up." Sometimes you do nothing but talk to another officer about it and maybe that officer will tell him if you're too shy. Or you can bring it up to a sergeant. It's not being a "rat" if it will cause a problem. If it's a minor thing and not a problem except among the officers involved, then it's a rat.

Another characteristic of correction officer group relationships that tends to indicate the inability of officers to derive satisfaction from associations with each other is the tendency of officers *not* to become involved with other officers outside of their work situation. Many feel that guards who "hang out together" tend to cause problems for the rest by giving guards as a group a bad name through their sometimes conspicuous presence during "barroom" altercations:

> As far as associations outside of work are concerned, the rule book says just work with them eight hours a day. It says nothing about outside. I pal around with a couple of guys or go to have a drink, but I try to keep my friends away from the prison. It's tough, though, in a city this size. I'm not against shop talk, provided it belongs, but you always talk shop when you're with hacks.

> I don't associate with officers outside of the institution. There's a few officers I don't like. A lot of them kid each other, fight now and then. There's always somebody at a party looking for a fight. It's not good to hang out with them. Some were my friends before they took the job.

Officers generally believe that those officers who "hang out" with other officers have a much greater tendency to become heavy drinkers, to become involved in gambling and to suffer marital problems:

> If I take the job home, I get a lot of strain. Six people who work there that I know got separations or divorces. If you get into the syndrome with other guards, drinking, going out; lots of separations and divorces of people I thought were happy.

Though not specifically asked, many officers indicated that they developed interests to which they devote a great deal of time outside of the institution. Some were involved in local government, many worked second jobs, while others were involved in sports activities. As one officer said, "You need outside things to keep you going." This tendency to avoid contacts that emphasize their work and to seek associations emphasizing totally different sets of concerns is illustrative of the general reference group shifting process described by Sherif, who points out that people dissatisfied with one group actively seek to attach themselves to another whose values they can accept.[3]

The tendency of officers not to derive satisfaction from associations with members of their work group and to dissociate themselves from that group does not mean that group sympathies do not exist. A vast majority of the officers indicate that a "kind of loyalty" exists among officers based mainly on the strength of their "working relationships." This is not a loyalty built by commitment to common goals and methods, but a loyalty mobilized by reactions to perceived threats emanating from one or another of the correction officers' two common enemies: the prison administration and inmates.

Based on observations made over a six-year period, it appears that attempts by the prison administration to alter conditions that adversely affect the general lot of officers are often met with united officer opposition. Rumors of nonviolent protests by inmates or of violent incidents involving inmates directed against officers quickly unite officers in opposition to the perceived threat.

ESTEEM AND SELF-RESPECT

In their efforts to satisfy their ego needs, it appears that correction officers are again on their own. Less than 16% of the officers are satisfied with opportunities for advancement and the possibilities of receiving recognition for the work that they do. Despite the many unsatisfactory conditions associated with their work, about three-fourths of these officers take "personal pride" in the work they perform. Though they believe they will not receive recognition from supervisors or other administrative or departmental personnel and that the quality of their work will not be a consideration in promotion decisions, the majority of the officers are able to find some aspect of their work of which they can be proud.

Personal Pride

The "pride" that officers take in their work is not related, except in a very few cases, to being an officer. Only two officers mentioned that they were proud to be officers. Most often officer pride is a generalized pride the individual would find in any activity in which he was involved. Such phrases as, "I do any job the best I can," and "I always take pride in what I do," suggest that the officer pride is less a reflection of the officer's position than it is a reflection of personal values.

That pride is an expression of individual values does not preclude the necessity that one's work provides one with opportunities to make valued contributions. Officers derive "personal pride" from various facets of their work. However, pride is most often expressed in the relationships officers manage to establish with inmates. Whether the emphasis is on maintaining order or on solving problems, officers measure pride in their work in terms of the responses they evoke in inmates:

> Most of all, the inmates know what I stand for. Not the hard-core type program that says things are definitely this way, and I don't say, "Anything you do is okay with me," either. I feel I allow myself flexibility to handle most situations and still maintain the respect of the inmates around me.

* * *

> Years ago there were no counselors that an inmate could go to to get a family problem straightened out. They always come to the officer. I always tried to get the man some satisfaction, to get an answer for him and not turn my back. They respect you for that. I never claimed to be Mr. Fix-It, but I always made an effort to solve problems.

Other officers find pride in the image they project and what they actually accomplish becomes less important than the fact that they are trying to accomplish something:

> You can tell if a person has pride by how he dresses, his attitude toward employees and inmates. You've got to strive to better yourself in the job and it makes it easier. Makes the job better. There's lots of self-pride. You set an example, you don't always get somebody to follow, but you just set an example. Inmates watch everything you do and remember everything you say. If you foul up outside or they smell booze on your breath, they know.

Even in performing routine tasks, officers tend to perform them as if inmates are the sole judges of their behavior:

> I take pride in frisking and packing inmates. I try to do it thoroughly but in such a way that the inmate can come in behind me and find things.

Those unable to take pride in their work alternatively blame "the system" for not providing opportunities or the inmates for not responding:

> There's not much room for it the way things are set up. I don't know if there's any place for it. There's not much to be proud of as far as doing something for somebody. The inmates don't appreciate it, that's for sure.

Others see any effort they might put forth to "help" inmates as futile, as making little difference in the inmates' lives:

> You know damn well some guys have records as long as your arm and there's not much you can do to stop them. Some first-timers, they needed money, they probably won't be back. Guys with chips on their shoulders, they'll be back. You get very little satisfaction; few guys will listen and understand.

Advancement

Only four officers referred to opportunities for advancement as the "best thing" about their jobs, none mentioned it as "the most satisfying aspect of their work" and only eight were satisfied with promotion opportunities.

Most have little incentive to become a sergeant, regardless of the opportunities. Becoming a sergeant would mean moving away from their established home to another institution for little pay increase. The disruption in their personal lives was often cited as a reason for not considering promotions.

Another reason for not wanting to become a sergeant is that their present positions as officers offer more flexibility in the hours and job assignments. The perceived position of a sergeant within the institution acts as a disincentive when compared to the benefits of the officer's job:

> I thought about it, but there's one drawback. Now I can work the shift and the job I want. If I advanced, I'd get one job and one shift. There's less variety when you work up.

Others indicate no desire for advancement because they believe advancement means involvement in the "politics" of institutional administration and a reduction in opportunities to make positive contributions:

> [Advancement] never crossed my mind. I don't want to get into the political in-fighting they carry on up there. And I don't see where a sergeant or lieutenant has anything to contribute in the sense of dealing with inmates.

A few officers rejected advancement, having considered their personal qualities and temperament determining that they were not suited for the positions:

> It's more responsibility and I'm more of a follower than a leader. I'm good at taking orders. I have to work at giving them.
>
> * * *
>
> The sergeant has lost responsibility. The higher up you get, the more responsibility you can put on somebody else. I have to do jobs myself. I can't depend on others to do things. I like to do things myself to see that it's done right. I would have trouble letting others do things.

The only advantage officers could see in becoming a sergeant is that one might have better access to information:

> You'd have more knowledge of the institution, you'd know what all the brass are doing and what the officers and inmates are doing, the mechanics of it.

In any event, opportunities for advancement were perceived as closed. While our research program was in progress, the validity of the civil service examination for the sergeant's position was in the process of being reviewed by the courts and no further exams were being scheduled.

Recognition

Most officers believe that their work lacks opportunities for recognition, which is often a source of discontent. When officers speak of recognition, they are not speaking about formal written recommendations. Many would settle for a simple "you've done a nice job" from somebody in authority. The lack of positive affirmation by others reportedly lowers morale and serves as a disincentive to positive action:

> Recognition is very poor down there. I've put on shows with inmates, but I got no recognition out of that. No "hey, you're doing a good job" kind of thing.

Not having one's value affirmed by others when one performs exceptional work often leads to the demise of the expectation of recognition:

> *Do you expect recognition?*
>
> No. Not any more. I did when I put on the shows. A lot of guys are like this. They should want to strive to get ahead and get recognition, but you just fall into a pattern and don't strive.
>
> * * *
>
> You don't get recognition and it's very bad. You may feel personally satisfied, but you don't expect recognition. You don't look for it because there's no reward for it. You can't get a better job and you can't get a promotion. When I was younger, I did expect it and I was chastised for what I did wrong. You're expected to do right, not wrong. The worst recognition you can get is if you do a job well and the inmates tell the brass that you did a good job. Then they say you're getting too close to the inmates and losing sight of your job.

Sometimes the expectation of not receiving recognition becomes so strong that officers come to reject the idea completely, preferring not to be noticed.

Self-Fulfillment

In examining the potential of the correction officer's job to provide opportunities for self-fulfilling behaviors, I asked if the nature of the work afforded the officers opportunities to "use their capabilities" and if they thought they "accomplished" anything in their work. In response to both questions, about two-thirds of the officers indicated that they did not contribute sufficiently, often citing the reluctance of the state to permit them to engage in more than menial tasks:

> The institutions and the state are reluctant to let the officer do more than watch, listen and observe. They say you're better trained and qualified, but they don't let you do anything. It would be a more interesting job if they let you use your abilities. I'm an official umpire and I often hear guys arguing. I'd like to step in, but the sergeant will say no and if I do, I'll get written up or fired. That I might be helpful to an inmate is beside the point.

Others point to the heavy burden imposed on their time by the routine duties of their assignment and the corresponding lack of time available for self-fulfilling behaviors. Most officers, however, are not bothered by the fact that their jobs fail to provide them with opportunities to utilize special skills, even though they would like to be able to deploy special skills that could be used in the institution. This may indicate that these officers have lowered their aspirations to what they can reasonably expect from their work:

> I think I've got more to offer than I'm called upon to do. In the service I was a supply clerk. I'm somewhat skilled in office procedures and skilled in inventory control and merchandising. I'm extremely handy with my hands, but these things aren't called upon in my work.
>
> *Does this bother you?*
>
> No. It doesn't bother me. One thing that does bother me though is that I'm a certified locksmith and I've made it known. When times come when they need one, no one ever calls me. It's a minor thing. A jammed lock and it slows the whole institution and I was never asked to fix it.

Some officers utilize their skills even though they're not called upon to do so. The following illustrates the extent to which some officers are willing to go to have opportunities to contribute:

> I fixed up lights and things in the shops. I was a repair technician before. You're supposed to go through channels. I could have probably gotten fired for doing it, but it makes you feel good to do something. I wanted to teach a course in washers and dryers; I thought it would go over good; I even talked to the head of the school about it, but he couldn't guarantee that I could stay on.

Though formal opportunities are generally not available for officers to contribute to helping inmates, those officers who experience feelings of accomplishment often gain such self-fulfillment from their informal interactions with inmates:

> They ask questions. A guy asked me about savings bonds. I explained them to him and he took them out. The guy said thanks. These guys surprise you sometimes.

Officers, however, often labor under the suspicion that no matter what they do, they may not "really" be accomplishing anything. It is difficult for them to evaluate the results of their actions and interactions.

SUMMARY—1976

The rewards of being a guard are few and basic. Job security and pay, factors that bring guards to their jobs, keep them working. They become dependent on their jobs and cannot afford to leave. While pursuing their careers, they lower their expectations and generally learn not to expect, and in some cases not to want, recognition, advancement or opportunities to make meaningful contributions. Even interpersonal relations with fellow officers appear incapable of providing feelings of belongingness or affection. Though generally satisfied with work relationships, personal relations among these guards are at times rather strained and "outside" associations cultivated. What higher-level rewards are provided by the guard's work appear to be self-generated, a sense of personal pride, or else conferred by inmates who provide opportunities for officers to make significant contributions.

FROM ALIENATION TO INVOLVEMENT: 1976-1986

While many of the negative features of correctional officers' work environment appear to have been ameliorated, many of the positive features have been enhanced.

Pay and Benefits

As in 1976, pay, benefits, and job security are the most often mentioned positive features of correctional officer work. By 1986, starting pay for correctional officers had risen to $18,000 and new salary scales brought officers to the top pay grade much faster. Improved medical plan and extended benefits have strengthened the degree to which officers' psychological and safety needs are satisfied. For the mid and late career officers, salary levels have allowed them to build and maintain a relatively high standard of living for the Auburn area. For these experienced officers the new salary scales (starting at $18,000, after three years at $25,000, and top pay after seven years) appears to have reduced the monetary incentive for remaining in correctional work past the minimum retirement age.

> The pay's decent. But they did the wrong thing with the pay structure. They changed it so the younger officers get more money faster to grab and keep new guys, and they've lost lots of the older officers. There's nothing to keep the older guy there. They retire and get out after twenty-five years.

For the younger officers coming in at 20 or 21 years of age, correctional officer pay means a much-improved life-style. As one officer with three years reports:

> The money is the best. Criminal justice jobs are generally not high paying, but we get paid pretty well. Lots of younger officers are into the stock market, nice houses, families, and cars.

Relations with Co-Workers

As in 1976, descriptions of correctional officer intergroup relations focused on the need for officers to support each other in the context of conflict with inmates. However, in 1986, the substantial number of officers hired since 1981 (in 1976, 19% had less than six years experience; by 1986, that percentage increased to 55%) appears to have created strong generational and shift divisions in the workplace. In addition, for the experienced officers there is a growing sense of officer anonymity. What in the context of the "old days" was seen as the "Auburn Family" is now being invaded by young outsiders. As one recently retired officer notes:

> It seems like there are barriers between the older and younger officers. There's not the closeness like there used to be. The officer who runs the front gate used to know everybody and their days off. I used to, too. Now you don't know anybody. But it's hard now, there are so many. Where there are ties, they're age group and shift ties.

* * *

> Officers are in their own cliques together. Some guys on sports, etc. It's changed. People used to go to retirement parties and Christmas parties. I would go and be with everyone. But now you can't get enough guys to go to these anymore. I don't know. Maybe it's just different officers. I don't know how guys from Syracuse and Utica and everywhere fit in. Most officers from Auburn have nothing in common with them.

Some of the younger officers report "hanging out" with officers from their cohort and shift. However, some younger officers and nearly all of the older officers still report their preference for avoiding close ties to correctional officers outside the workplace. Rather than reflecting an attempt to "disassociate" themselves from their jobs and "the undesirables" among correctional officers, the 1986 variant appears to represent the increased size and mobility of the guard force, in addition to changes in life-style accompanying ten years of aging.

Generational differences in shift assignment coupled with different levels and types of inmate activity across shifts have resulted in what both younger and older officers perceive as "two different institutions." As graffiti in the restrooms indicate, "The day shift gives it away and the night shift takes it back."

> There's two different groups set side-by-side according to shift. Older officers on days (7:00-3:00) and younger guys on nights (3:00-11:00). They're like night and day.

* * *

> The younger guys on 3:00-11:00 have a lot of ego. Think they have to save the institution because days gave it away. Their attitude is bad, high and mighty macho type.

Many older officers observe that they are more likely to give assistance to newer officers than experienced officers would give them when they broke in 15, 20 and 25 years ago.

> The new officer now can adjust more. Not like when we came in. They've been to the Academy to get basic knowledge, they got OJT in different areas. They rub elbows with experienced officers in all areas. It used to be older officers wouldn't talk to the younger ones. The old timers would say, "find out like I did," they had nothing to say. I don't do that. I show new officers anything I can on my job.

Many younger officers echo this 25-year veteran's words:

> In most cases years of experience don't matter. If you do the job right the older guys will help you out. They're very professional. Some of the old timers went on nights to get out, but many still in the same place, they've changed with the times. They've become more professional out of necessity.

Though the "training" aspect of experienced/new officer relationships appears to have improved, both newer and experienced officers noted a tendency among new officers to "play games" among each other and on newer officers.

> A lot of the younger officers are like little kids. Playing games with one another. The inmates are watching and losing respect for the CO's. The little immature things they push on one another.

One officer with seven years' experience describes the behavior of his younger colleagues:

> They play with each other. Tease, harass. All are good friends. They call up a buddy and tell him, "this is the Dep," and get him to do something. They're not supposed to do this, then after a while they call up and tell them it's a joke. Not anything to get anyone in trouble.
>
> * * *
>
> Holding on to your hat is difficult. I hang my hat on a hook, then went to take a call, come back and my hat was gone. I thought an inmate took it. I go to the Sergeant, fill out paperwork to report it missing. After one-half hour I found out that a young officer took it and put it in the lock box.

Though such behavior seems to represent a formal "hazing," the new cohort of officers is applying to entering officers, even older officers are not immune from such pranks. An officer with fifteen years' experience in "special housing" reports the following:

> The newer officers don't seem to care as much as the older ones. Two weeks ago, I had to help out feeding some inmates in the box (special housing). They've got six to eight officers up there now and they can't do the work we did with two a year ago. I ask one of these younger officers to help carry out some empty pans, he says, "It's not my job, my job is to watch C & D." So I told him to take care of that

> gate and I took care of the pans. I told his lazy ass. I told the Sergeant, too. When I was walking out these new officers were laughing. They were laughing about the badge on my hat. They had turned it upside down when I took my hat off. Two guards did that. Playing the kid games.

Finally a correctional officer group norm seems to be developing around the task-related theme of "do your job, help out, don't be lazy." This norm also seems to be communicated strongly across generations. For example, an officer with three years' experience describes how to become accepted.

> Dealing with guys with more years in terms of I'm learning from him, watch and learn. If he doesn't talk to inmates, I don't. If he says, "lock-in," that's what I do: You have to show guys with seniority respect. Do the job, show them you're willing to work and help out.

An officer with thirteen years' experience describes the same norm and the sanctions for its violation utilizing some prison argot (rare for these interviews):

> If you "hose" another officer you can get in trouble. Coming back in 40 minutes when you're supposed to be back in 20 minutes. Taking advantage of other officers like that.
>
> *What do officers do about this?*
>
> At lots of institutions they'd use the "parking lot scene" but at Auburn basically they'll "round on you," have nothing to do with you. Some harassment, snide remarks, graffiti. If you're in trouble, you'll read about it on the bathroom wall.

Recognition

Perhaps the greatest change in the officers' perceptions of the positive aspects of their work environment relates to increased opportunities for recognition for a job well done. Whether they experienced opportunities for specialized inservice training (e.g., drug detection and identification), participated in department-wide projects (e.g., Quality of Working Life in Corrections Program), received letters of commendation, read stories about officers in newspapers or union and/or departmental newsletters, or simply heard a good word from a superior, nearly every officer interviewed recognized that the Department of Corrections and the local administration was paying greater attention to officers' positive contributions.

> You see more recognition now. They've decided that it's a big factor for morale. People who put their lives on the line. Before, no one knew. The union puts things in the paper now. The administration will also acknowledge good work. Now they let you know. They just acknowledged an officer who quieted an inmate with a shive. He took his life in his hands.
>
> * * *
>
> Recognition is given a lot more freely now than before. Before it was only write-ups. Today they give commendations to officers who excel. One officer got recognized for being a good frisk officer.

For some officers, the attention to recognition appears to be going overboard and losing its meaning:

> At one time you'd never hear a word about it. Seldom an "atta boy." Now, everything you do, they try to blow it up in the newspaper, in journals; but it's not sincere. They go through the motions. I got a letter from the warden when I spotted an escape attempt. He sent letters to the guys who won the tug-of-war in the DOC Olympics. It sounded stupid.

Advancement Opportunities

Though most of the officers interviewed in 1976 did not see advancement as part of their career plans in 1986 and some reported getting on the Sergeant's list during the past ten years, almost all agreed that opportunities for the younger officers to advance were much greater than in the past. The opening of new facilities, and increases in the number of administrative slots at existing facilities had created possibilities that did not exist ten years ago.

As one 25-year veteran explains:

> If I had to do it over again, I probably would want to become a sergeant. I took the test once. But I'd become a sergeant only to get to be a lieutenant or captain. Sergeants are as bad as officers. In the middle on everything. I took Criminology at the community college. If I had pushed more I could have done it, become a Lieutenant, but I didn't put in the effort.

Many officers, however, were troubled by new departmental policy which allows officers to take the sergeant exam after two years' experience and makes them eligible for appointment after three years. In addition, the appointment of sergeants to maximum security institutions without maximum security experience was also seen as a problem.

> The new policies make more opportunities for advancement and make it faster. But it waters down the experience for a maximum security prison. They need at least five years' experience in a maximum security institution until they're ready to work there.

Interestingly, 11 of the officers in the 1976 sample became sergeants or lieutenants in spite of what officers generally perceived as poor opportunities in 1976. For each of these officers, promotion was something they were concerned about and for the sergeants interviewed the job was satisfying their individual needs. Freedom and greater opportunities to contribute are key qualities found in the new position:

> Basically there's more freedom as a sergeant. You're not contained in one area. You have more input to policy and procedure. When you're a CO it gets monotonous after a few years. After ten or 15 years you get burned out and stale. It's changed for me now; it's a lot better.
>
> For another, keeping busy and avoiding monotony provides his motivation.
>
> I went to sergeant because I was fed up with the job I had before. I wanted to be in the population but nobody else wanted to do my job so I was stuck. Always in the back of your mind there's the money and retirement benefits. But I tried sergeant more to change. That's why I've worked relief as a sergeant. The humdrum, same old things drive me crazy. There are different officers and inmates when you work relief. It keeps you active.

Pride and Self-Actualization

Though some officers still see little in the job besides their paycheck, and others still derive pride from appearance, new dimensions of self-evaluation and opportunities for self-actualization are emerging.

With increased specialization in job tasks and opportunities to work in specialized areas such as the new mental health unit, pride, opportunities to use personal skills and to contribute find their expression in performing the job assignment well. Officer recognition from the prison administration and peers from self-evaluation are often linked to the perception of the availability of self-actualizing opportunities.

> Yes, I have pride in what I do. In my area I've got it running smoothly. I get respect from the inmates, officers and civilians on the unit. Compliments from the unit supervisor. "You've got it cleaned up and running very well."
>
> I can use my abilities now because of the job I have. In the long run, for inmates, you don't change many, but in my location I can keep it running smoothly and that makes everyone comfortable.
>
> * * *
>
> In my job I have a lot of responsibility. When they (officers) need help, I know they're in trouble; I have to stay alert all the time. I cared less when I worked in my other assignment. But now I can't not care, I have to take the responsibility.

For other officers, pride is found not in their ability to "handle inmates" but rather in doing things in ways that get the task done, especially in comparison to how some "other officers" do things.

> I have pride in myself. I can do things other officers can't do. I'm the type who treats inmates like they'd want to be treated. I try to treat them as I'd want to be treated. I get along good where others don't. I'm ashamed of the way some guys operate.
>
> I've also developed skills in manipulating them (inmates) into doing things. Doing what they don't want to do. For me, it's a skill. Where before I said do this and that's all, now I can take and get it done. I've become a good talker.

Finally, among these experienced officers there is a distinct impression that they are now identifying more with their occupations, rather than disavowing their work.

> Lots of guys would rather quit at the end of the day as soon as they can. I go in at 7:45 a.m. and there are times I've worked to 4 p.m. and past. In the "box" I used to work until 5 p.m. and after almost everyday. If I'm going overboard to keep inmates in the "box" or where I work now, it's strictly business, part of the job.

For "newer" officers pride and opportunities to contribute appear to be derived from the realization that they can be "personally effective" in the prison world.

> It makes you feel great to see how you can run a block smoothly and wonder if you can keep it up.

* * *

> Where I can come into work and walk into the control center and look at inmates and they're reacting to *me*. Reacting to *my* program. Not horsing around. I can see them complying with my procedures. Inmates are calling me Mister and I don't even know them. From word of mouth inmates who I haven't worked with know me and my program. That gives you confidence when you come in. You know you're in control.

This "new officer" emphasis on order and control contrasted with the experienced officers' emphasis on "smooth operations" and helping inmates with problems is understandable when one realizes that these new officers entered correctional work during the "chaotic" period of Auburn during the early 1980s. Here we see institutional goals and concerns being translated into new officer self/task definition.

SUMMARY—1986

While salary and benefits have improved over the past ten years, increased opportunities for officers to satisfy "higher level needs" have increased the amount of satisfaction officers derive from their workplace. Improved advancement opportunities, the increased likelihood of supervisory, institutional and departmental recognition for the work officers do, and expanded opportunities for input have addressed many of the deficiencies identified by these officers in 1976. While these new conditions are certainly a *change* for these experienced officers, they form the basis of a different work-person relationship for *new* officers hired during the past five years. For these officers there are new sets of expectations and a *reduction* in opportunities for involvement in the future can be expected to have a more negative impact than the "uninvolvement" that existed in 1976. The links between generational change and organizational change again surface as an issue to be explored.

NOTES

[1]Maslow, Abraham. *Motivation and Personality*. New York: Harper and Row, 1954.

[2]Sherif, Muzafer. *Social Interaction*. Chicago: Aldine Publishing Company, 1967, p. 179.

[3]Ibid., p. 186.

GUARDS IN THE PRISON COMMUNITY

IV

The portrait which emerges from the collective experience of the correctional officers at Auburn gives shape, depth and substance to the traditional caricature of correctional officers as passive and manipulated prison operatives. The words of these officers provide us with a new view of the prison world from the officers' perspective. This view shows us that officers *act* as well as react; that they *manipulate* their environment as much as they are manipulated by others; that they *define their own tasks as much as their work is defined by their formal job descriptions;* that they *experience and cope with stress and derive rewards* from their work in ways far more complex and varied than the traditional anti-inmate correctional officer subculture description would lead us to expect. The material in this section attempts to access the impact of these findings on our understanding of correctional officers' contributions to life in the prison community.

Guards in the Prison Community

9

In the preceding chapters I have tried to portray the diversity and general character of the guards' tasks and work environment as guards perceive and experience them. In this final chapter I shall attempt to place this portrait within the larger context of the prison community as a whole. I will draw some conclusions and speculate about the significance of this portrait for our understanding of the correction officer's human relationships with both inmates and fellow officers and about the guard's contribution to the management of the prison.

HUMAN RELATIONSHIPS WITH INMATES

From an organizational perspective the correction officer's role in the prison community has traditionally been perceived in terms of custody. As members of a custodial staff, officers are concerned with maintaining institutional security, order and discipline, supervising inmates and enforcing rules. The Joint Commission on Correctional Manpower and Training found these activities to be characteristic of institutional correctional staffs.[1]

Where efforts are made to enhance or expand the correction officers' work role, these efforts focus almost exclusively upon behaviors designed to "change" inmates, or in some way influence inmates' postinstitutional life. For example, the Joint Commission on Correctional Manpower and Training observes that:

> The modern goals of rehabilitating the offender and facilitating his reintegration into the community make different demands upon the correctional system and its workers. They must accept the responsibility for developing a new repertory of change skills: skills to help offenders change through rehabilitation....[2]

By examining the correction officer's role from the officer's perspective, however, I found that neither the traditional custodial nor the proposed "change agent" roles adequately describe the guards' contribution to the life of the correctional community. While guards recognize the necessity of performing the role in custody and security functions and assume an inability to influence inmate rehabilitation, many officers appear to assume, at least partially, a role as the prison's "human services" worker. By defining *at least part* of their work in "human services" terms, officers concern themselves with the inmate's "here and now" institutional life, rather than his future outside the walls. As a human services worker, the officer responds to opportunities and occasionally seeks opportunities to ease the "pains of imprisonment" experienced by inmates. As a *provider of goods and services*, the officer lessens the inmate's material deprivation. As an *institutional referral agent or advocate*, the officer provides the inmate with a chance to exercise autonomy, albeit indirectly. If an inmate knows an officer will intervene on his behalf, the inmate can influence his environment by approaching an officer with a problem. At the same time, the officer lessens the inmate's frustration with the slowness of bureaucratic responses. The human services role also demands that the officer deal with the emotional and psychological problems of *inmate institutional adjustment*, including institutional concerns and conflicts, and personal or family problems.

That a substantial number of correction officers tend to define their work, at least in part, in "human services" terms, adds a new dimension to a conception of the "guards' function"—a dimension whose existence was previously assumed to represent exceptional correctional officer behavior or was implicitly denied.[3] However, human services appears to account for much of the "real substance" of correction officer work in prison. Human services behavior appears to arise spontaneously from the interaction of individual officers with inmates and the institutional environment. I suggest that it is precisely because such behavior lies outside of the formal institutional structure that its potential for easing the "pains of imprisonment" is enhanced. Inmate-officer interactions centering on a "human service" problem would seem to allow both officers and inmates an opportunity to meet as individuals, rather than as representatives of an organization or a "deviant" group. By acting as an "individual" rather than as an officer, the officer allows the inmate to drop the suspiciousness with which the inmate normally views the officer, thus enhancing the probability that the officer's intervention will have positive results.[4] The person-to-person rather than guard-inmate character of the relationship between prisoners and their keepers seems to extend for many officers into their experience of authority and the rule enforcement process as well.

With regard to the correction officer's experience of authority, for example, the assumption that officers possess authority merely because of their position and that authority is therefore something they must spend their time struggling to defend is called into question, at least from the perspective of a large number of officers. The assumption of "theoretical dominance,"[5] as Sykes describes it, may in fact be the antithesis of the manner in which many officers experience "authority." Some officers differentiate sharply between power and authority, viewing authority as something to be earned through the process of personal interaction with inmates. Authority as it is experienced by these officers is the "legitimate exercise of power," and the legitimacy they seek can be granted only by those over whom the power is exercised, the inmates. From the perspective of these officers, inmate-officer interactions not only provide inmates with oppor tunities to corrupt the authority of the officer, but they also provide the officer with an opportunity to legitimize his authority over inmates.

When a policeman makes a decision concerning *when* and *how* to enforce the law, his decision is viewed as an "exercise of discretion."[6] However, analogous correction officer behavior, decisions concerning *when* and *how* to enforce rules, is looked upon as an "exercise in corruption."[7] This perspective sees the decision *not to enforce rules* as a corollary of the necessity to gain inmate cooperation and insufficient power. Nowhere in the literature does one find a reference to correction officer discretion in rule enforcement, let alone descriptions of the factors involved in correction officer decision-making concerning when and how *to enforce* rules. However, examining rule enforcement from the guard's perspective revealed a number of realistic assumptions and positive motives involved in the officer's enforcement-nonenforcement decisions. The decision to enforce or not to enforce specific rules is related to specific situations, and the selection of an appropriate enforcement strategy is an extremely complex calculus, reflecting a number of interacting factors. The attitudes and needs of the officer, his views of past and future violations, his perception of the rule enforcement interaction, his assessment of situational factors, such as the location of the interaction, the time at which it takes place, the presence or absence of other inmates, and the demeanor of the inmate or inmates involved all play a part in determining whether and how an officer enforces an observed rule violation.[8] These findings raise questions concerning the validity of traditional assumptions concerning the dynamics of the correction officer's ability to manage inmate behavior in a prison setting.

The officer stands to gain much more than cooperation from his person-to-person interactions with inmates. With few opportunities to experience a sense of accomplishment from his work or to achieve recognition, confronted by feelings of powerlessness and isolation in his work environment, the officer finds in his relationships with inmates opportunities to fulfill his needs for meaning and self-esteem, to increase his sense of competency and to reduce his feelings of aloneness. Moreover, the officer's perception that he shares frustrations with inmates and occupies a position similar to the inmate in relation to the prison administration may enhance the amount of sympathetic understanding officers feel toward inmates. Social distance between an officer and an inmate might more accurately be perceived as the result of an interaction between the needs of the officer and the needs of an inmate, as well as a reflection of situational factors associated with specific job assignments, and not merely a reflection of the degree to which the inmate has managed to corrupt the officer.

GUARDS AS A "GROUP"

While a variety of factors brings guards and inmates closer together, forces also seem to be at work driving the guards apart from their peers. When I began this study I expected evidence of relatively strong group identification among correction officers—an identification characterized by uniform opinions focusing upon the virtues of solidarity and secrecy, with standardized sanctions imposed on those violating group norms. At Auburn, at least, it seems that correction officers generally experience a sense of group unity to the extent that they form a "work group." In the institution they are dependent on each other for support in times of crisis and at times for information and cooperation while they attempt to carry out their normal work duties. As recruits, however, these correction officers did not appear to benefit from close apprenticeship relationships with more experienced officers of the sort that have been found characteristic of the police. These correction officers most often learned how to do their jobs on their own after experiencing hostility, rather than cooperation, from more experienced officers. With the advent of a correction officers' training academy and the introduction of a bidding system for assigning institutional jobs, this initial period of isolation now appears to be diminishing.

The existence of a correction officer subculture capable of influencing the attitudes and behaviors of individual officers is not something that can safely be assumed, at least during periods of institutional normalcy. Rather than a cohesive group with widely accepted norms and strong sanctions for violations of such norms, the "regime of the custodians" appears to be a highly fragmented collectivity of individuals. Though their work sometimes requires interdependence, the correction officers at Auburn maintain a high degree of independence in both attitude and behavior. Rather than maintaining close personal relationships with other officers off the job, many correction officers go their own way, seeking to avoid personal contact with other officers outside of the institution.

A number of forces would seem to be at work at inhibiting tendencies toward group cohesion and identification. First, officers desire to be judged as individuals and seek ways to think of themselves as somehow different from other officers. Second, correction officers tend to accept the negative image attached to their profession and thus may not want to identify themselves with their job. By placing distance between himself and other officers, the individual also places himself apart from the stereotyped image traditionally associated with his job. In addition, the lack of functional interrelations among various job assignments tends to isolate most officers on their specific institutional tasks. That individual group ties among prison guards are weak is not surprising when one considers the lack of forces that theoretically tend to foster group cohesiveness.[9] They became members of the guards' group not because they desired to become "guards," but rather because they wanted to become "civil service workers" with job security and regular pay. There is no identification with "group goals" or "organizational goals" of the prison. Rather, work goals are individual expressions of the relationship between self-derived needs and the opportunities offered by specific job assignments. The guard's perception of leadership, decision-making and communication within the institution discourages active participation in his group and fosters an atmosphere of suspicion and distrust. Expectancies concerning what a guard can derive from his role are lowered the longer he remains a guard, and the guard remains a member of the group not because he prefers it to other alternatives, but rather because other alternatives are perceived as closed.

What group solidarity officers do experience appears to arise as a response to perceived threats from either inmates or correctional administrators. That group solidarity may quickly form on top of a general dissension of opinions might be partially explained by the existence of "pluralistic ignorance" among correction officers. That is, individual officers are of the opinion that officers as a group hold certain beliefs, though such generalized opinions do not exist, or at least did not seem to during my research. In response to a threat, however, assumed "group" beliefs, which few individuals actually hold, may form the basis of a group identity with which each feels the others agree.[10] In the ongoing life of the prison community, guard-inmate relations seem to be more salient and more positive than guard-"guard group" relationships—at least for the guards at Auburn.

GUARDS AND PRISON MANAGEMENT: INDUSTRIAL SABOTAGE IN PRISON

Traditionally the work goals of the correction officer are described as if they were the same as the conflicting goals ascribed to the organization for which he works.[11] Resolving conflicts between organizational goals is assumed to occupy much of the officer's time and to exert a strong influence on his behavior. At Auburn, however, these correctional philosophies have little relevance for the working officers who spend their time and effort pursuing their immediate, individually-defined goals. Officers desire to keep active, to maintain a degree of control over their work and to stay out of trouble and sometimes even to stay away from inmates. Faced with a work environment laden with fear, mental tension, uncertainty, isolation, inconsistency and boredom, correction officers are more motivated to develop strategies to cope with these conditions than to pursue management goals. Lacking institutionalized opportunities for achievement and recognition, correction officers interact with inmates and other parts of their work environment (e.g. their specific tasks) to create opportunities through which they can satisfy these personal needs.

From what I have learned it appears that the correction officer is an active participant in the community life of his institution. As an active participant, the officer is capable of both maintaining the community's ongoing processes or disrupting them. In this regard this research may have implications for the management of correctional institutions and for our understanding of the officer's role in the institution's changing social system. I hypothesize that a link between the correction officer's behavior and the maintenance or disturbance of the prison status quo can be found if one considers the analog of "industrial sabotage."

In industry, industrial sabotage produces damaged or faulty products or breakdowns which stop production. An HEW Task Force informs us that:

> In the production world where everything is alike, sabotage may be a distortion of the guild craftsman's signature, a way of asserting individuality in a homogeneous world—the only way for the worker to say, "That's mine." It may also be a way of striking back against the hostile, inanimate objects that control the worker's time, muscles and brain. Breaking a machine in order to get some rest may be a sane thing to do.[12]

At first glance this description of industrial sabotage may appear to have little relationship to the work of the correction officer. "People-work," after all, involves human beings who are not inanimate. However, from the description of work-related behavior and attitudes of correction officers provided above, one can appreciate the capability of officers to affect disruptively the "productive capacity" of correctional institutions.

One of the "products" produced by correction officers is smoothly functioning work areas. Order and security are maintained in such areas and few problems are generated. Smoothness in operation may result from a number of "informal accommodations" between inmates and officers, between officers and the institutional administration and between inmates and administration. It is with respect to these accommodations and the production of order and smoothness that correction officers may engage in behavior whose result, if not purpose, is to cause "institutional breakdowns."[13] Forcing breakdowns in the system may make the officer's job more difficult, but it also provides the officer with a sense of control over his environment, especially when there is an increment in the alienation and powerlessness experienced by many officers.

Sabotaging the status quo, however, makes the administrator's position more difficult than the officer's position; and it is the administrator who, in the final analysis, is responsible for the institution's functioning and thus becomes the inviting target of "sabotage" activities.

A number of examples of breakdowns in officer-administration accommodations can be found in the literature. Oscar Gursky, in a study of role conflict in a prison camp, describes the effects of a change in camp administration on the custodial staff. Here the change eventually developed into inmate hostility and violence. Gursky reports three staff reactions to the "tightening up" process:

1. A decline in old informal groups among staff;
2. An inability of the new supervisor to enlist the staff's cooperation in enforcing new policies because of his overcommitment to the custodial goal; and
3. The lack of direct communication channels from inmates to the guards and to the supervisor, resulting in a lack of knowledge by the chief policy-maker of the impact of his decisions.[14]

The staff at Gursky's camp failed to cooperate with the supervisor even though a disturbance eventually occurred as a result.

The Attica Commission reported that many experienced officers, knowledgeable in the ways of maintaining order in the prison, began to move to positions on wall posts as soon as the "bidding" system of job assignments was established. This movement out of the institution by experienced officers left the most inexperienced officers inside to deal with inmates. According to the Commission, the assignment of officers to blocks rather than specific companies also meant that inmates not only had to deal with inexperienced officers, but were faced with different officers nearly every day. These conditions, according to the Commission, were the result of officer reaction to changes that they perceived as adversely affecting their ability to manage their own affairs. According to the Commission, "most officers interviewed by the Commission now agreed that this movement was disastrous."[15]

At Auburn there is some evidence that correction officers react to dissatisfaction by engaging in "sabotage-type" behaviors, even during periods of relative institutional stability. For example, an officer may, as a general work strategy, attempt to adapt administrative directives affecting his work area to the "realities" of the situation. In doing so, he helps to maintain smoothness in institutional procedures by adjusting for circumstances of which the administrator was unaware. However, if conditions begin to change and if administrative directives come to be perceived as severely impinging on the officer's ability to control his work environment, the officer's belief that he has no opportunity to provide input into that decision may lead him to abandon his attempts to fit directives to the "realities" of his job. The administrator does not anticipate the difficulties that flow from his directives because the officer previously had managed to prevent such difficulties from surfacing. However, as the officer's discontent increases, he may engage in the sort of rigid behavior of which he normally does not approve. The officer justifies such action by arguing, "It's not my responsibility"; "If that's the way *they* want to do it, it's okay with me. Let them pay for it." This would seem to confirm Merton's hypothesized "bureaucratic" response.[16]

I hypothesize that a link between the conditions that produce job dissatisfaction among correction officers and the occurrence of behavior contrary to the officer's sense of "effective" behavior (effective because it minimizes difficulties), might be found in the officer's perception of his "responsibility" and in conditions that lead the officer to assume or divest himself of the responsibility for activities in his area. By manipulating "the burden of responsibility" the correction officer is able to accept personal responsibility for his work under normal conditions while placing the responsibility for problems on the prison administration when normal conditions are upset. In this way the officer finds "sanctions" for behavior of which he generally does not approve.

When it comes to the correctional administrators, we find that it is easy for officers to look upon them as the "outgroup"—referred to as "they" and "the people up front." Lack of meaningful contact with administrators places the administrators apart. The "administration" takes on a stereotyped image of "callous, calculating manipulators," attempting to intervene in the officer's work environment, usually to his detriment, with motivations that are generally perceived as suspect. Contact between officers and "higher-ups" is not seen as contact between equals. The officer may say that he is being "treated like a child" or "like a number," feeling "dehumanized by the administration."[17]

During his "normal" work situation, the goals of the organization for which he works appear to have little meaning for the officer. As most officers perceive them, organizational goals are often unclear and sometimes contradictory. When an officer says, "I really don't know what they're [the administration] trying to do" or "Their policies really have no effect on me doing my job," he appears to be saying that he performs his duties in ways which fulfill more immediate personal goals.

However, when the status quo becomes upset and organizational goals begin to change from, say, custody to treatment or treatment to custody and such changes begin to upset the officer's ability to pursue *his* goals in the usual fashion, I suggest that officer may react by choosing one of many organizational goals available (not necessarily the ones the organization desires to pursue at the moment) and substitute such goals for his own. To the extent that there is conflict over goals in the prison administration, conflict may be enhanced at the line-officer level, as different officers align themselves with different factions. I would hypothesize that the behavior of the individual officer pursuing a segmental organizational goal may contribute little to disrupting the institutional routine; but many officers working at cross-purposes may magnify the extent of "institutional breakdown."[18]

SUGGESTIONS FOR ADMINISTRATORS

Job dissatisfaction among correction officers can create problems for institutional administrators and for the officers themselves. Worker absenteeism and "sabotage activities" can limit the effectiveness of institutional programming and potentially lead to institutional disruptions. To the extent that a relationship exists between absenteeism and job dissatisfaction and to the extent that speculations about industrial sabotage are true, the alleviation of correction officer job dissatisfaction should be a major priority of the correctional administrator.

Correction administrators often consider the potential reaction of the inmate population to correctional policy decisions and occasionally provisions are made to allow inmate participation in some of the decisions that affect their lives. The theory behind such practices is that inmates who participate in decisions will have a stake in seeing that decisions are effectively carried out.[19]

Correction officer participation in decision-making, however, has not been seen as essential to the implementation of correctional decisions. Perhaps this is the case because the officer has long been perceived by administrators as the "foot soldier" in a military-style organization of the prison's staff. Being the foot soldier, the officer's job is to follow orders, not to participate in their formulation. The spread of public employee unionization, to be sure, is beginning to reduce the comfort with which correctional administrators can maintain this view.[20] Where employees' grievance procedures are utilized as an alternative to participation in planning, an adversary relationship between employee and management is apt to develop, and where such procedures are viewed by the employee as ineffective, they become another source of worker discontent, increasing the feelings of impotence they were designed to alleviate. If correction officer dissatisfaction is to be accepted as a problem in need of a solution, and if the perceptions and feelings associated with that dissatisfaction are to be addressed, one must consider enhancing collaborative relationships between correctional administrators and correction officers.

Traditional in-service training courses generally attempt to enhance skills that correction officers are called upon to perform frequently or which will be needed in emergencies. Report-writing, inmate-packing techniques (preparing inmates for transfer or discharge), security procedures and first-aid training are an important part of a correction officer's repertoire of job-related skills. However, by focusing in-service training programs upon such traditional goals and skills, their potential benefit to institutional management and to the officers involved is severely limited. Training sessions designed to encourage officers to share information concerning what they find to be successful methods of dealing with inmate problems would seem to be appropriate. Techniques such as the "critical incident" approach would appear to be appropriate in helping to focus officer attention on issues relevant to their jobs.[21] Even if officers failed to learn new techniques from discussion, such training sessions help to break down the isolation experienced by many officers and can decrease their alienation from their work and their workplace. They might also provide the prison administration with valuable insights into the "reality" of policy implementation. In-service training courses can also serve as a vehicle to increase correction officer participation in decisions that affect their work situation.

To come to terms with correction officer work concerns, training sessions might reveal problems related to the implementation of administrative policy and can be aimed at developing solutions to such problems. Duffee describes experimental training programs in which officers studied the organizational operations and structure of a minimum security institution and tried to identify and solve problems in the day-to-day operations of the institution.[22] Ultimately, the success of such programs depends on the willingness of the institutional administration to accept officer suggestions for procedural improvement. However, the potential for reducing correction officer job dissatisfaction by increasing their sense of competency, participation and work-related self-esteem ("the administration thinks I'm worthy of being listened to"), as well as in improving the problem-solving skills of officers, would suggest that such training schemes are worthy of wider application and implementation.

SUGGESTIONS FOR FUTURE RESEARCH

Having described correction officer behavior at Auburn in a wide variety of work situations and officer reactions to the environment in which they work, it remains to be seen whether these findings reflect the experience of other officers in other maximum security institutions or in other types of correctional settings. Should further studies be done, it will be necessary to account for similarities and differences that may exist.

This research highlights a number of areas descriptively, such as inmate-officer interactions resulting from the officers' attempts to deal with rule violations. The characteristics of the inmates and officers involved in the situations I describe might be examined to determine the effects of actor variation on the outcome of the interaction. The varieties of inmate-officer interaction occurring in cell blocks, industrial areas, the yard or other institutional locations and their outcomes might be analyzed to determine what influence ecological factors have on both officer and inmate behavior.

In this regard the effects of both inmate and staff turnover rates on the character of different prison communities also merits exploration. It may be that staff turnover is high in locations where alternative employment opportunities are readily available—for example, in prisons located in large urban areas. With high turnover rates there exists the possibility that human ties between staff and inmates may be weaker than in institutions with low turnover rates. Also, turnover rates *within* a prison may affect a prison's sense of community. Frequent changes in correction officer or inmate work assignments may have a destabilizing effect or prevent the development of institutional stability.

Variations in the relative strengths of interpersonal relationships among officer groups in various institutions also need to be examined and accounted for. The effects of correction officer unionization on the behavior of correction officers must be determined. A study of officer "grievances" and their disposition might serve to shed light on the possibilities of reducing conflict between line officers and the correctional administration.

Where officer attitudes have been examined, they were usually scrutinized to highlight differences between the perceptions of correction officers in different institutional settings, between correction officers and treatment staff or supervisors or between correction officers and inmates toward various treatment programs or correctional goals.[23] This examination of correction officer job satisfaction and dissatisfaction suggests that the attitudes of correction officers are themselves a worthy subject for future examination. My findings suggest that correction officer attitudes are more complex and variable than previously thought.[24] I found that correction officers perceive and evaluate different aspects of their work environments differently. What is important for one officer may not be important for another; what is perceived negatively by one officer may be perceived positively by another. Further research into correction officer attitudes might seek to establish the relationships among the various dimensions of correction officer perceptions of his environment. In addition, the relationships between attitudinal measures and correction officer behaviors (rule enforcement styles, social distance patterns) also merit further attention.

Our findings relative to the relationship between job location and officer work concern, rule enforcement and social distance also highlight the need for further research into the effect of ecological factors on officer perceptions and behavior and on inmate attitudes and behavior. It may be that officer perception of inmates and their behavior toward inmates are less dependent on generalized officer attitudes than they are on situational factors governing the varying contexts within which officers and inmates interact.

CHANGE WITHOUT CHAOS: 1976-1986

Between 1976 and 1986 the place of the correctional officer in the community life of Auburn Prison underwent some subtle and not so subtle shifts. As these officers see it, behavioral changes in the inmate culture, the intrusion of the state-level bureaucracy into institutional affairs, and a growing and increasingly youthful and non-local officer corps, are altering the ways correctional officers at Auburn relate to inmates and to each other. In addition, improved communication, greater opportunities for providing input and receiving recognition and increased structure in determining the details of job assignments have reduced the levels of institutional paranoia and alienation and have helped correctional officers begin to identify more closely with their occupations.

From Discretion To Structure and Accountability

In 1976, correctional officers exercised a great deal of discretion in determining the shape of the tasks required on specific job assignments and in their helping and rule enforcement dealings with inmates. Officers learned the ins and outs of specific tasks through experience and this experience was or was not passed on informally in ways determined by individual officers. In their human services role informal mechanisms and networks dominated, as individual officers served as gate-keepers between the inmates and a variety of institutional services and as informal therapists helping troubled inmates cope with their institutional problems. Though formal procedures existed to link inmates to services it was often the discretion of individual officers that determined whether these procedures worked smoothly or not. The discretion officers exercised and its human services content provided officers with a sense of control and purpose in their work.

By 1986, both officer task definition and inmate service provision had become more structured. Redeployment, with its emphasis on detailed written job descriptions, reduced the amount of behaviorally-measured creative task development demanded from officers. However, to the extent that redeployment involved officers in preparing written descriptions of their work, it fostered greater understanding of specific job assignments. The development and implementation of written policy and procedure to govern both officer and inmate behavior and the communication of these new guidelines to both officers and inmates formalized service provision networks. Again, officer participation in the process of policy and procedure development and change allowed officers to develop increased feelings of competency and opportunities to demonstrate those competencies in meaningful ways. Greater inmate awareness of their "rights" under the guidelines and increased officer clarity concerning job expectations are providing structure and predictability in officer-inmate relationships where informal officer discretion previously dominated.

Rather than reacting negatively to this reduction of discretionary decision-making power, the officers at Auburn appear to have embraced the structure provided by procedural guidelines and job assignment descriptions. It is less likely now that officers will be asked to justify "their" individual/personal decisions. Challenges to authority are less likely to be interpreted as challenges to "personal authority." Now, more and more, authority is becoming "legalistic." The increased availability of middle-level supervisors and grievance procedures makes officers much more accountable for their actions. This is especially true in rule enforcement practices. Infraction reports are reviewed by supervisors before submission and officer decisions can be challenged by inmates who have assistance in challenging, and hearings which establish the validity of officer complaints. From the perspective of these experienced officers, structure and accountability are preferable to discretion. Structure lessens the likelihood that officer inmate interactions will become "personal" confrontations and reduces opportunities for officer/inmate conflict.

From Human Services To Law Enforcement And Security

Perhaps the most distressing characteristic of Auburn in 1986 is the diminution of officers' focus on human services work, especially as it manifests itself in helping inmates cope with the pains of imprisonment. While written guidelines were beginning to structure and formalize officer/inmate interactions, changes in the nature and prevalence of inter-inmate violence and the increased availability of drugs have led many correctional officers to re-emphasize institutional security (focusing on reducing incidents of violence *not necessarily helping individuals*) and law enforcement (rule violation) aspects of their work. Drugs, contraband weapons, extortion and protective custody have become central concerns. Rather than acting as brokers for services or helping inmates cope with the "pains of imprisonment," through *personal interventions*, frisks, drug testing and violence prevention became ways of monitoring and controlling the increasingly predatory character of the inmate society as a whole. Though human services activities as described in 1976 still occupy some officer time, changing conditions have reduced their relative saliency for these correctional officers.

From Human To Bureaucratic Relations

From the officers' perspective in 1976 it was clear that much of what characterized officer/inmate relations was not determined by formal demands of the role. Rather, the lack of formal training, the reluctance of experienced officers to assist new ones and positive initial contacts with inmates led many officers to define their relationships with inmates in *human* terms. The relatively atomized inmate world, characterized by self-oriented coping strategies, permitted officers to contribute readily to the inmates' adjustment to confinement. The perceived unpredictability and unresponsiveness of formal "helping services" reinforced the feeling that informal assistance to inmates was an appropriate response. In addition, the perception that inmates rejected formal concern of counselors as "paid for" and, therefore, "not real," made the officers feel that their informal assistance was more valued.

By 1986, however, the spread of formal training to all incoming officers in the mid-1970s, assistance from experienced officers and an emphasis on formal job assignment descriptions and formal procedures have created a work atmosphere more likely to produce formal, bureaucratized officer/inmate relations. Emphasis on accountability and improved inmate access to counseling services and the inmates' ability to handle personal problems utilizing telephone and visits have reduced likelihood that officers will perceive that the "human" touch officers previously contributed will be needed. Finally, the increase in predatory group-oriented inmate violence and changes in rule enforcement procedures have shifted the officers' interpretation of inmate rule violation behavior from a "personal failure" to a more legalistic failure to comply with the rules.

ORGANIZATIONAL CHANGE AT AUBURN 1976-1986

Many of the officers re-interviewed in 1986 were quite surprised to find themselves describing how Auburn and the Department of Corrections had changed in the previous ten years. They were also dumbfounded to realize that Auburn still functioned rather smoothly despite all the changes, especially those that resulted in more benefits for inmates and more controls on and reduction in officer discretion. In addition, as these officers have seen Auburn's population change[25] to one with a higher proportion of "troublesome" inmates, they believe Auburn is gaining a reputation as an institution which handles the most troublesome inmates with the fewest problems and still maintains high-intensity inmate programming.

If one reads the literature on prison change one might expect that such changes would be associated with organizational turmoil. Jacobs,[26] Irwin,[27] and DiIulio[28] each describe the impact of administrative and court-ordered change on the prisons and prison systems they studied. As these changes related to prison staff, Jacobs, for example, describes the response of Stateville's staff to the emergence of professional administration (1970-1975) as follows:

> Staff demoralization and disorganization resulted in the demise of security within the prison. Violence escalated. Between 1971 and 1972, four inmates escaped from Stateville. The old Reganites saw their world collapsing around them.
>
> The disorganization was so great that the capacity to complete basic tasks was reduced. Inmates did not get showers; the food areas did not get cleaned; lawyers were made to wait hours because tickets could not get delivered.[29]

This does not seem to have been the case at Auburn. Though violence in terms of inter-inmate assaults has increased and changed its nature, this appears mostly to be a reflection of changes in the inmate population and culture rather than administrative chaos. Though changes in the relative saliency of bureaucratic and humanistic approaches to correctional officer work may have contributed somewhat to this increase of inmate assaults, the basic functioning of the institution (as reflected in correctional officer order maintenance activities) appears to have gone on as always. How can this be?[30]

Conditions of Change

Unlike the prisons and prison systems described by Jacobs, Irwin and DiIulio, the conditions at Auburn between 1976 and 1986 reflect a high degree of organizational and administrative stability. Robert Henderson has been superintendent at Auburn since 1972. Thomas Coughlin has been Commissioner since 1978. In this respect, these administrators have been able to oversee the process by which "...correctional philosophy can be translated into policy decrees and then into a bureaucratic routine of administrative action..."[31] and they appear to have done so without developing the "cult of personality" so evident in DiIulio's descriptions of Texas, California, Michigan and Jacobs' discussion of Stateville.

Secondly, many of the conditions that accompanied staff demoralization and disorganizations in the other systems and institutions seem to have been absent from Auburn during this period (and in all probability in the preceding years). Auburn's correctional officer corps was and still is characterized by racial homogeneity. Ethnic heterogeneity and status cliques and hierarchies often reflected divisions in the officer corps with the pre-1976 era. By 1986, the invasion of younger officers and "non-Auburnians" had lessened the saliency of ethnic identification. In 1976, Auburn's officers were not particularly loyal to either the institution or to the warden,[32] though they did manifest a certain degree of pride in their belief that Auburn was recognized as the state's "educational" institution. Though some officers described their loyalty to specific supervisors, the relative autonomy of the officer and supervisor made such loyalty more a reflection of friends working together to keep their area running smoothly than of comrades in arms working together to control a recalcitrant inmate population.

In part, the generally positive approach of Auburn's staff to change can be seen to have resulted from absence of change in the racial makeup in the officer corps (an important factor at Stateville and in California), and in the long-term stability in departmental and institutional leadership. In addition, the general lack of paramilitary and stereotypical anti-inmate attitudes and behaviors, and the relative autonomy of officer task definition and behavior allowed officers to react to changes individually rather than as a group. This occurred in spite of Auburn's unionization and the officer strike of 1979. Thus, the set of starting conditions at Auburn was substantially different from that of institutions and systems that faced turmoil.

The Change Process

Though these structural and attitudinal factors explain part of what happened at Auburn, I believe it is the processes of change and the attitudes toward change described by the officers and the Administration that differentiate Auburn from other institutions. As one officer who became a sergeant describes it:

> The department depends on how the pendulum swings. But I think it keeps going and they keep giving and giving. If years ago you said they'd have trailers and visits with wives and girlfriends... Who would have thought? What will it be next month? Like the telephones, now they can call anybody. At Auburn you don't like the policies but you will do them anyway. If this were Attica, and they said to give the keys to the inmates, they'd have a strike. At Auburn, if they told us to do that, we'd give the keys to the inmates.
>
> *How do you deal with this?*
>
> You don't. It's policy. It comes down and you have to comply with it. It's hard for some of the older officers to do that. They just look at things and shake their heads.
>
> *Does it affect the way you do your job?*
>
> No. You just do things. That's the way it is here. Something new will come along next week and you do that too. You don't have much opposition to change here; it's more or less accepted as part of what goes on.

This officer's comment (and those of many others) gives the distinct impression that *change* rather than *stability* has become institutionalized at Auburn. Innovation has been part of the institution's history and innovation has become part of what these officers expect. Auburn's administration and its staff reflect Gareth Morgan's analysis of "Organizations as Flux and Transformation." According to Morgan,

> One of the strengths of the theory of autopoiesis (the idea that "...systems can be recognized as having environments, but that relations with any environment are *internally* determined")[33] is that it shows us that while the preservation of an identity is fundamental for all living systems, there are different ways in which closure in relation to the environment can be achieved. When we recognize that the environment is not an independent domain, and that we don't necessarily have to compete or struggle against the environment, a completely new relationship can develop. Organizations committed to this kind of self-discovery are able to develop a kind of systemic wisdom. They become more aware of their role and significance within the whole, and of their ability to facilitate patterns of change and development that will allow their identity to evolve *along with* that of the wider system.[34]

In effect, the independent discretionary nature of task definition performance of officers in the pre-1976 period, their alienation from their work and the administration, their lack of training and lack of social interaction with their peers, their frustration with the lack and inconsistency of direction and clear communication enhanced the skills and knowledge base of these officers when their frustration was taped in the redeployment and policy procedure development process. This allowed these officers and the administration at Auburn to search for ways to incorporate the environment into their daily activities. Central office direction, court decisions, inmate and officer grievances now are perceived as part of the institution's internal environment rather than as threats. To the extent that problems resulting from institutional policy and procedures create problems which further policy and procedure development can address, the staff and administration at Auburn is demonstrating its organizational ability to learn to learn. In this way, the organization is ensuring its survival.

SUMMARY—1986

From the perspective provided by the experiences of the correctional officers at Auburn, it is clear that correctional reform does not have to be a painful, conflict-laden process. With involvement of and support for all parties, with open, clear and frequent communication, both planned (legal and administratively mandated change) and unplanned (changes in the inmate culture) variations in prison environments can be accommodated and accepted.

NOTES

[1]Joint Commission on Correctional Manpower and Training. *Perspectives on Correctional Manpower and Training*. Washington, DC: Joint Commission on Correctional Manpower and Training, 1970, p. 127. See also *Correction Officers Training Guide*. College Park, MD: The American Correctional Association, 1975, for a description of the correctional officers traditional functions.

[2]Joint Commission on Correctional Manpower and Training. *Perspectives on Correctional Manpower and Training*, p. 99.

[3]The denial of "human service" functions has also been characteristic of police work. See Goldstein, Herman. *Policing a Free Society*. Cambridge, MA: Ballinger Publishing Company, 1977, pp. 21-44. For an exception to this in the correctional literature see Toch, Hans. *Police, Prisons and the Problems of Violence*. Washington, DC: U.S. Government Printing Office, 1977.

[4]This observation regarding correction officer behavior is similar to observations made by Glaser:

> The more comprehensive and non-ritualized the duties of an employee become in dealing with inmates, the more he is inclined to treat them on the basis of their personal attributes toward them based on their class or social status, and inmates are inclined to reciprocate in kind.

Glaser, Daniel. *The Effectiveness of a Prison and Parole System*. Indianapolis, IN: Bobbs-Merrill Company, 1969, p. 88.

[5]Sykes, Gresham. *The Society of Captives*. New York: Atheneum, 1970, p. 94.

[6]See, for example, Davis, Kenneth Culp. *Police Discretion*. St. Paul, MN: West Publishing Company, 1975; Skolnick, Jerome N. *Justice Without Trial*. New York: John Wiley and Sons, 1966; Wilson, James Q. *Varieties of Police Behavior*. New York: Atheneum, 1971.

[7]See, for example, Sykes, Gresham M. *the Society of Captives*. Princeton, NJ: Princeton University Press, 1958; McCorkle, Lloyd M. "Guard-Inmate Relationships," in *The Sociology of Punishment and Correction*, edited by Norman Johnston, Leonard Savitz and Marvin M. Wolfgang. New York: John Wiley and Sons, 1962, pp. 419-422.

[8]These factors are similar to those involving police-juvenile interactions described by Werthman, Carl and Piliavin, Irving. "Gang Members and Ecological Conflict," *The Police*, edited by David J. Brodua. New York: John Wiley and Sons, 1967, pp. 56-98, and Piliavin, Irving and Briar, Scott. "Police Encounters with Juveniles," *American Journal of Sociology*, Vol. 70 (1964), pp. 206-214. See also Bittner, Egon. "The Police on Skid-Row: A Study of Peace Keeping," *American Sociological Review*, Vol. 32 (1967), pp. 699-715.

[9]See Cartwright, Dorwin. "The Nature of Group Cohesiveness," in *Group Dynamics*, edited by D. Cartwright and A. Zander. New York: Harper and Row, 1968, pp. 91-110.

[10]See Janis, Irving L. "Group Identification under Conditions of External Danger," in *Group Dynamics*, edited by D. Cartwright and A. Zander. New York: Harper and Row, 1968, pp. 80-90.

[11]Cressey, Donald R. "Contradictory Directives in Complex Organizations," in *Prison Within Society*, edited by Lawrence Hazelrigg. Garden City, NY: Anchor Books, 1968, pp. 477-496.

[12]*Work in America*, p. 88.

[13]See Wright, Erik Olin. *The Politics of Punishment*. New York: Harper and Row, 1977, p. 141.

[14]Gursky, Oscar. "Role Conflict in Organizations: A Study of Prison Camp Officials," in *Prison Within Society*, p. 466.

[15]New York State Special Commission on Attica. *Attica: The Official Report of the New York State Special Commission on Attica*. New York: Bantam Books, 1972, p. 126.

[16]See Merton, Robert K. "Bureaucratic Structure and Personality," in *Complex Organizations*, edited by Amitai Etzioni. New York: Holt, Rinehart and Winston, 1965, p. 66 for a description of this behavior in the "bureaucrat."

[17]See Duster, Troy. "Conditions for Guilt-Free Massacre," in *Sanctions for Evil: Sources of Social Destructiveness*, edited by Nevitt Sanford and Craig Comstock. Boston, MA: Beacon Press, 1971, pp. 25-36 for a discussion of conditions which allow military and police personnel to divest themselves of responsibility and engage in behavior they normally consider improper.

[18]From my experiences as a correctional worker, and observations of correctional workers made over the years, it became evident that the multiplicity of prison "goals" makes it possible for the individual worker to justify nearly every action in terms of some institutional goal. Goffman makes similar observations concerning the effect of multiple goals in "total institutions":

> It is less well appreciated that each of these goals of charters seems admirably suited to provide a key to meaning—a language of explanation that the staff, and sometimes the inmates, can bring to every crevice of action in the institution.
> (Goffman, Erving. *Asylums*. Garden City, NY: Anchor Books, 1961, p. 83.)

[19]Bennis, Warren. *Changing Organizations*. New York: McGraw-Hill Book Company, 1966, p. 136.

[20]A 1972 survey of correctional agencies reports that 38% of 53 adult correctional agencies indicated that they were negotiating a contract or presently operating under a contract negotiated with an employee organization. Morton, Joann B. and Beadles, Nicholas. "Collective Bargaining Activities in State Correctional Agencies," in *Readings in Public Employee/Management Relations for Correctional Administrators*. Athens, GA: Southeastern Correctional Management Training Council, University of Georgia, 1973, p. 87.

[21]Katsampes reports successfully utilizing this method to increase officer awareness of inmate problems. See Katsampes, Paul. "Changing Correction Officers: A Demonstration Study," *International Journal of Criminology and Penolgoy*, Vol. 3, No. 2 (1975), pp. 123-144. See also Toch, Hans, Grant, J. Douglas, and Galvin, Raymond T. *Agents of Change: A Study of Police Reform*. New York: John Wiley and Sons, 1975, for an application of this technique in the police sphere. See also Milan, M.A., Wood, L.F. and McKee, M. "The Correctional Officer as a Behavioral Technician," *Criminal Justice and Behavior*, Vol. 3, No. 4 (1976), pp. 345-360, for a discussion of a training project designed to instruct correction officers in the utilization of behavior modification techniques.

[22]Duffee, David. *Using Correctional Officers in Planned Change*. Washington, DC: National Institute on Law Enforcement, National Technical Information Service, 1972.

[23]See, for example, Mang, J. and Zastrow, L. "Inmates' and Security Guards' Perceptions of Themselves and Each Other: A Comparative Study," paper presented at meeting of American Criminological Society, Chicago, 1974. O'Leary, V. and Duffee, D. "Managerial Behavior and Correctional Policy." Albany, NY: School of Criminal Justice, 1970 (mimeograph); Brown, B., DuPont, R., Kozel, N.J. and Spevacek, J.D. "Staff Conceptions of Inmate Characteristics: A Comparison of Treatment and Custodial Staffs of Two Differing Institutions," "Role Conflict in Correctional Communities," in *The Prison: Studies in Institutional Organization and Change*, edited by Donald R. Cressey. New York: Holt, Rinehart and Winston, 1961, pp. 229-259.

[24]Our findings in this regard are similar to those of Regoli who suggests that Niederhoffer's Police Cynicism Scale is actually multidimensional. Regoli identifies five dimensions subsumed under Niederhoffer's general cynicism scale: cynicism toward relations with the public, toward organizational functions, about police dedication to duty, about police social solidarity and toward education and training. Regoli, Robert M. "An Empirical Assessment of Niederhoffer's Police Cynicism Scale," *Journal of Criminal Justice*, Vol. 4, No. 3 (1976), pp. 231-241.

[25]In discussing changes at Auburn with Superintendent Henderson in August of 1988, he informed me that inmates had to apply for transfer to Auburn during the 1960s and early 1970s. The school programs were for inmates who wanted a good education, the license plate shop for inmates who wanted to work and make some money. Because of the attractiveness of these programs, transfers to Auburn were made on a more selective basis. In the late 1970s and early 1980s, this policy changed as "quality" inmates were now placed in medium and minimum security institutions and "problem" inmates were now distributed across the maximum security system rather than concentrated in one or two institutions as was done in the 1960s and early 1970s. Thus, by the mid-1970s Auburn's population also included larger numbers of "problem" inmates. Now, in the 1980s, Auburn's reputation according to the officers reflects two central themes: 1) when the State wants to try out a program, Auburn is the first place it is put into effect; 2) Auburn handles the most troublesome inmates with the fewest problems, all while maintaining high intensity inmate programming (8/8/88—Personal Interview).

[26]James Jacobs, *Stateville*. Chicago: University of Chicago Press, 1977.

[27]John Irwin, *Prisons in Turmoil*. Boston: Little, Brown, 1980.

[28]John J. DiIulio, *Governing Prisons*. New York: The Free Press, 1987.

[29]Jacobs, *op. cit.*, p. 85.

[30]Many who have described prison change (for example, J. Irwin, *Prisons in Turmoil*, Boston: Little, Brown, 1980; J. Jacobs, *Stateville*, Chicago: University of Chicago Press, 1977; and J. DiIulio, Jr., *Governing Prisons*, New York: The Free Press, 1987) view the changes in prison regimes brought about by increased penetration of state bureaucracies into local prison affairs and court decisions in terms of the dynamics and distribution of power, authority and control among inmate, officer, administrative and central corrections department authorities. This "power" perspective may be

entirely correct with regard to the "politics" of prison change (a politics of change and crisis so important to the late 1960's and 1970's period they describe). However, from a behavioral perspective, an exclusive focus on power and authority may lock our understanding of prison dynamics into the stereotyped responses so evident in the classic Stanford Prison Experiment.

In listening to the correctional officers at Auburn discuss change, prison liberalization, court interaction, increased inmate autonomy a concern for the "loss of power" is surprisingly absent. One has the feeling that in spite of everything, officers at Auburn feel they are generally in control. What has changed for them is not their ability to control, but rather the manner in which they do it. Auburn officers seem to understand that while their discretionary decision making power was being limited in certain areas (particularly rule enforcement and control over formal human services functions), their ability to maintain order and control in the institution was not being destroyed.

[31]DiIulio, *op. cit.*, p. 241.

[32]See DiIulio, *op. cit.*, for a description of impact of institutional and personal loyalty in Texas, and Jacobs, *op. cit.*, in Stateville.

[33]Gareth Morgan, *Images of Organization*. Beverly Hills, CA: Sage, 1986, p. 238.

[34]Ibid., p. 245.

Appendix A

January 19, 1976

TO: ALL CORRECTION OFFICERS, AUBURN CORRECTIONAL FACILITY

FROM: ROBERT MALONEY

RE: RESEARCH ON VIEWS OF CORRECTION OFFICERS

During the next few months Mr. Lou Lombardo will be contacting some of you and asking for your cooperation in a research study he is conducting. His study is concerned with the work you do, your feelings about your work, the satisfactions and dissatisfactions you have with your work, the ways in which you handle your various duties and your general feelings about being a correction officer.

Mr. Lombardo is a full-time teacher at the Osborne School at Auburn Correctional Facility and is working on his Ph.D. degree at the School of Criminal Justice, SUNY, Albany. The help and information that you provide will help him to complete his degree requirements.

I believe Mr. Lombardo's research is unique and potentially very helpful to us as individual correction officers and as a union. Because he is coming directly to correction officers, instead of inmates or reformers, his research will give us an opportunity to influence correctional policies and practices as they relate to our jobs.

In order to gather the information he is seeking, Mr. Lombardo is asking you to participate in an interview. In order to minimize interference with your institutional work assignments and Mr. Lombardo's teaching schedule, the interviews will have to be conducted during both your and Mr. Lombardo's off-duty hours. Mr. Lombardo has assured me that your identities and any information you provide will be kept strictly confidential.

This research has been approved by Deputy Commissioner Quick and Deputy Commissioner Stanton of the Department of Program, Planning and Evaluation in Albany, and by Superintendent Henderson.

Since I believe that this research is in our interest as a union and in your interest as individual officers, I am asking you to give your fullest cooperation to Mr. Lombardo's research effort.

Sincerely yours,

Robert Maloney
President Local 1447
V.P. for Correction, Council 82 AFSCME

Appendix B

April 6, 1976

TO:

FROM: LOU LOMBARDO

, as Bob Maloney informed you in a letter he sent out last month, I am conducting a research study for my doctorate degree dealing with correction officers and their feelings toward their work. In order to do a thorough job, I am trying to interview as many officers as possible with all levels of experience and from all job assignments.

The interview generally lasts about two hours and covers a wide variety of subjects from what you like and don't like about your job to how inmates feel about officers. Most officers have found it convenient to be interviewed at Cayuga County Community College in Frank Sikora's office. Although either my home or the officer's home have sometimes proved better.

So that I can set up an interview schedule for the coming weeks, please indicate at the bottom of this sheet if you are willing to participate in this research and a good day and time for an interview. I am free any time except Monday thru Friday from 8 A.M. to 4 P.M., when I am teaching in the school. However, from April 15 to April 25 I am free all day. If you would like to be interviewed during this period please let me know. Also give me your phone number and when you can be reached so that I can contact you and set up a firm date.

Please fill out the bottom of this sheet and return it in my box (Box "L" in the institution mailboxes).

Thank you very much for your cooperation. I hope this research proves valuable for all concerned.

Yours truly,

Lou Lombardo

Best day of the week for an interview: ____________________

Best time of the day for an interview: ____________________

Preferred location for interview: ____________________

Phone number: ____________ Time when can be reached: ____________

Appendix C
Background Data Sheet and Interview Guide

1. AGE ________
2. EDUCATION: 1 = high school 4 = bachelor's degree
   2 = some college 5 = bachelor's degree plus
   3 = associate's degree 6 = master's degree
3. Number of college courses since becoming an officer ________
4. Educational level when became an officer ________
5. Number of weeks training before put on job ________
6. Number of in-service training courses completed ________
   Valuable? ________

WORK EXPERIENCE

1. Number of years as correction officer ________
2. Number of years at Auburn ________
3. Other institutions worked at: 1. ________ years ____
   2. ________ years ____ 3. ________ years ____
   Present job assignment ________ Shift ____
   a. Time on assignment ________ Bid? ____
      Why bid?
   b. Previous job assignments: 1. ________ Shift ____ years ____
      2. ________ Shift ____ years ____
      3. ________ Shift ____ years ____
   c. Preferred job assignment ________ Why? ____
   d. Job assignment least preferred ________ Why? ____
   e. Preferred shift ________ Why? ____
   f. Least preferred shift ________ Why? ____
   g. Determinant: Job ________ Shift ________ Why? ____
   h. Hours overtime 1975: ________

UNION ACTIVITY

Union member: Yes ____ No ____

Number of meetings attended 1975 ____

Number of grievances filed 1975 ____ Topics: a. ____________________

b. ____________________

c. ____________________

Is or was union officer: Yes ____ No ____

FAMILY BACKGROUND

Born in Auburn area: Yes ____ No ____

Other family members working at prison: Yes ____ No ____

RECRUITMENT

1. How did you come to be a correction officer?
2. Did you have any friends or relatives working there when you began work there?
3. What jobs did you hold before?

INITIAL EXPECTATIONS

a. What did you think about the prison before you began working there?
b. Did you find what you expected? How was it different?
c. What did you think the correction officer's job was like before you started?
d. Did you find what you expected? How was it different?
e. What did you expect convicts would be like before you started?
f. Did you find what you expected? How were they different?

JOB DESCRIPTION

If you had to describe to someone who did not know anything about your work, what you do as a correction officer, what would you tell him?

If you were to tell this person about the way inmates behave in prison, what would you tell him?

What's the biggest problem you have in doing your job?

What's the most difficult thing about your job?

JOB SATISFACTION

1. If some guy were thinking about becoming a correction officer and he asked you what the *BEST THING* about the job was, or what you found most satisfying, what would you tell him?
   Did you have any idea things would be this way when you started?
2. Are you satisfied with your pay?
   Is this a major concern of yours?

3. How about job security, are you satisfied with that?
   Is this a major concern of yours?
4. How about your personal relationships with other officers? How would you characterize these?
5. How about *opportunities to be recognized* for the job you do?
   Do you expect to be recognized for what you do?
6. How about feelings of *personal pride* in what you do?
   Do you expect that you would find personal pride?
   From what do you take personal pride?
7. How about opportunities for advancement?
   Is this a major concern of yours in your work?
8. How about opportunities to use your full capabilities? Do you have them? When does this happen?
   Is this a major concern of yours in your work?
   Do you feel you are accomplishing something in your work? What?

JOB DISSATISFACTION

1. If some guy were thinking about becoming an officer, and he asked you what the *WORST THING* about the job was, or what you found most dissatisfying about it, what would you tell him?
   How do you deal with this?
2. How about *what the department is trying to do*? Do its policies bother you in any way?
   How do you deal with this?
   Do they affect the way you do your job?
3. How about the *administration of this institution*? Do its policies *toward inmates* bother you?
   How do you deal with this?
   Do they affect your job in any way?
4. How about the *administration's policies toward officers*? Do they bother you?
   How do you deal with this?
   Does this affect the way you do your job?
5. How about your *immediate supervisors*? Do you have any problems with them?
   How do you deal with this?
   Does this affect the way you do your job?
6. Do you have any problems with the *routine* of the job?
   How do you deal with this?
   Does this affect the way you do your job?

7. Do you ever find your job *boring*?
   Does this bother you?
   Does this affect the way you do your job?
   How do you deal with this?
8. Do you ever feel that *different people expect different things of you*? How?
   Does this bother you?
   How do you deal with this?
9. Do you ever have any problems reconciling your *role as a security officer* and your *role as a counselor*?
   How do you deal with this?
10. How about finding out what's going on in the institution. How do you get information?
    Is it prompt?
    Is it accurate?

HELPING INMATES WITH PROBLEMS

What do you do when an inmate comes to you with an *institutional* problem?

How about if an inmate comes to you with a *personal* problem?

Do you ever find yourself discussing institutional problems you're experiencing with inmates?

Do you ever find yourself discussing your personal problems with inmates?

Do you ever try to find out if particular inmates are having problems? Seek out inmates with problems?

RULE ENFORCEMENT AND DEALING WITH INMATES

1. What things do you consider to be minor rule violations?
2. Suppose you observed an inmate violating one of these rules. What would you generally do about it?
   Why would you handle it in that way? What do you hope to gain by it?
3. What generally happens in a situation where you write a man up for a minor rule violation?
   How do you know when to write a man up, and when not to?
   How many write-ups last year? Last month?
4. What do you think the primary purpose of institutional rules is?
   How do you think inmates feel about rules?
   How about the way they're enforced?

5. If a new officer was coming into the institution, what would you tell him about maintaining authority and establishing authority over inmates?
   Where does your authority come from?
   Were you ever in a situation where you felt your authority challenged by an inmate? What happened?
   What did you do?
   How did the inmate react?
   Do you feel your *authority* slipping?
   How can you tell?
   Does it affect the way you do your job? How?
   What do you do when this happens?
6. How does an officer get the *respect* of inmates?
   Do you feel that inmates respect you? How can you tell?

GROUP ASPECTS

a. How do officers generally get along with one another?
b. Do you feel officers feel a loyalty toward one another?
c. Suppose that a new officer is coming into the institution now. How does he go about becoming accepted by other officers?
d. When you began as an officer, was it easy to become accepted by other officers? What was it like?
e. What kinds of things can get an officer into trouble with other officers?
f. What do other officers do about this? Do they treat him any differently? How?
g. Do you feel other officers feel about the things we've been talking about the way you do?
   In what ways are they different?
   In what ways are they the same?
h. Does pressure from other officers ever make you do things you wouldn't do otherwise? Like what?

REACTIONS OF PUBLICS

a. What do you think inmates generally think about correction officers?
b. How about the general public? What do you think they generally think about correction officers?
c. How does your family feel about your being a correction officer?

TREATMENT OF DEVIANTS

a. How do officers generally treat homosexuals here?
b. How do you deal with militant inmates? What are militants like anyway?

Appendix D
Tables

Table 1. Length of Experience for Comparison of Final Sample with Entire Officer Population

Months experience	Number in final sample	Number in population	Percent of population
1–48	8[a]	46	13
49–108	15[a]	136	38
109–168	7	45	13
169–228	10	68	19
229+	10	64	18
	50	359	101[b]

[a] As our interviews proceeded, a decision was made to increase the number of officers to be included in the lowest experience stratum (1-48 months) and to decrease the number in the 49-108 month stratum. This was done to increase the amount of information we might obtain concerning training academy experiences. Difficulties in setting up interviews with two of these less-experienced officers by the time interviews were suspended allowed us to increase the number of officers in this group by only one.

[b] Percentage greater than 100 due to rounding.

Table 2. Distribution of Work Assignments[a]: Final Sample and All Officers Assigned 12/3/75

Location	Number in final sample	Number in population	Percent of population
Wall Post	7	26	9
Work Gang	5	23	8
Block	10	40	14
Relief	10	81	28
School and Industry	2	28	10
Administration Building	6	43	15
Yard	8	21	7
Miscellaneous	(3)[b]	20	7
Kitchen and Mess Hall	2	10	3
	50	292[c]	101[d]

[a] This represents the officer's permanent job assignment on the day he was interviewed.

[b] Three of the officers working in the yard were assigned to miscellaneous yard duty. The item in parentheses was not counted in the total.

[c] This number is less than the total 359 officers in the entire population, since on any one day for which the "job plot" was obtained a certain number of officers would not be scheduled to work, being on vacation or on their regular day off.

[d] Percentage greater than 100 due to rounding.

Table 3. Number of Officers Holding Particular Job Assignments With Varying Amounts of Experience

Months experience	Work gang	Wall post	Adminis-tration building	Industry and school	Cell blocks	Relief	Miscel-laneous	Kitchen mess hall	Yard	Total
1–36	—	1	2	—	2	6	9	2	7	29
37–72	—	5	8	3	5	29	7	5	7	69
73–108	3	3	4	8	6	15	3	2	3	47
109–144	—	1	1	4	8	2	—	—	3	19
145–180	2	3	2	4	8	8	1	1	—	29
181–216	2	3	7	6	7	11	—	—	1	37
217–254	11	5	12	3	3	7	—	—	—	41
255+	5	5	7	—	1	3	—	—	—	21
Total	23	26	43	28	40	81	20	10	21	292[a]
$\bar{X}$ months experience	208.8	178.1	165.3	138.4	124.6	114.3	75.7	73.7	60.2	
$\bar{X}$ years experience	16.7	14.8	13.8	11.5	10.4	9.5	6.3	6.2	5.0	

[a] This number is less than the total 359 officers working at Auburn, since on any one day for which the "job plot" was obtained a certain number of officers are not scheduled to work, being on vacation or on their regular day off.

Table 4. Previous Occupations of Officers in Sample

Occupation	N
Factory workers	28
Construction trades	6
Truckers	4
Hospital workers	4
Taxi drivers	4
Restaurant work delivery, bartenders	4
Family businesses	3
Directly from college	3
Other prison jobs	2
Security guards	2
Farmers	2

Table 5. Themes Associated With Recruitment

Theme	Number of officers mentioning theme[a]	Percent
Security	34	68
Pay and benefits	15	30
Alternative to police work	5	10
Friends worked there	3	6
Alternative to factory	3	6
Talked into it	3	6
Just a job	2	4
Others	3	6

[a] Question: How did you come to be a correctional officer?

Table 6. Motivational Concerns By Job Preference (Number of Officers Mentioning)[a]

Mentioned as preferred job		Motivational Concern					
		Activity	Control	Help	Away	Other	Total
With inmates	Block	5	2	5	—	—	12
	Gang	3	5	1	—	—	9
	Shop	2	—	—	—	—	2
Away from inmates	Yard	—	—	1	—	—	1
	Administration building	3	2	—	6	—	11
	Wall	2	1	—	5	1	9
		15	10	7	11	1	44

[a] 11 officers mentioned no jobs as preferable. Marginal totals are unequal, since three officers mentioned two locations and one motivation and one officer mentioned one job with two motivations.

Table 7. Motivational Concerns of Officers Who Bid on Present Jobs

Motivational concern		Number of officers
Noninstitutional		2
Intrinsic to Job		15
a. Activity	4	—
b. More helpful	1	—
c. Control	6	—
d. Get away	4	—
Shift	—	6
Weekends off	—	4
Other	—	2
Total	—	29

Table 8. Work Locations of Officers Not Bidding on Present Jobs

	Held job prior to bidding	Given job after bidding
Block	5	—
Gang	2	—
Administration building	5	—
Wall	2	—
Vacation relief	—	6
Miscellaneous	—	1
	14	7

Table 9. Frequency Distribution—Themes Correction Officers Associate with Their Work

Functional theme	Number of officers mentioning theme	Percentage of officers mentioning theme[a]
Human services	25	50
Order maintenance	22	44
Security (guard function)	13	26
Supervision	11	22
Rule enforcement (police function)	11	22

[a] Theme occurrence total is greater than 100% because of the responses of many offices contained more than one theme. Nineteen mentioned one theme; 15, two themes; 13, three themes; 3, four themes.

Table 10. Correction Officer Views on Source of Their Authority[a]

Source of authority	Number mentioning[b] N=50
Personal (way officer handles himself)	32
State	6
Rules	12
Being an officer	9

[a] *Question: Where does your authority come from?*

[b] Total greater than 50 since ten officers mentioned more than one source.

Table 11. Number and Percent of Officers Referring to Reason for Enforcement Strategy by Enforcement Strategy
(Question: Why do you handle things as you do?)

Reason for enforcement strategy theme	Enforcement strategy		Total	
	Tell inmate	Ignore[a]	*N*	%
Unnecessary rules	8	5	13	26
Fairness	7	3	10	20
Take it personally	9	1	10	20
Functional	18	3	21	42
a. Inmate-oriented	6	2	8	16
b. Officer-oriented	8	1	9	18
c. Institution-oriented	4	0	4	8
Total	42[b]	12[b]	54	

[a] Though no officer mentioned "ignore" as his only strategy, ten officers did indicate that they sometimes ignored certain violations.

[b] Two officers in each strategy group mentioned two reasons for enforcement themes, raising the total number of responses above 50. In all four cases, unnecessary rules and fairness were linked.

Table 12. Distribution of Officers According to Rate of Absenteeism[a]

$\bar{X}$ Sick days[b,c] used per month (1976)	Number of officers
0–0.5	28
0.6–1.0	14
1.1–1.5	2
1.6–2.0	2
2.1+	4
	50

[a] Data on individual officers provided by the institution's Deputy Superintendent for Administration.

[b] Combines days designated as used for personal sickness and those designated family sickness. (*Note:* Officers generally receive a full day's pay when they use sick leave. They accumulate sick leave at the rate of four hours per semimonthly pay period).

[c] $\bar{X}$ $(N=50)=0.88$ days per month
$\bar{X}$ $(N=49)=0.68$ days per month (excluding one officer absent 120 days due to heart attack).

Table 13. Distribution of Correction Offices by 1976 Earnings[a]

Earnings[b]	Number of officers
$12,000–13,999	8
14,000–14,999	22
15,000–15,999	5
16,000–16,999	4
17,000+	11

[a] Data provided by Deputy Superintendent for Administration, January, 1977.

[b] Officers' income ranged from $12,543 for an officer with two years' experience and no overtime to a high of $20,164 for an officer with 18 years' experience who worked 476 hours overtime.

Table 14. Correction Officer Norm-Violating Behaviors[a]

Behavior	Number mentioning ($N=50$)
Dealing in contraband	14
Does not do his job	9
Fails to assist in fight	6
"Rats" on other officers	6
Bends rules too much	4
Too friendly with inmates	3
Changes other officer's directions to inmates	3
"Plays games" with people	2
Gossips	2
Abuse of sick time	2
Argues in front of inmates	1
Enforces rules too much	1
Off-work behavior bad	1
Gets other officers in trouble	1
Too much "mouth"	1
Lying about officers	1
Starts rumors	1
Don't know	7

[a] *Question: What kinds of things can get an officer into trouble with other officers?*

Table 15. Inmate Population and Turnover Rates 1976-1986

	Monthly Inmate Population			Monthly Turnover Rates		
Year	High	Low	X̄ Monthly	High	Low	X̄ Monthly %
1976	1595	1537	1572	24.4	8.2	14.1
1977	1566	1595	1580	36.5	9.6	18.4
1978	1571	1590	1582	24.6	8.6	15.6
1979	1567	1599	1583	19.1	10.3	13.3
1980	1555	1592	1572	24.8	10.9	16.4
1981	1569	1664	1608	15.2	9.2	12.8
1982	1622	1677	1661	16.4	8.5	12.2
1983	1623	1683	1640	18.9	11.4	15.1
1984	1638	1692	1677	18.4	9.7	13.8
1985	1631	1684	1674	18.8	10.7	14.8

Table 16. Percent of Each Year's January Seniority List by Years of Experience

		# Years of Experience				
Year	N	0-3	4-6	7-12	13-18	19+
1976	359	11	8	36	21	23
1977	NA*	NA	NA	NA	NA	NA
1978	379	16	9	34	12	27
1979	NA	NA	NA	NA	NA	NA
1980	391	15	11	34	9	30
1981	407	24	9	26	13	28
1982	403	24	14	24	13	24
1983	NA	NA	NA	NA	NA	NA
1984	502	44	5	18	16	17
1985	516	35	20	15	17	14

*NA = Seniority lists for these years not available.

Table 17. Percent of Officers Indicating Positive Responses to Problem-Sharing Situations

Problem Initiating Officer/ Inmate Relationship	I Original Sample (N=50) 1976	II (N=25)[b] 1986	III New Sample[a] (N=23)[c]	II+III Total 1986 (N=48)
Inmate Institutional	88%	88%	47%	69%
Inmate Personal	58%	52%	26%	39%
Finding out if problem exists	60%	44%	39%	42%
Sharing officers institutional	48%	24%	17%	21%
Sharing officers personal	12%	24%	13%	19%

[a] Officers hired after 1976.

[b] Combines 17 interviews and 8 questionnaires.*

[c] Combines (5) interviews and (18) questionnaire responses* (hired since 1976).

* On questionnaire officers were to indicate their agreement or disagreement with the following statements:
Inmate Institutional Problems: "If an inmate that I know comes to me with a problem like needing a new pair of shoes, I generally call around to see if I can help him out."
Inmate Personal Problems: "It's best never to offer any advice to an inmate who comes to you and talks about some sort of family problem."
Seeking Out Inmates with Problems: "It's a good idea to try to find out if an inmate's having some kind of problem rather than waiting for the inmate to come to you."
Officer Institutional Problem: "I sometimes find myself talking to inmates that I know about problems I experience in the institution."
Officer Personal Life: "I sometimes talk with inmates about what's going on in my personal life."

Table 18. Measures of Inmate Behavior:* Number of Rule Violations for Selected Offenses 1976-1985

Year	Fights[a]	Attack on Officer[b]	Self-Directed Violence[c]	Drugs[d]	Sex Offenses[e]	Order Maintenance[f]
1976	267	77	14	7	5	2242
1977	399	56	36	13	15	2651
1978	443	92	24	64	23	3425
1979	457	58	26	66	14	2711
1980	436	93	25	111	31	2677
1981	456	73	37	71	17	3003
1982	490	88	52	87	41	3099
1983	429	77	42	98	39	2935
1984	478	92	65	116	42	3797
1985	481	74	72	113	50	3406

* Data gathered from institution's "The Daily Journal of Infractions" 1976-1985. This includes reports filed by *all* institution's officers, not only officers in sample.

[a] *Fights with inmate* includes: reports written for fighting, wrestling, heated arguments, assaults with injuries.

[b] *Attack on officer* includes: reports written for attack on officer, assault on officer, hitting officer with thrown object or substance, physical contact with officer.

[c] *Self-directed violence* includes: suicide attempts, self-inflicted injury, cutting up, cut wrists or arms, any self-inflicted injury not specified suicide attempt.

[d] *Drug offense* includes: reports written for possession of marijuana, heroin, cocaine.

[e] *Sexual offenses* include: homosexual offenses, masturbating, exposing self to officer.

[f] *Order maintenance* includes: loitering on gallery, not locking in, delaying company, skipping school, no sneakers on gym floor, refusal to work, refusing frisk, insolence, etc.

Table 19. Order Maintenance Reports[a] by Location[b] 1976-1985
Number and percentage of Total Reports

			Blocks	Yard	Shops	School	Gym/ Lib	SHU	Kitchen /MH	Visiting Room
Year	Total	% With Location	N (%)	N (%)	N (%)	N (%)	N (%)	N (%)	N (%)	N (%)
1976	2442	(52)	612 (27)	52 (2)	76 (3)	170 (8)	48 (2)	50 (2)	144 (6)	11 (1)
1977	2651	(44)	519 (20)	98 (4)	43 (2)	117 (4)	41 (2)	186 (7)	156 (6)	19 (1)
1978	3425	(39)	598 (17)	94 (3)	64 (2)	119 (4)	59 (2)	197 (6)	143 (4)	28 (1)
1979	2711	(54)	689 (25)	106 (4)	27 (2)	223 (8)	69 (3)	122 (5)	203 (8)	31 (1)
1980	2677	(70)	928 (35)	113 (4)	44 (2)	178 (7)	54 (2)	178 (7)	309 (12)	48 (2)
1981	3303	(57)	1097 (37)	115 (4)	61 (2)	128 (4)	83 (3)	146 (5)	219 (7)	21 (1)
1982	3099	(70)	1120 (36)	163 (5)	48 (2)	244 (8)	160 (5)	107 (4)	322 (10)	16 (1)
1983	2935	(72)	1105 (38)	158 (5)	32 (1)	172 (6)	121 (4)	108 (4)	398 (14)	19 (1)
1984	3797	(42)	855 (22)	113 (3)	23 (1)	178 (5)	79 (2)	159 (4)	172 (5)	27 (1)
1985	3406	(38)	663 (20)	65 (2)	37 (1)	164 (5)	35 (1)	122 (4)	172 (5)	27 (1)

[a] Data gathered from institution's "Daily Journal of Infractions."

[b] Violations in subenvironment include:

Blocks: Loitering, throwing things on gallery, not locking in, opening cells, things on bars, on wrong company, delaying company, talking after quiet bell, any other non-violent, non-contraband, from block, gallery or company.

Yard: Disobey direct order, failure to provide ID, any other non-violent, non-contraband from yard.

Shops: Sneakers in shop, refusal to work, any other non-violent, non-contraband in shops.

School: Skipping school, loud talking in class, out of place, any other non-violent, non-contraband in school.

Gym/Library: Smoking in gym, shoes on gym floor, illegal entry, out of place, any other non-violent, non-contraband in gym/library.

Kitchen/Mess Hall: Refusal to work, not wearing whites, food serving violations, taking food, stealing food, any other non-violent, non-contraband in mess hall or kitchen.

Visiting Area: Insolence, fondling, petting, kissing, sitting wrong, creating disturbance.

SHU: Throwing materials from cell, disruptive, noisy behavior, any non-violent, non-contraband from SHU.

Other order maintenance (location not specified): Sick call, phone privileges, abusive language, vile language, abuse, out of place, refusing order, refusing frisk, interference as in-state employee, harrassment, lying, refusal to work, refusal to accept assignment.

Appendix E

The exploratory nature of this research required that the variety of work experiences found in the sample be maximized. The first step in the sampling process involved dividing the entire officer population into strata based on months of experience. Prior to making the decision to fill quotas based on experience alone, two lists were obtained from the institutional administration: a seniority list of all officers working at Auburn and a listing of job assignments held by individual officers on a particular day. These two lists were cross-classified to determine if sampling based on seniority alone (the only variable for which accurate information was readily available on all officers) would be likely to yield an overall sample sufficiently diversified in specific task-related experience as well (See Table 3, Appendix D). Tendencies highlighted by the arrangement of the data on this table enhanced my confidence that it would.

To ensure that the sample was representative of the institutional population as a whole and to obtain a number of officers I could deal with practically, approximately 15% of each stratum was set as a quota to be obtained for each stratum, yielding a total sample size of 52.

With quotas determined, each officer on the alphabetized seniority list was assigned an identification number and placed into the appropriate stratum. The officers within each stratum were then arranged by random assignment in the order in which they would be contacted for interviews. In the event that substitutions were needed to fill quotas, the officer whose name occurred next to the list within a particular stratum was contacted. (Tables 1 and 2, Appendix D, indicate the degree to which the final sample is representative of officers population in terms of experience and job assignment.)

Bibliography

Annual Reports of the Prison Discipline Society of Boston, The Twenty-Nine Annual Reports of the Board of Managers (1826-1854), Volumes 1-6. Montclair, NJ: Patterson-Smith, 1972

Argyle, Michael. *The Social Psychology of Work*. New York: Taplinger Publishing Company, 1972

Barnes, Harry E. *A History of the Penal, Reformatory and Correctional Institutions for the State of New Jersey*. Trenton, NJ: MacCrellish and Quigly Company, 1918.

Bates, Sanford. "Institutes and Schools for Prison Officials," *Proceedings of the National Conference on Social Work*, Vol. IX (1931), pp. 421-429.

Berkman, Alexander. *Prison Memoirs of an Anarchist*. New York: Schocken Books, 1970.

Bidwell, C.E. "The Young Professional in the Army: A Study of Occupational Identity," *American Sociological Review*, Vol. XXVI (June 1961), pp. 360-372.

Bluhm, Hilde O. "How Did They Survive? Mechanisms of Defense in Nazi Concentration Camps." *American Journal of Psychotherapy*, Vol. II (1948), pp. 3-32.

Bogardus, Emory S. "Social Distance Scale," *Sociology and Social Research*, Vol. XVII (1932), pp. 55-62.

Brady, J.C., Brodsky, L.L. and Grenfall, J.E. "Evaluation of Semantic Differential Changes in Correctional Training Officer Attitudes," *Journal of Correctional Education*, Vol. XXI (1968), pp. 4-6.

Briggs, Dennie L. and Dowling, John M. "The Correction Officer as a Consultant: The Emerging Role in Penology," *American Journal of Correction* (May-June 1964), pp. 28-31.

Brown, B.S. DuPont, R.L., Kozel, N.J. and Spevacek, J.D. "Staff Conceptions of Inmate Characteristics: A Comparison of Treatment and Custodial Staffs at Two Differing Institutions," *Criminology*, Vol. IX (1971), pp. 316-329.

Carroll, Bonnie. *Job Satisfaction*. Ithaca, NY: New York State School of Industrial and Labor Relations, Cornell University, 1973.

Chang, Dae H. and Zastrow, Charles H. "Inmates and Security Guards' Perceptions of Themselves and Each Other: A Comparative Study," *International Journal of Criminology and Penology*, Vol. 4, No. 1 (1976) pp. 89-98.

Cheatwood, A.D. "The Staff in Correctional Settings: An Empirical Investigation of Frying Pans and Fires," *Journal of Research in Crime and Delinquency*, Vol. II, No. 2 (1974), pp. 173-179.

Cohen, Stanely and Taylor, Laurie. *Psychological Survival: The Experience of Long-Term Imprisonment*. New York: Vintage Press, 1973.

Cormier, Bruno M. and Williams, P.J. "The Watcher and the Watched," *Annales Internationales de Criminologie (Annals of International Criminology)*, Vol. IX (1971), pp. 447-452.

Cormier, Bruno M. *The Watcher and the Watched.* Plattsburg, NY: Tundra Books, 1975.

Cressey, Donald. "Contradictory Directives in Complex Organizations," in *Prison and Society*, edited by Lawrence Hazelrigg. New York: Anchor Books, 1968.

Cressey, Donald. "Limitations of Treatment," in *The Sociology of Punishment and Corrections*, edited by N. Johnston, L. Savitz and M. Wolfgang. New York: John Wiley and Sons, 1970, pp. 501-508.

Cullen, F. *Reaffirming Rehabilitation.* Cincinnati, Ohio: Anderson Publishing Co., 1983.

DeBerker, Paul. "Staff Strain in Institutions," *British Journal of Delinquency*, Vol. VI, No. 4 (1956), pp. 278-284.

DeBerker, Paul. "The Sociology of Change in Penal Institutions," in *Changing Concepts of Crime and Its Treatment*, edited by Hugh J. Klare. London: Pergamon Press, 1966. pp. 139-154.

Diedrick-Snoek J. "Role Strain in Diversified Role Sets," *American Journal of Sociology*, Vol. XXI (1966), pp. 363-372.

DiIulio, John J. *Governing Prisons.* New York: The Free Press, 1987.

Duffee, David. "The Correction Officer Subculture and Organizational Change," *Journal of Research on Crime and Delinquency*, Vol. II (1974), pp. 155-172.

Duffee, David. *Using Correctional Officers in Planned Change.* Washington, D.C.: National Institute of Law Enforcement, National Technical Information Service, 1972.

Evans, A.A. "Correctional Institution Personnel—Amateurs or Professionals," *Annals*, Vol. 293 (May 1954), pp. 72-77.

Farmer, R.E. "Cynicism: A Factor in Corrections Work," *Journal of Criminal Justice*, Vol. 5, No. 3 (1977), pp. 237-246.

Fish, N. "Institutional Paranoia," *Group Analysis*, Vol. V, No. 1 (1972), pp. 27, 28.

Fogel, David. *"...We Are the Living Proof..."; The Justice Model for Corrections.* Cincinnati, OH: Anderson Publishing Company, 1975.

Fox, Vernon. "Prison Disciplinary Problems," in *The Sociology of Punishment and Corrections*, edited by N. Johnston, L. Savitz and M. Wolfgang. New York: John Wiley and Sons, 1970, pp. 393-400.

Garabedian, Peter G. "Social Roles and Processes of Socialization in the Prison Community," in *The Sociology of Punishment and Corrections*, edited by N. Johnston, L. Savitz and M. Wolfgang. New York: John Wiley and Sons, 1970, pp. 484-496.

Galliher, John F. "Change in a Correctional Institution: A Case Study of the Tightening-Up Process," *Crime and Delinquency*, Vol. XVIII, No. 3 (July 1972), pp. 263-270.

Galliher, John F. "Naming Behavior and Social Interaction in Prisons," *British Journal of Criminology*, Vol. XII, No. 1 (1972), pp. 167-174.

Gillin, John L. "The World's Oldest Training School for Prison Officials," *Journal of Criminal Law*, Vol. XXIII (May 1932), pp. 101-102.

Glaser, Daniel. *The Effectiveness of a Prison and Parole System*. Indianapolis, IN: The Bobbs-Merrill Company, 1969.

Goffman, Erving. *Asylums*. Garden City, NY: Anchor Books, 1961.

Goffman, Erving. "On the Characteristics of Total Institutions: Staff-Inmate Relations," in *The Prison: Studies in Institutional Organization and Change*, edited by Donald Cressey, New York: Holt, Rinehart and Winston, 1961, pp. 68-106.

Gooding, Judson. *The Job Revolution*. New York: Collier Books, 1972.

Gursky, Oscar. "Role Conflict in Organization: A Study of Prison Camp Officials," in *Prison Within Society*, edited by Lawrence Hazelrigg. Garden City, NY: Anchor Books, 1968.

Hart, Hastings H. *Training Schools for Prison Officers: Plans and Syllabi of the United States Training School for Prison Officers; The New York City Keepers' Training School;* and *The British Training School for Prison Officers*. New York: Russel Sage Foundation, 1930.

Hartman, C. "The Key Jingler," *Community Mental Health*, Vol. V, No. 3 (1969), pp. 199-205.

Hawkins, Gordon. *The Prison: Policy and Practice*. Chicago, IL: University of Chicago Press, 1976.

Haynes, Gideon. *A Historical Sketch of the Massachusetts State Prison*. Boston, MA: Lee and Sheppard, 1869.

Heim, Richard B. "Prison Personnel: A Review of the Literature," *American Journal of Corrections*, Vol. 286, January-February (1966), pp. 14-20.

Hendry, C.H. and Twomey, J.F. "Staff Interpersonal Ratings of Inmate Relationships," *Journal of Correctional Education*, Vol. XXI, No. 1 (1969), pp. 8, 9.

Herzberg, Frederick. *Job Attitudes: Review of Research and Opinion*. Pittsburgh, PA: Psychological Service of Pittsburgh, 1957.

Herzberg, Frederick. *Work and the Nature of Man*. Cleveland, MO: World Publishing, 1966.

Hindman, R.L. "Inmate Interactions as a Determinant of Response to Incarceration," *British Journal of Criminilogy*, Vol. XI, No. 4 (1971), pp. 382-390.

Hoppock, Robert. *Job Satisfaction*. New York: Harper and Row, 1935.

Irwin, John. *Prisons in Turmoil*. Boston, MA: Little, Brown, and Company, 1980.

Jacobs, James B. *Stateville: The Penitentiary in Mass Society*. Chicago, IL: University of Chicago Press, 1977.

Jacobs, James B. "What Prison Guards Think: A Profile of the Illinois Force," *Crime and Delinquency*, Vol. 24, No. 1 (1978), pp. 185-196.

Jacobs, James B. and Grear, M. P. "Drop-Outs and Rejects: An Analysis of the Prison Guard's Revolving Door," *Criminal Justice Review*, Vol. 2, No. 2 (1977), pp. 57-70.

Jacobs, James B. and Retsky, Harold G. "Prison Guard," *Urban Life*, Vol. IV, No. 1 (April 1975), pp. 5-29.

Jacobs, James and Zimmer, Lynn. "Collective Bargaining & Labor Unrest," in *New Perspectives on Prisons & Imprisonment*, edited by James Jacobs. Ithaca, NY: Cornell University Press, 1983.

Jayewardene, C.H.S., McKay, H.B. and McKay, B.E.A. Krug. "In Search of a Sixth Sense: Predictors of Disruptive Behavior in Correctional Institutions." *Crime and/et Justice* (formerly *Criminology Made in Canada)*, Vol. 4, No. 1, pp. 32-39.

Johnson, Elmer H. "Roles and Rules in the Correctional Community," *American Journal of Corrections*, Vol. XXXI (1969), pp. 48-52.

Johnson, Robert. "Ameliorating Prison Stress: Some Helping Roles for Custodial Personnel," *International Journal of Criminology and Penology*, Vol. 5, No. 3 (1977), pp. 263-273.

Kahn, Robert L., Wolfe, D.M., Quinn, R.P., Snoek, J.D. and Rosenthal, R.H. *Organizational Stress: Studies in Role Conflict and Ambiguity*. New York: John Wiley and Sons, 1964.

Katsampes, P. "Changing Correction Officers: A Demonstration Study," *International Journal of Criminology and Penology*, Vol. 3, No. 2 (1975), pp. 123-144.

Katz, Daniel and Kahn, Robert L. *The Social Psychology of Organizations*. New York: John Wiley and Sons, 1966.

Kehle, M. "Prison Officers: The Inside Story," *New Society*, Vol. 44, No. 879 (1979), pp. 272-295.

Kronstadt, Sylvia. "The Prison Guards: An Unhappy Lot," *New York Affairs*, Fall (1974), pp. 60-77.

Lawes, Lewis E. *Twenty Thousand Years in Sing-Sing*. New York: Blue Ribbon Books, 1932.

Loeb, M.B. and Smith, H.L. "Relationships Among Occupational Groups in a Mental Hospital," in *The Patient and the Mental Hospital*, edited by M. Greenbladt, R.H. Williams and D.J. Levinson. Glencoe, IL: Free Press of Glencoe, 1957.

Luden, Walter. *The Prison Warden and the Custodial Staff: Problems of Tenure and Turnover of Wardens and Custodial Offices in Federal and State Prisons in the United States and Canada*. Springfield, IL: Thomas Charles Company, 1965.

Lundberg, Donald E. "Methods of Selecting Prison Personnel," *Journal of Criminal Law*, Vol. XXXVIII (May 1947), pp. 14-39.

Lundberg, Donald E. "Some Aspects of the Job of Prison Guard," Ph.D. thesis, Cornell University, 1946.

Mang, J. and Zastrow, L. "Inmates' and Security Guards' Perceptions of Themselves and Each Other: A Comparative Study," paper presented at the Meeting of American Criminological Society, Chicago, 1974.

Martin, John Bartlow. "The Riot at Jackson Prison," Part 1, *Saturday Evening Post,* Vol. 225, June 6 (1953); Part 2, ibid, Vol. 225, June 13 (1953); Part 3, ibid., Vol. 225, June 20 (1953); Part 4, ibid., Vol. 225, June 27 (1953).

Martinson, Robert. "Social Interaction Under Close Confinement," Berkeley, CA: Institute of Social Sciences, University of California, 1966 (mimeographed.)

Maslow, Abraham. *Motivation and Personality*. New York: Harper and Row, 1954.

Mathiesen, Thomas. *Defences of the Weak*. London: Tavistock Publications, 1965.

May, Edgar. "A Day on the Job—In Prison," *Corrections Magazine,* Vol. 2, No. 6, December (1976), pp. 6-11.

Maxim, P. "Treatment—Custody Staff Conflict in Correctional Institutions: A Re-Analysis," *Canadian Journal of Criminology and Corrections,* Vol. 18, No. 4 (1976), pp. 379-385.

McCleery, Richard. "Conflict and Accommodations in a Penal Institution," paper presented at the Annual Meeting of the American Political Science Association, St. Louis, MO, September, 1958.

McCorkle, Lloyd W. "Guard-Inmate Relationships," in *The Sociology of Punishment and Corrections,* edited by N. Johnston, L. Savitz and M. Wolfgang. New York: John Wiley and Sons, 1970, pp. 419-422.

McCorkle, Lloyd W. and Korn, Richard. "Resocialization Within Walls," in *The Sociology of Punishment and Corrections,* edited by N. Johnston, L. Savitz and M. Wolfgang. New York: John Wiley and Sons, 1970, pp. 409-418.

Meaden, W.D. "Duties of Prison Officers," in *Papers and Discussions on Punishment and Reformation Being the Transactions of the Third Department of the National Association for the Promotion of Social Science*. London: Victoria Press, 1862.

Montalvo, B. and Paulin, S. "Faculty-Staff Communications in a Residential Treatment Center: Wiltwyck School for Boys, New York, New York," *American Journal of Orthopsychiatry,* Vol. XXXVI, No. 4 (1966), pp. 706-711.

Morgan, Gareth, *Images of Organization*. Beverly Hills, CA: Sage, 1986.

Morris, Norval. *The Future of Imprisonment*. Chicago, IL: University of Chicago Press, 1974.

Motivans, Joseph J. "Occupational Socialization and Personality. A Study of the Prison Guard," in *Proceedings of the 93rd Congress of the American Correctional Association* (1963), pp. 186-196.

National Advisory Commission of Criminal Justice Standards and Goals. *Corrections*. Washington, D.C.: U.S. Government Printing Office, 1973.

Niederhoffer, Arthur. *Behind the Shield: The Police in Urban Society*. Garden City, NY: Doubleday and Company, 1967.

O'Leary, V. and Duffee, D. "Managerial Behavior and Correctional Policy," Albany, NY: School of Criminal Justice, 1970 (mimeographed).

O'Neill, Michael W. "The Role of the Police—Normative Role Expectations in a Metropolitan Police Department," unpublished Ph.D. thesis, SUNY at Albany, NY, 1974.

Palola, Ernest and Larson, William P. "Some Dimensions of Job Satisfaction Among Hospital Personnel," *Sociology and Social Research,* Vol. XXV, Spring (1972), pp. 65-73.

Philiber, Susan. "Thy Brother's Keeper: A Review of the Literature on Correctional Officers," *Justice Quarterly,* Vol. 4, No. 1, 1987, pp. 9-37.

Piven, Herman and Alcabea, Abraham. *The Crisis of Qualified Manpower for Criminal Justice.* Washington, D.C.: U.S. Department of Health, Education and Welfare, 1969.

Pogrebin, Mark. "Role Conflict Among Correctional Officers in Treatment Oriented Correctional Institutions," *International Journal of Offender Therapy and Comparative Criminology,* Vol. 22, No. 2 (1978), pp. 149-155.

Potter, Joan. "Guards' Unions: The Search for Solidarity," *Corrections Magazine* (New York), Vol. 5, No. 4 (1979), pp. 25-35.

President's Commission on Law Enforcement and the Administration of Justice. *Task Force Report: Corrections.* Washington, D.C.: U.S. Government Printing Office, 1967.

"Professional Training of Prison Officials," *Journal of Criminal Law,* Vol. II, May (1911), pp. 121-230.

Report from the Correction Officers Training Seminar. Topeka, KS, 1968.

Reynolds, John N. *The Twin Hells: A Thrilling Narrative of Life in the Kansas and Missouri Penitentiaries.* Chicago, IL: M.A. Donahue and Company, 1890.

Rice, Ronald G. "A Scale for Measuring Attitude Changes Among Inmates of Local Jails and Among Correctional Workers," unpublished Ph.D. thesis, University of Florida, 1971.

Rothman, David J. *Discovery of the Asylum.* Boston, MA: Little, Brown, and Company, 1971.

Roucek, J. "Sociology of the Prison Guard," *Sociology and Social Research,* Vol. XX (1935), pp. 145-151.

Sandhu, Harjit S. "Perceptions of Prison Guards: A Cross-National Study of India and Canada," *International Review of Modern Sociology,* Vol. II, March (1972), pp. 26-32.

Schlenker, Barry R. and Tedeschi, James T. "Interpersonal Attraction and the Exercise of Coercive and Reward Power," *Human Relations,* Vol. XXI, November (1972), pp. 427-429.

Sellin, Thorsten. "Historical Glimpses of Training for the Prison Service," *Journal of Criminal Law, Criminology and Police Science,* Vol. XXV, November (1934), pp. 594-609.

Sherif, Muzafer. *Social Interaction*. Chicago, IL: Aldine Publishing Company, 1967.

Shoom, S. "Authority: One Aspect of the Correctional Worker-Client Relationship," *Canadian Journal of Corrections*, Vol. XIV, No. 2 (1972), pp. 181-184.

Smith, R.S., Milan, M.A., Woof, L.F. and McKee, J.M. "The Correction Officer as a Behaviorial Technician," *Criminal Justice Behavior*, Vol. 3, No. 4 (1976), pp. 345-360.

South Carolina Department of Corrections. *Collective Violence in Correctional Institutions*. Columbia, SC, 1973.

Special Task Force to the Secretary of Health, Education and Welfare. *Work in America*. Cambridge, MA: Massachusetts Institute of Technology Press, 1973.

Stutsman, Jesse O. *Curing the Criminal: A Treatise on the Philosophy and Practice of Modern Correctional Methods*. New York: McMillan, 1926.

Stutsman, Jesse O. "The Prison Staff," *Annals*, Vol. 157, September (1931), pp. 62-71.

Sykes, G. "The Corruption of Authority and Rehabilitation," *Social Forces*, Vol. XXXIV (1956), pp. 257-262.

Sykes, Greshan. *The Society of Captives*. New York: Atheneum, 1970.

Sykes, Gresham and Messinger, Sheldon L. "The Inmate Social Code," in *The Sociology of Punishment and Corrections*, edited by N. Johnston, L. Savitz and M. Wolfgang. New York: John Wiley and Sons, 1970, pp. 401-498.

Teeters, Negley K. and Shearer, John D. *The Prison at Philadelphia, Cherry Hill: A Separate System of Penal Discipline, 1829-1913*. New York: Columbia University Press, 1957.

Terkel, Studs. *Working*. New York: Pantheon Books, 1972.

Teske, R.H.C., Jr. and Williamson, H.E. "Correctional Officer Attitudes Toward Selected Treatment Programs," paper presented at the 28th Annual Meeting of the American Society of Criminology, Tucson, AZ, November 4-7, 1976.

Thomas, J.E. *The English Prison Officer Since 1850: A Study in Conflict*. London: Routledge and Keegan Paul, 1973.

Thomas, N. "Inmates' Role in Staff Orientation," *American Journal of Corrections*, Vol. XXXI, No. 4 (1969), p. 34

Toch, Hans. *Living in Prison: The Ecology of Survival*. New York: Free Press, 1977.

Turner, Ralph H. "Role-Taking, Role Standpoint, and Reference Group Behavior," *American Journal of Sociology*, Vol. LXI (1956), pp. 316-328.

Wallack, Walter M. *The Training of Prison Guards in New York State*. New York: Bureau of Publications, Teacher's College, Columbia University, 1938.

Walsh, R.T. "Researcher-Participant Collaboration in Corrections Research," *Canadian Journal of Criminology and Penology*, Vol. 18, No. 4 (1976), pp. 387-404.

Ward, Richard J. and Vanderyoot, David. "Correctional Officers with Case Loads," *Offender Rehabilitation,* Vol. 2, No. 1 (1977), pp. 31-38.

Weber, George H. "Emotional and Defensive Reactions of Cottage Parents," in *The Prison: Studies in Institutional Organization and Change,* edited by Donald Cressey. New York: Holt, Rinehart and Winston, 1961, pp. 189-228.

Wheeler, Stanton. "Role Conflict in Correctional Communities," in *The Prison: Studies in Institutional and Organizational Change,* edited by Donald Cressey. New York: Holt, Rinehart and Winston, 1961, pp. 229-259.

Whiteley, Sutard, Briggs, Dennie, and Turner, Merfyn. *Dealing with Deviants: The Treatment of Anti-Social Behavior.* New York: Schocken Books, 1973.

Wickersham Commission Reports. *Report No. 9, Report on Penal Institutions, Probation and Parole.* Montclair, NJ: Patterson-Smith, 1968.

Wilsnack, Richard and Ohlin, Lloyd. "Pre-conditions of Major Prison Disturbances," Harvard University, 1974 (mimeographed).

Wilson, James Q. *Varieties of Police Behavior.* New York: Atheneum, 1971.

Zeno. *Life.* New York: Stein and Day, 1968.

Zimbardo, Phillip G. "The Psychological Power and Pathology of Imprisonment," a statement prepared for the U.S. House of Representatives Committee on the Judiciary, October 25, 1971.

For Product Safety Concerns and Information please contact our
EU representative GPSR@taylorandfrancis.com Taylor & Francis
Verlag GmbH, Kaufingerstraße 24, 80331 München, Germany